ISRAEL
NATIONAL PARKS &
NATURE RESERVES

AZARIA ALON

A CARTA GUIDE

2008 First English Edition
Translated by Paul King

Our special thanks to the Israel Nature and National Parks Protection
Authority for placing at our disposal the information needed to publish
this book.

Great care has been taken to ensure that the information presented
here is up-to-date and accurate. We shall be grateful for pointing
out any errors, omissions or incomplete information. Please address
all comments to Carta, Jerusalem. Due amends will be made in the
following edition.

ISBN: 978-965-220-705-0

Carta books are available at special discounts for bulk purchase for sales
promotions, premiums, fund-raising, or educational use. For details,
contact:
        Carta, Jerusalem
        18 Ha'uman Street, POB 2500
        Jerusalem 91024, Israel
        E-mail: carta@carta.co.il
        Website: www.holyland-jerusalem.com

Printed in Israel

Greetings to all our readers!

Israel is blessed with panoramic landscapes, hundreds of historical sites and a wide variety of nature reserves, national parks and open areas, where the visitor can enjoy an abundance of antiquities and a rich world of wild flora and fauna. Each and every one of these sites is part and parcel of our country's cultural and historical assets, and, with the public's help, is preserved and treasured by the Israel Nature and National Parks Protection Authority.

This Guide offers the reader innumerable hiking trails amidst all of Israel's vast splendor. You are invited to use these trails to help you actively partake in the joy of Israel's nature and history, to travel to the different sites and participate in the many activities offered by the nature reserves and national parks.

The touring trails in the Guide are designed for families and individuals alike, and for all ages. Thus, everyone can find the most suitable tour from the wide variety offered.

With the help of this Guide you can also learn about some of our country's rich history throughout the ages, understand a little more about the mysteries of nature that surround us, and experience each and every visit to the fullest extent possible. Even the "armchair travelers" can enjoy a "virtual tour" of every site by reading the rich descriptions and perusing the maps that accompany each area.

Our employees at the sites and in the field are more than happy to assist you with information, guidance and any service you may need in preparation of or during your visit at the nature and historical sites.

Here's a warm welcome to all the sites of Israel's Nature and National Parks Protection Authority!

Eli Amitay
Director General
Israel Nature & National Parks
Protection Authority

4

Guidelines for the Visitor

As you set out on your tour, be sure to follow safety and other on-site rules. The following instructions are intended to protect your life and well-being, and to safeguard nature, landscapes, and the natural heritage.

◆ Carefully read and follow all signs in the area.
◆ Walking and driving are permitted on designated routes only.
◆ Do not go close to the edge of cliffs or descend cliffs.
◆ Do not roll or throw rocks down inclines.
◆ Descending (rappelling) or climbing cliffs is allowed in designated areas, and only individuals who have undergone appropriate training and use proper equipment, may do so.
◆ Do not climb walls of ancient structures and do not enter ruins or buildings unless entry is explicitly permitted.
◆ Staying overnight is permitted at authorized campsites only.
◆ Do not use natural water sources for drinking. Most water in the riverbeds is not potable. Bring your own drinking water.
◆ Trips in areas designated as military firing zones require written permission from the Israeli Defense Forces (IDF).
◆ Always wear proper attire, hiking shoes, and head covering.
◆ Always carry some type of signaling device (flashlight or matches) or a communications device (cell phone, walkie-talkie).
◆ Harming anything at the site is strictly prohibited, as are defacements of any kind: writing, painting, or chiseling graffiti.
◆ Keep the area clean. Do not burn or bury trash; take it with you.
◆ The use of dry foliage for campfires is strictly prohibited, except at camping grounds or other designated sites.
◆ Report any safety hazard to the Telephone Report Center of the Israel Nature and National Parks Protection Authority: tel. 02-5005444.
◆ Attention all visitors: safety rules must be conscientiously observed. Infringements will be vigorously investigated and/or prosecuted.

Key to Map Symbols

Battle site, Field school, Parking lot, Bird lookout, Water fountain, Muslim site, Antiquities, Christian site, Outdoor recreation, Hiking trail, Jewish site, Lookout point, Covered pool, National Park, Souvenir shop, Hospital, Beach, Showers, Restrooms (WC), Restaurant, Snack bar, Telephone, Sound & light show, Picnic site

Accessibility Information

This Guide pays particular attention to persons with mobility limitations and/or physical disabilities. Each site is rated for accessibility, based on the facilities available and their accessibility.

- ♿ Wheelchair-accessible route
- 🚶 Cane- or walker-assisted route
  - [1] Inaccessible site
  - [2] Partly accessible or accessible with light assistance
  - [3] Accessible site; does not meet approved standards
  - [4] Accessible site meeting approved standards

Parking, public restrooms, and food facilities are specially marked, with their level of accessibility.

- **P** Parking lot / car park
- 🚻 Public restrooms
- 🍴 Food facilities
  - ✔ Good accessibility
  - ✗ Partly accessible or light assistance required
  - ✗ Inaccessible

Guide dogs for the blind are permitted everywhere by law, except religious sites and sites containing animals.

- 👁 Special arrangements for the visually impaired.

The trails in most nature reserves are usually not accessible for individuals with disabilities.

 This information is a service provided by Access Unlimited, The Society for the Advancement of Accessibility in Israel, 17 Bilu Street, Kfar Saba 44413. Tel: 09-7658394; fax: 09-7650340; website: www.access-unlimited.co.il.

GLOSSARY OF TERMS

Be'er — well
Ein(ot) — spring(s)
Gebel — mountain (Arabic)
Giv'a(t) — hill
Har(ei) — mountain(s)
Hof — beach

Horba(t); pl. Horvot — ruin(s)
Ketef — mountain flank
Khirbe(t) — ruin (Arabic)
Ma'aleh — ascent
Matzuk (pl. Metzukei) — cliff(s)
Mehlaf — interchange

Metzad; Metzuda — fort; fortress
Mitzpeh — lookout
Nahal — stream, riverbed
Tel — archaeological mound
Tzomet — junction
Wadi — riverbed (Arabic)

Information | Museum | Guest house | Lookout tower | Play-ground | Hostel | Kayaking | Airport | "Tower & stockade" settlement | Overnight camping | Scuba diving | Swimming

First aid | Sports hall | Water slide | Marsh | Fish pond | Bungalow | Ball field | Amphi-theater | Fortress

Gilboa iris | Carob tree | Cliff | Spring | Mountain | Cave | Ruin / Tel

KEY MAP

Names Parks & Reserves

Location on map and
page number in guide 54 86

Borders

.... International border

══════ Separation of Forces Line 1974

Autonomous Areas

☐ Area A

☐ Area B

▨ Nature Reserve

```
0          10          20
                          km
```
1 kilometer = 0.621372 mile

Rosh Hanikra

Achziv 140

Nahariya

**Acre
(Akko)**

Nahal Na'aman & Ein Afek 146

Kiryat Yam

Haifa   Kiryat Bialik

Kiryat
Motzkin

Kiryat
Ata

Carmel Wildlife Preserve 244

244 Carmel   Kiryat
Tiv'on

Isfiya

Beit She'arim 224

Daliyat el Karmil

Hof Dor–Habonim 252

238 Nahal Me'arot

Yokne'am

**Zichron
Ya'akov**

Nahal Taninim 260

Umm el
Fahm

Binyamina   Kafr
Qari

Caesarea 266

**Pardes
Hana–
Karkur**   Ar'ara

Sharon 280 **Hadera**   Baqa el
Gharbiya

Nahal Alexander 274

Mediterranean Sea

18 Hermon
34 Nahal Hermon
26 Nimrod Fortress
68 Nahal Iyon
60 Tel Dan
54 Hurshat Tal

LEBANON

Kiryat
Shmona

Golan

120 Nahal Betzet
126 Nahal Keziv
126 Montfort
108 Bar'am
74 Hula
80 Tel Hazor
Hatzor
Haglilit
134 Yehi'am Fortress
134 Nahal Yehi'am
114 Mt. Meiron
Safed
86 Jordan Valley
98 Nahal Amud
40 Yehudiya Forest
Karmi'el
92 Chorazin
48 Gamla
Sakhnin
152 Capernaum

G a l i l e e
*Sea of
Galilee*
156 Kursi
Shfar'am
Tiberias
162 Hamat Tiberias
216 Tzipori

Migdal
Ha'emek
Natzrat Ilit
Nazareth
Afula
Ilit
Afula
170 Nahal Tavor
230 Tel Megiddo
178 Kochav Hayarden (Belvoir)

184 Ma'ayan Harod
Beit
She'an
190 Gilboa
208 Beit She'an
202 Beit Alfa Synagogue
196 Gan Hashlosha
Jenin
Jordan River
Border Crossing

JORDAN

© Carta, Jerusalem

Tulkarm

Tubas

Tayiba

Tira

Ra'anana Qalqilya

Nablus

S a m a r i a

Kfar Saba
Hod
Hasharon

Rosh Ha'ayin

Ari'el

Adam Bridge
Border Crossing

Petah Tikva
Kiryat Ono
Yehud
Or Yehuda

Lod

Ramla

Modi'in

El Bira

Ramallah

Allenby Bridge
Border Crossing

Jericho

Jerusalem

Ma'aleh
Adumim

Abdullah
Bridge
(defunct)

Ein Hemed
308 312 Castel
302 Sorek Cave

318 Jerusalem (around City Walls)

350 Qumran

Bethlehem

Einot Tzukim 356

Dead Sea

344 Herodion

J u d e a

328 Beit Guvrin–Tel Maresha

Hebron

Kiryat
Arba

Ein Gedi
364

364 Ein Gedi Antiquities

© Carta, Jerusalem

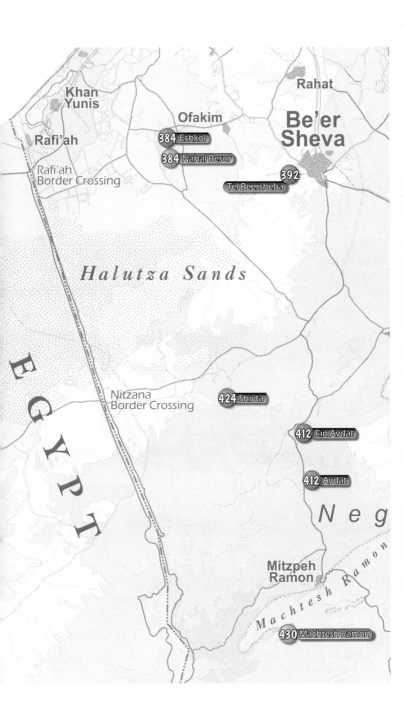

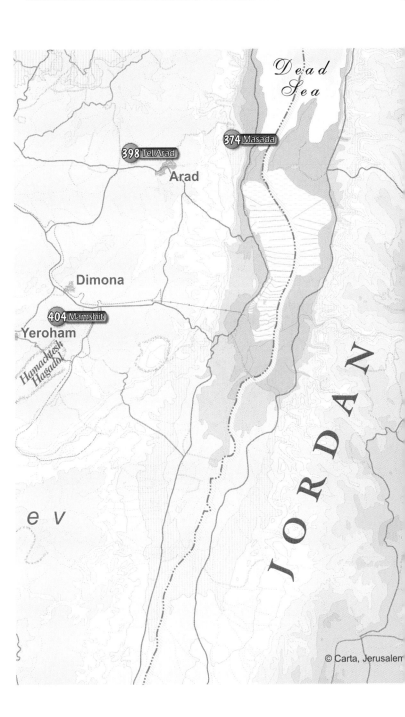

Dead Sea

374 Masada

398 Tel Arad

Arad

Dimona

404 Mamshit

Yeroham

Hamachtesh Hagadol

e v

JORDAN

© Carta, Jerusalem

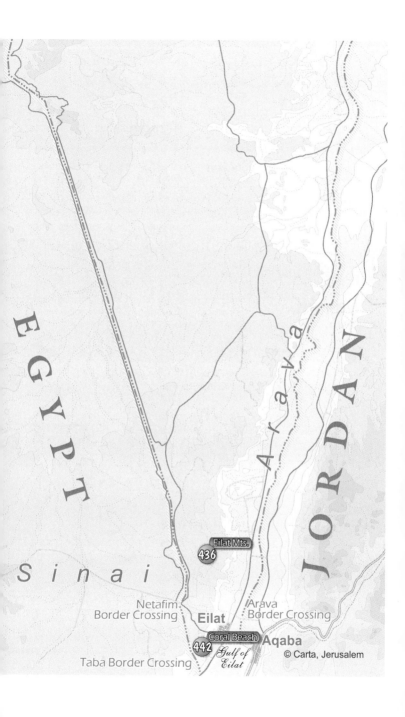

EGYPT

JORDAN

Arava

Sinai

Eilat Mts.
436

Netafim
Border Crossing

Arava
Border Crossing

Eilat

Aqaba

Coral Beach
442

Gulf of
Eilat

Taba Border Crossing

© Carta, Jerusalem

CONTENTS

Nature Reserve is indicated in green.
National Park is indicated in red.
Italics refer to sites outside the Nature Reserve/National Park

16

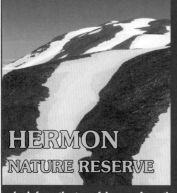

Location: end of Route 98, about 12 km north of Majdal Shams
Tel.: 04-6981337
Ski resort (in season):
  Tel.: 03-6025405
Entrance fee

...look from the top of Amana, from the top of Senir and Hermon... (Song 4:8)

Skiing | Hiking trail | Lookout point

WC | Restaurant | Snack bar | Telephone

Accessibility Rating

♿ 2   🚹 3

P ✔ 🚻 ✔ 🍴 ✔

Most of Mt. Hermon, including the summit, is situated in Syria and Lebanon. Only the southern section of the mountain range, with the Shlagim [Snow] observation point at its peak (alt. 2,224 m), is within Israeli-controlled territory. Almost the entire Israeli area, excluding the ski resort, but taking in Mt. Shaked and Mt. Habushit, is a nature reserve. Due to security considerations, important areas of this reserve are military zones, closed to the public.

The Hermon Nature Reserve comprises three main mountain ridges that run from the north-east to the south-west and are separated by gorges: the eastern ridge is Ketef (=flank) Hermon running from the Shlagim (Snow) Observation Point in the direction of Neveh Ativ. Nahal Ar'ar and the Man Valley separate it from the Shirion spur. Nahal Si'on divides the Shirion spur from the Ketef Si'on flank. Nahal Guvta separates Mt. Hermon from the rest of the Golan Heights. Despite their proximity, the Hermon and the Golan have markedly different geological compositions.

The Hermon is familiar to the public principally by virtue of its snow-capped peak, which dominates the Hula Valley and most of the Upper Galilee. For several months of the year, snow falls on the mountain at altitudes beyond 1,000 m and at the higher altitudes remains for several months. Wind and sun precipitate the melting of the snow. The wind turns the snow

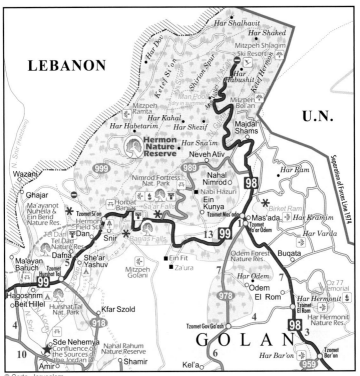

© Carta, Jerusalem

Mt. Hermon — snow-covered Man Valley.

into slush along the length of the valleys where it slowly melts and is absorbed into the ribbed and multi-furrowed mountain. The water emerges from springs at the bottom of the mountain forming the Hermon, Dan and Snir streams. The Jordan River begins at the confluence of these three streams.

VEGETATION

With the melting of the snow, the flora of the mountain comes to life. There is a sparse selection of conifers, mainly species of juniper which maintain their greenness under the snow. Most of the mountain's trees are deciduous, consisting of species of oak and trees from the *rosaceae* family: pear, plum and crab-apple; they leaf and blossom following the spring thaw. At the same time, bushes and dwarf-shrubs renew their growth. Along the margins of the melting snow emerge weeds and geophytes. As the snow melts, beginning in the lower areas and continuing up the slopes, vegetation takes root. The Hermon is the only place

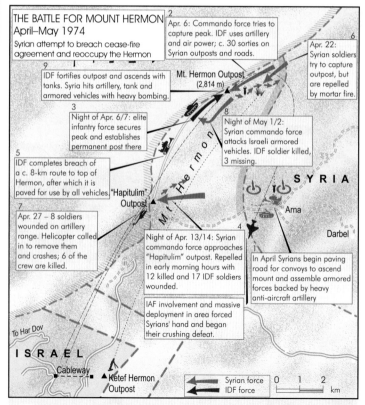

THE BATTLE FOR MOUNT HERMON
April–May 1974
Syrian attempt to breach cease-fire agreement and reoccupy the Hermon

2
Apr. 6: Commando force tries to capture peak. IDF uses artillery and air power; c. 30 sorties on Syrian outposts and roads.

6
Apr. 22: Syrian soldiers try to capture outpost, but are repelled by mortar fire.

9
IDF fortifies outpost and ascends with tanks. Syria hits artillery, tank and armored vehicles with heavy bombing.

Mt. Hermon Outpost
(2,814 m)

3
Night of Apr. 6/7: elite infantry force secures peak and establishes permanent post there

8
Night of May 1/2: Syrian commando force attacks Israeli armored vehicles. IDF soldier killed, 3 missing.

5
IDF completes breach of a c. 8-km route to top of Hermon, after which it is paved for use by all vehicles.

"Hapitulim" Outpost

Mt. Hermon

S Y R I A

Arna

Darbel

7
Apr. 27 – 8 soldiers wounded on artillery range. Helicopter called in to remove them and crashes; 6 of the crew are killed.

4
Night of Apr. 13/14: Syrian commando force approaches "Hapitulim" outpost. Repelled in early morning hours with 12 killed and 17 IDF soldiers wounded.

1
In April Syrians begin paving road for convoys to ascend mount and assemble armored forces backed by heavy anti-aircraft artillery

IAF involvement and massive deployment in area forced Syrians' hand and began their crushing defeat.

To Har Dov

I S R A E L

Cableway
Ketef Hermon Outpost

Syrian force
IDF force

0   1   2
km

Area conquered by IDF in Yom Kippur War   Road breached to Mt. Hermon outpost in the country in which 4 zones of vegetation exist, changing gradually as one goes up the mountain. Many of the plants are also known from other areas of the country: for example, sections of the mountain below the snow line have vegetation similar to that found in the Galilee hill range. However, most vegetation above the snow line is unique to the Hermon. Space does not permit a full enumeration, but worth noting are species of tulips, the Lebanese Foxtail lily (*Eremurusnlibanoticus*), the Blue Desert lily (*Ixiolirion tataricum*), and the Mesopotamian iris (*Iris mesopatamica*). The higher one climbs the mountain in the spring and summer, the lower, it seems, one retreats in the seasons of the year; in August, the mountain's upper heights look like its lower slopes in April, blossoming and colorful. In the 1,500 to 2,000 m range, a unique pattern of vegetation may be found, namely, thorny pillows in the shape of halved balls known as *tragacantic* vegetation, a hardy plant that can withstand the snow. At altitudes above 2,000 m vegetation struggles for existence and at the summit the ground is almost barren.

FAUNA

In the fauna world, there are species unique to the Hermon. The yellow squirrel (*Sciurus anomalus*), now extinct in the

Young Hermon viper.

Cherry blossom.

thickets of the Galilee, may still be found here, as well as other mammals such as wild boar in the valleys, hares, hyrax, and tiny rodents. There are bird species such as the rock nuthatch (*Sitta neumayer*) and the horned lark (*Ermophila alpestris*), snakes such as the Hermon viper, and various insects. Poaching has harmed animal life and overgrazing, mainly of goats, has damaged the living environment, especially the trees and shrubs.

STRUCTURAL FEATURES AND HISTORICAL REMAINS

Most of the mountain is rocky, built of chalk from the Jurassic age and is not suitable for human settlement, although there are settlement remains and cultic sites such as Mt. Habetarim.

Mount Habetarim and the Abrahamic Covenant (Genesis 15:7–18)

The mountain reaches an altitude of 1,296 m. On the southern slope, which descends to the Si'on stream, there is a holy site that the Arabs call "Makam Ibrahim el Khalil" (the holy site of Abraham the Friend). According to tradition, this is the place where God made a covenant with Abraham (Genesis 15:18). A domed structure beside a water reservoir may be found here among the ancient oak trees.

OUTSIDE THE NATURE RESERVE

The Ski Resort

The ski resort is outside the nature reserve. It reaches an altitude of 2,000 m. The site has nine cable systems providing tows and

Mt. Hermon, looking southeast.

Ski resort on Mt. Hermon.

lifts for a variety of slopes that respond to the skills of skiers at all levels of the sport. Skiing and related snow activities take place only during the winter.

THE SETTLEMENTS ON THE SLOPES OF THE HERMON

Three Druze villages are on the south-east side of Mt. Hermon: Majdal Shams, Mas'ada, and Ein Kunya. To the south is the Jewish settlement of Neveh Ativ which operates the Hermon ski resort.

Majdal Shams

This village is situated on the southeast slopes of Mt. Hermon at an altitude of 1,150 m above sea level. The name Majdal Shams means "tower of the rising sun," and implies that in gratitude to its elevation, the rays of the sun arrive early. It was annexed to Israel in the context of the Knesset's Golan Law (14 December 1981). The northern part of the village is built upon the ruins of a settlement dating from 2nd to 3rd century CE. On this site may be found the foundation and remains of ancient structures, as well as burial caves which the local population refers to as "tombs of the Jews." At the village center is a statue of the Sultan Pasha al-Atrash, leader of the Druze uprising against the French in 1915.

Mas'ada

Mas'ada is a Druze village situated at an important road juncture called the Masa'da intersection. From here, roads lead in different directions to Quneitra, Banias, Majdal Shams

Hermon tulip.

(West). East of the village is the Ram Pool and beside it a restaurant and observation point which overlooks the Sa'ar spring and the Hermon slopes to the north, as well as the Odem forest to the south.

Ein Kunya

This Druze village is 3 km northwest of the Mas'ada intersection. Within the village there is a special tomb attributed to the sister of Nebi Shu'eib (Jethro, father-in-law of Moses). Within the borders of the village, there is also an ancient archaeological mound [tel] which was inhabited during the Canaanite period and much later during the Talmudic period. A new bridge replacing the one destroyed by the Syrians in the Six-Day War (June 1967) has been constructed on the bank of the ravine to the south of the village. It has been named "The Bridge of Friendship" to signify the amity between Israelis and the Druze.

Neveh Ativ

A collective settlement 8 km east of the Banias springs, named after 4 soldiers from the Egoz Patrol who fell on the Golan Heights during the Six-Day War. The letters in "Ativ" are taken from the first initials of the soldiers' names: Abraham, Tuvia, Yair, and Benjamin. The village was founded in 1969 within the jurisdiction of the

Druze on the Golan Heights.

Syrian village of Jubata ez Zayit whose inhabitants fled during the Six-Day War. At the time it was given the name Ramat Hashalom (Peace Heights). Initial attempts at Jewish settlement failed and in its place Neveh Ativ was established in 1971. The residents of Neveh Ativ operate the Mt. Hermon ski site. The village also has many guest rooms.

Mt. Hermon, looking east.

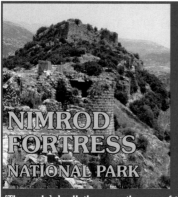

Location: access from Route 989 that branches to the NE from Route 99 (Kiryat Shmona–Mas'ada Junction), near Sa'ar Falls

Best season: year-round
Length of visit: 2 hours
Tel.: 04-6949277
Entrance fee

[The eagle] dwelleth...upon the crag of the rock, and the strong place (Job 39:28)

 Muslim site
 Antiquities
 Lookout point

Accessibility Rating

 Snack bar
 WC

At the foothills of the Hermon, perched on top of a steep rise which is clearly separated from the surrounding environment, are the remains of a fortress built towards the beginning of the 12th century CE. The fortress is known by several names: Metzudat (= fortress) Nimrod in Hebrew and Qal'at Nimrud in Arabic. Nimrod is mentioned in the Book of Genesis (10: 8) as "a mighty hunter before the Lord" and his legendary exploits have roots in an anterior Mesopotamian tradition. Among other things, this fortress is attributed to him, ignoring the large time gaps between the supposed dates of his life and the dates which archaeologists ascribe to the foundations of the fortress. In the Muslim tradition, superhuman exploits are also attributed to Nimrod. The fortress has two additional names: Qal'at es Subeiba in Arabic, corrupted to Asbiba in the Crusader literature; Qal'at Banias after the nearby stream and falls.

HISTORY

Who built this fortress, and when? The area was witness to many clashes between the Crusaders and the Muslims with the fortress changing hands a number of times. It is situated on the frontier between the Crusader Kingdom of Jerusalem and the Golan Heights. The mixed architectural styles are evidence of its changing hands several

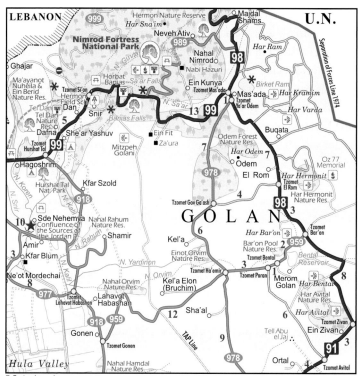

© Carta, Jerusalem

Rush broom.

Black-seeded centaury.

times. Recent excavations have revealed that it was initially built by the Crusaders in about 1129. After several failed attempts, the Muslims captured the stronghold on 18 October 1164. For the next hundred years, the Muslims reinforced the position and prevented the Crusaders from retaking it. In 1260, with most of the country under Mameluke domination, most of the Crusader fortresses were destroyed in order to prevent any attempts at recapture. The Nimrod citadel, however, was abandoned until the present, when the Israel Nature and National Parks Protection Authority undertook partial renovations.

THE FORTRESS

The site chosen for the fortress is an isolated incline with a sharply delineated and narrow head. The fortress itself is long and narrow with strongly-constructed citadels at either end. The southern wing, which overlooks the route from the Golan to west of the Jordan River, is extensively fortified, consisting of a strong wall and watchtowers. In the west, beside today's main entrance, is the first citadel, built by the Crusaders. In the northeast, at its highest point, there is a large citadel which was built by the Muslims. Various sections of the structure exhibit all the contemporary characteristics of a fortress: living quarters, various service rooms, slit-wall firing positions, and so forth. The principal purpose of the fortress was military oversight of the entire area of the Hula Valley to the west. Even today, in its role as a tourist site, the visitor is impressed by the panoramic view it provides.

Nimrod Fortress — general view.

Nimrod Fortress — view of the remains.

THE WALKING TRAIL

1. The Northwest Tower

The tower has an impressive gate which bears an inscription in Arabic of the Ayyubid ruler el-Aziz Uthman from 1230. The "terrace" in front of the gate is part of a room renovated by the Sultan (ruler) Bilikh. He also restored the tower and added two floors to it. Through an opening on the ground floor, there is access to a cistern and above it a shaft reaching a height of more than 7 m through which water reached the upper floor. In 1759 an earthquake destroyed large sections of the structure.

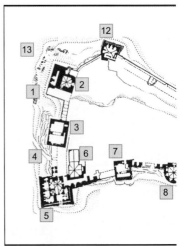

© Carta, Jerusalem

2. The Baybars Inscription

El Malik ez Zahir Baybars (1260–1277) was a Mameluke ruler who conquered the country in 1275. The inscription lavishes praise on the Mameluke sultan. It was apparently written on the front of the second story, the apparent residence of Baybars' lieutenant, who was in charge of the renovation operations.

3. The Western Tower

This tower has not yet been excavated.

Members of the Israel Nature Society gather at Nimrod Fortress.

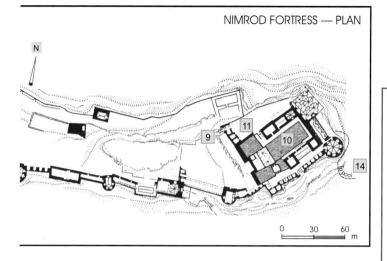

NIMROD FORTRESS — PLAN

1. NW tower	6. Large reservoir	11. Lookout from top of
2. Baybars inscription	7. Trough	dungeon
3. W tower	8. "Beautiful Tower"	12. N tower (prison tower)
4. (service corridor)	9. Moat	13. Hidden passage
5. SW tower	10. Dungeon (keep)	14. Pool

4. The Service Corridor

A modern path which passes through a breach in the wall and leads to the fortress.

5. The Southwest Tower

This tower affords a view of the Galilee, the Hula Valley and the slopes of the Golan. Steps lead to an inner chamber which was the original tower. Evidence for this comes from the embrasures interspersed on the exterior wall. Baybars enlarged the tower and added embrasures.

6. Large Water Reservoir

The reservoir is 24 × 9 m wide and 7 m high. A system of canals channeled rainwater into it but it has been destroyed. The reservoir

may be seen from a later breach in the southern wall.

7. Trough

On the eastern side of the reservoir is a trough, a facility for drinking water. In 1240, Fakhr ed Din Hassan restored the trough and placed an inscription above it.

8. The "Beautiful Tower"

Built by Baybars, this tower juts out from the wall in a sort of semicircle. Originally, the interior was octagonal, but now it consists of seven sides. The construction is of exceptional quality.

9. The Moat

The moat separates the fortress

from its dungeon. Today, one can cross the moat in its western sector where it is filled in; in the past there was a wooden bridge. At the edge of the moat by the southwest corner of the dungeon may be found the most ancient inscription on the grounds of the fortress dating from the ruler el-Aziz Uthman (1228).

10. The Dungeon (Keep)

A vast, strongly fortified area which overlooks the fortress. Soldiers retreated to this area when the lower defensive system was overrun. The entrance gate is located in the northwest corner. Square towers were built on the four corners of the structure.

11. The Observation Point from the Top of the Dungeon

This observation point offers a view of the Hermon, the Golan, the Galilee, and the Hula Valley.

12. The Northern Tower (Prison Tower)

It appears that this structure was also built by Baybars. The tower is well-preserved and consists of a central chamber and stairs that lead to the roof. From the top of the tower one can see Mt. Hermon and Mt. Dov. In the 15th century it apparently was used as a prison.

13. Hidden Passage

In the "terrace" corner within the northwest tower (1) there is a graduated hidden passageway leading north. It is 27 m long by 1.8 m wide and has a high-vaulted ceiling. On the ceiling, one can detect a row of stones that have been shunted aside

Nimrod Fortress and the Hermon.

from their original position by an earthquake. The passage ends in a hidden aperture located at the bottom of the exterior wall of the northern city wall that is concealed on the outside by a pile of rocks.

14. The Pool

A trail for experienced hikers leads from the fortress to the pool. It measures 26 m × 54 m and reaches a depth of at least 5 m. It was designed to collect rainwater for the inhabitants of the fortress and may also have been used for agriculture.

OUTSIDE THE NATIONAL PARK BOUNDARIES

Hiking Trail: Nahal Hazur and Nahal Guvta

An intermediate-level hiking trail which begins at the road ascending from the Banias to the Nimrod Fortress and continues to Neveh Ativ. The path begins at the parking lot beside the statue of the sheikh holy to the Druze, Uthman el-Hazuri. The blue-marked path follows Nahal Hazur (see the map containing path markers for the Golan, Hermon and Upper Galilee). The blue-marked path ends at the Nimrod Fortress and a black-marked path leads on through Nahal Guvta to the sources of the Banias. In years with heavy rainfall, the streambed is filled with water and passage requires long leaps from boulder to boulder.

Nahal Nimrod

It is located close to the national park. At the settlement, there is a dairy specializing in cheeses, a restaurant, and guest rooms.

Rock lizard.

Location: on Route 99 (Kiryat Shmona–Mas'ada), E of Kibbutz Snir

Best season: year-round

Length of visit: ½–2 hours

Tel.: 04-6902577

Fax: 04-6904066

Entrance fee (combined ticket may be purchased for Nahal Hermon/Nimrod Fortress)

...on this side Jordan, from the river Arnon unto mount Hermon. (Deut 3:8)

Christian site	Outdoor recreation	Antiquities	Lookout point	Picnic site

Accessibility Rating

WC	Snack bar	Restaurant	Souvenir shop

Nahal Hermon is the most eastern of three water sources for the Jordan River. Its volume is smaller than the other streams but it is noteworthy for several unique environmental features. The derivation of its waters are entirely from the run-off of melting snow on the Hermon; the mountain acts as a gigantic sponge, absorbing the melting snow on the slopes and discharging it from springs at its base. Nahal Hermon emerges from beneath a large cave. There are grounds for assuming that in prehistoric times the stream gushed forth from inside the cave itself until an earthquake changed its course. In ancient times the place was holy—for the Canaanites it was a place of worship to the god Baal-gad, and during the Hellenistic period to the shepherd god, Pan.

The Nahal Hermon reserve, which includes the stream and its banks up to the head of the channel, continues with the stream until it exits on the plain north of Kibbutz Sde Nehemya. At this juncture it meets Nahal Dan, and within a kilometer, Nahal Snir, to form the head of the Jordan River. However, two kilometers downstream, beside Kibbutz Kfar Blum, the river splits into two channels that only rejoin below the Hula conservation area.

The volume of water collected by Nahal Hermon is not great: it reaches full strength in winter and spring and diminishes

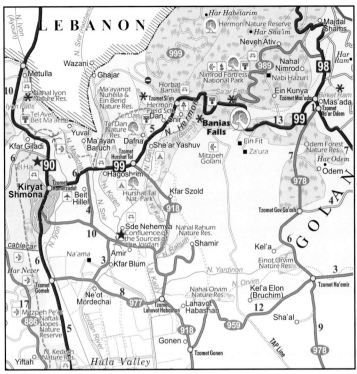

© Carta, Jerusalem

considerably in the summer and in years of drought. Nevertheless, the stream with all its strong current, waterfalls, cliffs, and trees constitutes an important component in what has been coined "a land of many streams" in the area north of the Hula.

HIKING IN THE RESERVE

Hiking Trail No. 1
(see map on p. 37)

From the main parking lot at the entrance to the Banias reserve ascend the wide steps to the cave of Pan. On the wall, beside the cave, there are carved niches into which were placed statues of the god Pan. A city was built here beside the water source by Philip, son of Herod the Great, and was called Caesarea Philippi, but over the years this name fell into disuse and it was called by its earlier name of Panias after the god, Pan. (In Arabic, there is no 'p', hence it is pronounced 'Banias'.) Josephus states that an underground aqueduct linked the source of the stream to the Ram Pool, which was the true source of the Jordan River. He recounts that straw was thrown into the Ram Pool and that it came out in the Banias cave. This location is also regarded as a holy site

Cave of the god Pan and carved niches.

in Islam: at the top of the cliff is a grave holy to Muslims—Nabi Khadr.

The cave with niches on its sides, the crystal-clear water that flows from beneath the mountain, the surrounding trees —all this makes for a pastoral environment. Close by are the ruins of the ancient settlement of Panias, which has been partially excavated.

Route 99, which ascends from the Galilee to the Golan Heights, traverses the streambed below the spring. This was the former Tyre–Damascus route. Following the demand of the French at the time that borders were determined between the French and British Mandates after WW I, it remained within the French Lebanese zone, along with the source of the Hermon. On the other side of the road, water enters the riverbed created from the meeting of the two streams descending from the Golan: Nahal Guvta and Nahal Sa'ar. Both are dry during the summer, but water flows in the winter and spring; the Sa'ar waterfall is one of the most impressive in the Golan.

Hiking Trail No. 2

South of Route 99, Nahal Hermon continues in a south-westerly direction. Its path cuts the Banias in its western section and reaches the Officers' Pool (Breichat Haketzinim). This is a concrete-reinforced pool whose spring-fed waters are warmer

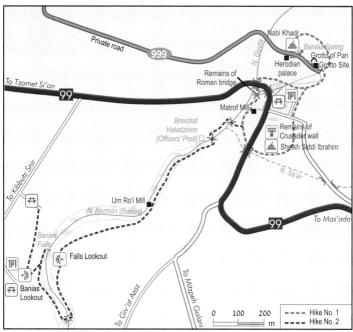

© Carta, Jerusalem

than the waters of the Banias, and that is the reason it served the Syrian army officers stationed in the area prior to the Six-Day War—hence its name. Today, it is used as a fish hatchery.

Nahal Hermon continues through a narrow fissure. In this section there is an impressive view of cliffs and gushing water accompanied by an abundance of trees and plant life. North of

Nahal Hermon, near the waterfall.

here, situated on a small table of land named "Banias plateau," is Kibbutz Snir and the field school of the Israel Nature Society. This area was designated as part of the British Mandate in Palestine but was occupied by the Syrians. Even though it was officially declared an Israeli demilitarized zone after 1948, it was held by the Syrians until the Six-Day War (1967).

Opposite Kibbutz Snir, Nahal Far'a plunges into a fissure which has a beautiful waterfall during the rainy winter and spring season. However, the waterfall in this area is the Banias, situated to the north of it. A special path leads to it, also from route 99. The waterfall is not high—no more than 10 meters—but it is strong, noisy and foamy. At the top of the falls an Oriental plane tree, growing from a rock, divides the current into two separate streams. The falls are surrounded by large trees. Arriving here one feels as if he has entered a savage and primordial setting.

OUTSIDE THE NATURE RESERVE AREA

The Odem Forest Nature Reserve

Over human history, the Golan was settled intermittently and sometimes hundreds of years passed without human habita-

tion. During such periods, the Golan was pasture land in which nomads wandered with their flocks without setting up permanent occupancy. This itinerant lifestyle probably spared many of the trees on the Golan and as a result one finds not only isolated trees but sections of forest. One of these is the Odem Forest.

The Odem Forest extends over several thousand acres west of route 98 between Kibbutz El Rom and the Druze village of Mas'ada. It is characterized by a dense concentration of Kermes oak (*Quercus calliprinos*) with a scattering of terebinth (or Atlantic pistachio). This particular wooded area is constantly reinvigorated and always green; many of its trees are well-defined without producing thickets. In

Grotto of Pan.

the spring, the forest floor bursts into blossom. The most notable displays emanate from the Greek cyclamen, a flower which is considered rare in other places, and various kinds of orchids. Access is quite easy since route 98 passes alongside the Reserve, and route 978 from Mas'ada to the Gov–Ga'ash and Ha'emir junctions cuts through the middle of it.

One element that sets this Reserve aside from others is the scattered presence of large pits. These are karst formations which descend deep into the earth.

The Ayalim [deer] Forest is situated close to the Odem settlement. It has a concentration of wild animals and there are activities for visitors.

Birket Ram (Ram Pool)

Birket Ram is a natural water formation which measures 600 × 900 meters, reaches a depth of 6 to 10 meters, and holds about 3 million cubic meters of water. The pool has the appearance of a crater and is at an elevation of 940 meters. It contains sweet water fed by underground springs and rain. Geologists believe that the pool was formed by volcanic activity in which the peak of the mountain blew off leaving a crater.

Waterfall in Nahal Far'a.

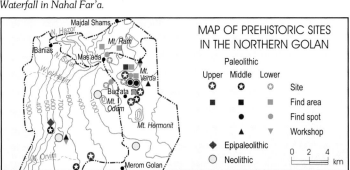

MAP OF PREHISTORIC SITES IN THE NORTHERN GOLAN

© Carta, Jerusalem

Location: bounded on the E by Rte. 808; W—Rte. 888; N—Rte. 9088 (the Katzrin road); S—Rte. 869

Best season: Spring through Fall

Length of visit: 2 hrs to a day

**Tel.: 04-6962817
04-6963043**

Information office at car-park

Entrance fee (includes parking)

...and Golan in Bashan out of the tribe of Manasseh. (Josh 20:8)

 Hiking trail Outdoor recreation Lookout point Picnic site

Yehudiya Parking Lot Accessibility Rating
(reserve's nature trails unsuitable for handicapped)

 3 3  ✔ ✔ ✔

 Snack bar Telephone WC Camping

 2 3 ✔ ✗

The Yehudiya Forest is the largest nature reserve on the Golan and the most multifaceted because of the elements which comprise it. Its main botanical feature is the oak forest which grows on the plateaus and slopes in the central sector of the Golan. The Tabor oak forest, of which the nature reserve is part, once extended over large areas of both banks of the Jordan River: in the west it continued from the Hermon foothills through the eastern section of the Upper Galilee and into the Lower Galilee, the western part of the Lower Galilee and onto the coastal plain up to the Yarkon River. Throughout this vast area there are extensive remains in the form of small wooded areas such as Hurshat Tal (the Tal Grove) and clumps of trees. To the east of the Jordan it spread over parts of the Golan and onto the Gilead mountain range. The Yehudiya Forest, as mentioned, is part of this forest complex.

The Tabor oak forest is of the type called "park forest" and is different from the groves of Kermes Oak (*Quercus calliprinos*) and the Terebinth (*Pistacia palaestina*). The latter type is a thicket grove, in which trees touch each other, sometimes becoming entangled, while bushes climb around them, turning the grove into a thicket, and thus often making it impassable. In a park forest, the trees stand as individual entities, each with its own trunk, and

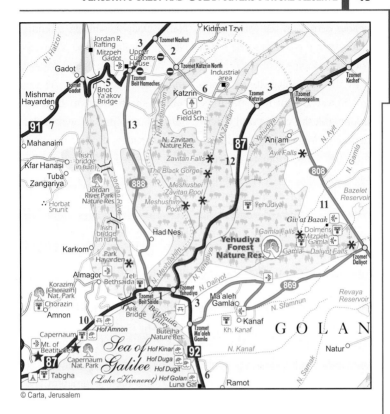

© Carta, Jerusalem

space between them for large animal and human passage. The Tabor oak is a deciduous tree native to the Mediterranean area, more adaptable than the Kermes Oak to the moderate temperatures and extended seasons without rainfall. The tree is resilient when cut or toppled by natural causes and will often renew itself even when cut off at the base of its trunk; it is also well-protected when enveloped by forest fires. Fires caused through human carelessness or natural causes burn the leaves and treetops but the trunk and branches, covered in a tough bark which is not flammable, often renews its foliage after the fire.

Because the forest is bereft of leaves in the winter months, the ground is exposed to the direct rays of the sun and this generates the growth of herbaceous plants and related shrubs which produce a colorful floral display. Among them are anemones and the rare Golan iris. In the spring, the oak leaves appear in an invigorating green and become darker as summer approaches. The weeds wither providing a yellow carpet on the forest floor. Thus, with the seasons, the forest is ever-changing.

In the Yehudiya forest many trees grow out of rock mounds. In general, the young and tender acorns falling to the ground from the oak trees have difficulty overcoming the surrounding vegetation, but in this area the rock mounds provide cover and protection for them.

The central bloc of this forest covers an area reaching an elevation of 400 m northeast of the Sea of Galilee. As the Yehudiya Reserve also includes a good part of the rivers or streams originating in the Golan, it sends extensions beyond the central bloc—each one includes a part of the Nahal channel. The main Nahals in this nature reserve are:

Golan iris.

Nahal Daliyot, with its tributary, Nahal Gamla; Nahal Yehudiya with its tributaries; Nahal Zavitan; and Nahal Meshushim. All four Nahals share much in common but each also has its own distinct characteristics. Route no. 808, aptly named "the waterfalls route," traverses the eastern side of the nature reserve. On the western side, gorges twist and turn in descent, creating a series of waterfalls. The most prominent among them in the reserve are Daliyot Falls; Gamla Falls, which is the highest in the Golan; Ayit Falls, which is also called Ani'am; and Zavitan Falls. In almost all the gorges there are canyons, of which the most prominent may be seen in Nahal Yehudiya and Nahal Zavitan. The well-known Meshushim Pool (Hexagonal Pool) is in Nahal Meshushim. It was formed from a prehistoric volcanic crater, whose center solidified in prismatic shapes of large and upright basalt rock. Later, it was carved out by the Nahal, which exposed the hexagonal prisms and created a pool within the crater.

Within the nature reserve are many residues of human activity. There are a number of large dolmens—tombs in the shape of a table, from prehistoric times (two large basalt stones and a third stone placed on top of them).

In the period of the Mishna and the Talmud (c. 200 BCE–300 CE), a flourishing Jewish town existed here, evidence for which are the remains of several synagogues and the ruins of the city of Gamla (see Gamla, p. 48). In addition, there are the remains of several Arab villages which were inhabited until the Six-Day War.

The town of Katzrin, as well as several Jewish villages, is located at the fringe of the reserve.

Route no. 87 cuts through the middle of the Reserve. There are several access routes to the Nature Reserve. The main starting point is the Yehudiya parking lot, at the center of the Reserve on route 87.

Meshushim Pool.

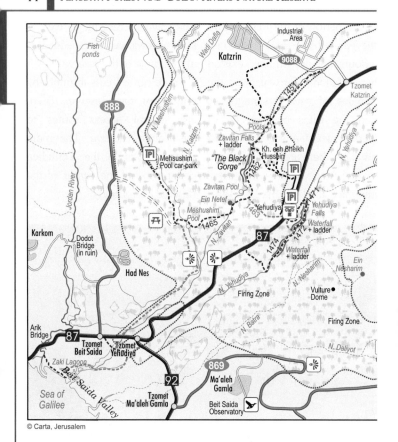

© Carta, Jerusalem

HIKING TRAILS IN THE NATURE RESERVE

Gamla

See the Gamla Nature Reserve on p. 48.

Upper and Lower Nahal Yehudiya

Both trails are circular, for good hikers who also know how to swim. Both begin at the Yehudiya parking lot on route 87 (Yehudiya–Katzrin junctions).

The Upper Trail. The red trail (1471) passes by the abandoned Syrian village of Yehudiya, turns northeast above the bank of Nahal Yehudiya, and then descends in a sloping path to the pool at the bottom of the Yehudiya Falls. It then continues along the riverbed beside the stream. In order to traverse the second waterfall, the hiker must descend a 9-m metal ladder and swim across a deep-water pool. Where the path splits into two, take the green trail to the right which returns to the Yehudiya reserve parking lot.

The Lower Trail. This hike also begins on the red-marked

trail (1471) from the Yehudiya reserve parking lot but the hiker turns right before the abandoned Arab village of Yehudiya and descends to the streambed on the green-marked trail (1474). At the bottom of the canyon, one encounters a red-marked trail (1472). Turn right and descend the length of the slope of the Nahal. This hike also requires a ladder descent of 5 meters and a swim across a pool. The red-marked trail leads back to route 87. Turn right at this road and return to the parking lot.

Gamla Falls.

Nahal Zavitan

The hiking trails in Nahal Zavitan are graded moderate and difficult.

Upper Nahal Zavitan. This trail begins on the Katzrin road before the Katzrin junction (9088). A red-marked path (1451) descends the Nahal slope in a southwesterly direction passing by some beautiful, large and deep pools surrounded by basalt pillars. This path leads to a vantage-point overlooking Zavitan waterfall (the Copper falls), which reaches a height of about 28 m. From this vantage-point, one can descend to the waterfall and the pool below it via a sloping, blue-marked path. The path returns via the ruins of the Khirbet esh Sheikh Hussein village, and from there by a paved road to route 87 (Yehudiya–Katzrin junctions).

Lower Nahal Zavitan. This trail, for skilled hikers, starts at the Yehudiya nature reserve parking lot. A green-marked trail (1463) leads to the Nahal Zavitan riverbed. Arriving at the red-marked road (1462) turn right, and after about a 15-minute walk, turn left and continue up to the black-marked trail. Continue here along the Nahal Zavitan bed and after a few hundred meters turn right and ascend on the red-marked path, which leads

Daliyot Falls.

to the Meshushim pool. Before ascending the red-marked path, it is recommended to continue another 10 minutes along the present trail to the Ein Nataf springs.

The Meshushim Pool

It is also possible to reach this pool by motor vehicle from a road that links into route 888 ascending from the Beit Saida junction. At the end of the road there is a shaded parking lot. The red-marked trail leads directly to the Meshushim (Hexagon) pool. The hike, of moderate difficulty, takes about one-and-a-half hours.

The walls of the pool are built of basalt pillars in the geometric shape of a hexagon created through a cooling of the lava flow. Volcanic eruptions were the origin of the lava flow.

Nahal Daliyot

A red-marked trail suitable for family hikes. The trail begins at a eucalyptus grove close to the Daliyot junction and ends at the Gamla parking lot. Length of hike: about 2 hours.

Yehudiya Forest.

**GAMLA
NATURE RESERVE**

**Location: from Route 808 (Hamapalim–Magshimim junctions), c. 2 km N of Daliyot Junction, going W.
Best season: year-round; Daliyot trail recommended only in Spring.
Recommended hours— morning or afternoon.
Length of visit: 2 hours
Tel.: 04-6822282
Entrance fee**

For from the top of the rocks I see him, and from the hills I behold him... (Num 23:9)

Jewish site	Christian site	Antiquities	Lookout point	Picnic site

Snack bar	Souvenir shop	WC

Accessibility Rating

The Gamla nature reserve is part of the Yehudiya forest, but constitutes a separate entity. The city of Gamla put up stiff resistance and was finally captured by the Romans in the great Jewish revolt in 67 CE. A detailed description of the city, the siege and its bitter end is given by Flavius Josephus but years of archaeological searching failed to locate it among the many sites found on the Golan Heights. After the 1967 Six-Day War, the Israeli archaeologist, Yitzhaki Gal, suggested that the ancient Gamla site was on a spur beside the ruins of Deir Qeruh. Shmaryahu Gutman supported this idea on the basis of his fifteen years of seasonal excavations.

HISTORY

Following the construction or capture of the city of Gamla by Alexander Jannaeus in 81 BCE, it grew and was fortified in its distinctive location on a narrow spur between Nahal Gamla and Nahal Daliyot. Its conquest by the Romans in 67 CE was a difficult undertaking because of its naturally fortified position. The city was finally captured amidst extensive carnage. According to Josephus' eyewitness account of the battle, 4,000 defenders were killed and another 5,000 leapt to their deaths in the gorge below. Nevertheless, it would be unjustified to refer to call Gamla "the Masada of the Golan," because it was a living

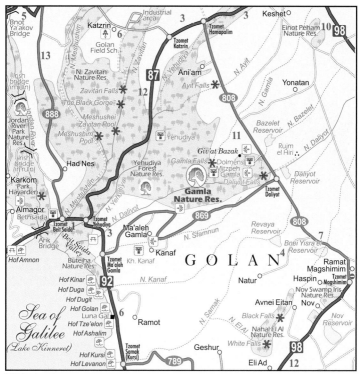

© Carta, Jerusalem

city and not an isolated fortress like Masada.

Since its destruction, it has not been rebuilt and it has disappeared from the visible landscape.

ARCHAEOLOGICAL EXCAVATIONS

The excavations began in the right location, in the eastern wall of the city, and immediately brought impressive results: part of the city's wall was exposed, as well as a lavish structure, the community's synagogue; Roman ballista stones and arrowheads give evidence for Josephus' battle account. Continued excavation unearthed houses and streets providing further confirmation of a thriving city. Over 6,000 coins were found dating from the Hasmonean dynasty to the time of the city's destruction. Among those whose busts appear on the coins are John Hyrcanus, the high priest and head of the Jewish commonwealth; Judah Aristobulus, and Alexander Jannaeus (Jonathan). Two coins from Gamla's last year of existence have the inscription "for the salvation of holy Jerusalem."

Hoard of silver shekels discovered near the entrance to the olive press at Gamla.

SITES TO VISIT AT GAMLA

The Ancient Synagogue

This is one of the earliest synagogues in the country. It served the Jewish community before the destruction of the Second Temple in 70 CE. It is in the shape of a rectangle, 16 m × 20 m, and its back wall was part of the city's wall.

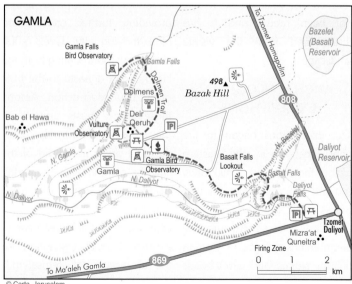

© Carta, Jerusalem

Deir Qeruh

Situated north of Gamla on the northern bank of Nahal Daliyot, this site was built in the Byzantine period during the fourth century CE. A church and a monastery dedicated to Saint Gregory were built here. Remains of these structures from the sixth century are present, as well as installations such as an olive press.

Dolmens

The dolmens are ancient remains of tombs which date from the beginning of the middle Canaanite period. They have the shape of a table, hence their name, which derives from the Celtic language and has become an international loanword for this funereal structure. The dolmen is built from two or more upright stones with a large stone slab capped horizontally on top of them. Approximately 700 dolmen formations have been found in the Gamla area alone.

Gamla Falls

The falls are situated after a vulture observation post on the northern bank of Nahal Gamla. The marked path leads to an observation point from which there is a view of the falls. At 51 meters, the Gamla Falls is the highest in Israel. From this point, Nahal Gamla forms a deep canyon, with steep, clifflike banks.

TYPES OF BIRD-LIFE

The canyon of Nahal Gamla serves as a home for wildlife

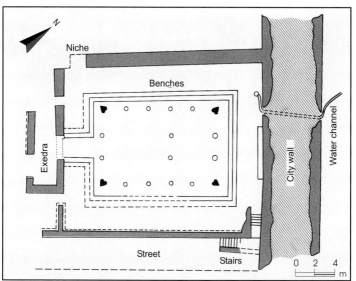

Plan of the synagogue at Gamla.

© Carta, Jerusalem

and a nesting ground for various birds of prey, mainly vultures. The birds lay their eggs in the rocky clefts and ledges of the canyon, locations inaccessible to humans or animal predators. To view these nests observation points are located at appropriate places along the trail. Flights of the vultures and nursing of their young are among the most impressive sights in the Gamla nature reserve.

Other birds of prey in the Gamla Reserve include:
• The Egyptian vulture (*Neophron percnopterus*), which nests and departs during the migration season;
• The short-toed eagle (*circaetus gallicus*) that nests in the summer;
• The long-legged buzzard (*buteo rufinus*) which is generally present all year round but can also depart in the migrating season.

FAUNA

There are numerous animals in the Gamla nature reserve. Many of them are well-camouflaged in their environment and difficult to see; others are only active at night. Among the animals present here are wild boar,

Olive press, from Khirbet Deir Qeruh.

Nahal Gamla.

turtles, porcupines, rats, hyrax, jackals, foxes, and wild cats.

OUTSIDE THE NATURE RESERVE TRAILS

The Nahal El Al Nature Reserve

Entrance to the reserve is from Moshav Neveh Eitan, which may be reached via route 98 between the Afik and Magshimim junctions. There is an observation point at the beginning of the trail which gives a view of the Galilee and the Golan settlements. The marked trail follows the length of Nahal El Al, passing Black Falls which plunges from a height of 8 meters to a pool below, and farther on bypasses White Falls which cascades from a height of 14 meters. Descend to the pool via a winding stair path. From the pool the trail continues south to the settlement of Eli Al.

Location: on Route 99 (Kiryat Shmona–Mas'ada), near Kibbutz Dafna.

Best season: year-round

Length of visit: 2 hours to a day

Tel.: 04-6951579

Entrance fee

HURSHAT TAL
NATIONAL PARK & NATURE RESERVE

As the dew of Hermon that descended from the mountains of Zion... (Ps 133:3)

 Camping   Outdoor recreation   Swimming   Showers   Picnic site

 Snack bar   Restaurant   Telephone   WC

Accessibility Rating

   2   3

   P ✔ ♦♦ ✔ 🍴 ✔ ≈ ✔

According to a Muslim legend, ten friends of the prophet Mohammed rode north until nightfall where they found themselves not far from Nahal Dan, one of the sources of the Jordan. They stuck their sticks into the ground in order to tie their horses to them. The sticks took root and grew into large trees which came to be known as "the Grove of the Ten." Today, the grove far exceeds the original ten trees of the legend. The Hebrew name is Hurshat Tal (The Dew Grove) which draws upon the biblical verse in Psalms 133:3: "As the dew of Hermon, that descended upon the mountains of Zion."

Part of the forest grove is under the auspices of the national parks authority and the remainder is a nature reserve.

The National Park is designated as a place for public enjoyment and recreation. Various rivulets, constituting branches of Nahal Dan, flow through the Park. Pools have been constructed, as well as various sport facilities. Grass has been planted and additional shrubbery and landscaping has been added to the native vegetation. On the grassy plots there is room for 150 tents. There are also 50 bungalows and guest rooms, as well as picnic sites.

PARK TREES

Most of the trees in the grove are Tabor oak (additional trees were

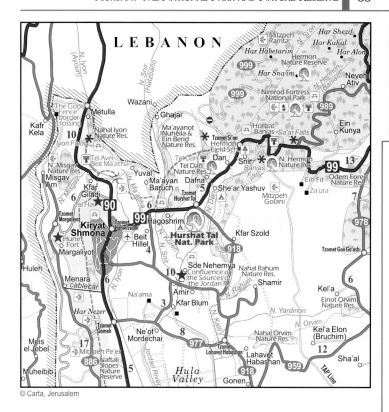

© Carta, Jerusalem

planted in the National Park, many not native to the country). These trees are hundreds of years old and they have been spared harm because they are regarded as sacred: popular belief holds that anyone who damages a sacred tree will be severely punished by heaven; a tragedy will befall him, or a member of his family, and he will not live out the year. This grove is one of the remaining woods from the large forest of Tabor oak that once populated a vast area of the country west of the Jordan. It ranged from the foot of the Hermon and traversed the eastern Upper Galilee, the central area of the Lower Galilee, the western part of the Jezreel Valley, the plains of Manasseh, the areas of *kurkar* (fossilized dune sandstone), and finally reaching the sands of the coastal plain up to the Yarkon River. Only several blocs have survived from this great forest, mainly the Solelim–Shfar'am bloc where there are sacred trees and other scattered trees. It is possible to determine the extent of this ancient forest on the basis of these arboreal remains. The

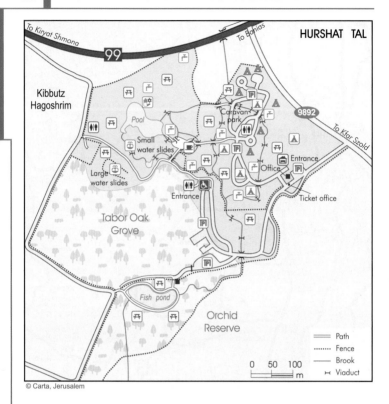

© Carta, Jerusalem

Tabor oak may also be found on the Golan Heights (the Yehudiya Forest) and in the Gilead region. Interspersed among the oak are Atlantic Terebrinth, a tree which is thinly distributed from the Hula Valley to the Negev highlands.

The Hebrew words for oak and terebrinth are *alon* and *ela*, respectively. The prefix "*el*" is "god" in Hebrew and thus points to the sacred associations of these two trees. Indeed, earlier language derivations for these words suggest that godlike qualities were ascribed to these trees. Their size and longevity undoubtedly contributed to ascriptions of holiness but an additional factor should be noted: dead branches fall from elderly trees. At the location where the branch joins the trunk, these species exhibit a self-renewing capacity of their tissue and the small area where the break occurs often appears in the observer's interpretation as the facial image of a man or monster. The phenomenon is quite impressive, and can leave a fearful imprint upon children. Thus, prehistoric man may also have seen spirits or deities emerging from the tree.

Management of the grove is

Oak trees in Hurshat Tal.

carried out on the basis of the park's needs. This area is not intended for recreation, and accordingly park policy allows the vegetation to pursue its natural course. The main tree species here, too, is the Tabor oak but there is a rich ground layer of vegetation, especially climbers, weeds, and flowery shrubs.

THE ORCHID RESERVE

Southeast of the fish pond there is an area surrounded by a cattle fence. In order to maintain its pristine nature, there are no walking paths through it. A rich variety of flowers blossom here in the winter and spring, the most noteworthy of which are several from the 32 known species of wild orchids in the country: for example, the Bug orchid (*Orchis coriophora*), the Punctate orchid (*Orchis punctulata*), and the *Orchis israelitica*, an indigenous species of orchid. The National Park and Nature Reserve constitute a sanctuary even in the Hula Valley, which is rich in water, vegetation and scenic terrain.

OUTSIDE THE PARK BOUNDARIES

Kayaking at Kfar Blum

Kayaking on the Jordan River and additional attractions such as bicycling routes and jeep tours, pony rides for children, a snappling park, archery range, an artificial mountain-climbing wall, and other nature recreation activities.

The Jordan River Promenade

This is a paved and floodlit promenade along the eastern

bank of the Jordan, between Kibbutz Kfar Blum and Kibbutz Amir.

The Nahal Orvim Nature Reserve

This Nahal is a winding canyon-shaped streambed, which flows westward from the area around Mt. Bental. The section from the gas pipeline to Lahavot Habashan has been declared a nature reserve. Access is from route 959 (Ha'emir junction to Gonen junction). During the winter months, there is a waterfall and water flows through the Nahal. Descent into the Nahal is from the north bank along a red-marked path. Birds of prey nest along the cliffs. Hikers may complete their walk at the lookout point where there is a view of the falls, or continue into the bed of the Nahal which has about 200 varieties of plant life.

Sde Nehemya

This kibbutz is on the northern edge of the Hula Valley. It has a park with an exhibit of reptiles and a rich display of animal life.

Cranes.

Eurasian Scops owl.

...and called Leshem, Dan, after the name of Dan their father. (Josh 19:47)

Jewish site | Antiquities | Lookout point | Outdoor recreation | Souvenir shop

Hiking trail | Picnic site | Snack bar | Telephone | WC

Accessibility Rating

♿ 3   🧍 3

P ✔   🚻 ✔

At Tel Dan only the short trail is accessible for individuals with disabilities.

Nahal Dan is the shortest water course among the three sources of the Jordan, but the one that contains the greatest volume. The biblical city of Dan, also referred to as Laish or Leshem in antiquity, is mentioned in the books of Joshua and Judges. In Arabic the spring is called Ein el-Dan ("spring of the Dan"), and the tel (archaeological mound) beside it is known as Tell el-Qadi ("the Judge's mound"). There are grounds for assuming that these names are preserved from earlier times.

Nahal Dan is situated in the heart of an area known as "the land of streams and rivers," and indeed, in the Nahal and along its margins, water and vegetation are present in abundance. The Nahal has a single principal source but it is also fed by dozens of smaller springs. Walking in this environment one has the feeling of springs emerging everywhere. All this water has its origin from the winter snows on Mt. Hermon. The snow melts slowly, seeps into the sponge-like earth of the mountain, and emerges in the foothills. The water flows quietly from the springs, but it continues down an ever-increasing slope, turning into a torrent and generating standing waves and foam. When the stream emerges from the nature reserve, it splits into several rivulets which rejoin when it encounters Nahal Hermon to form the Jordan River.

Walking through the reserve,

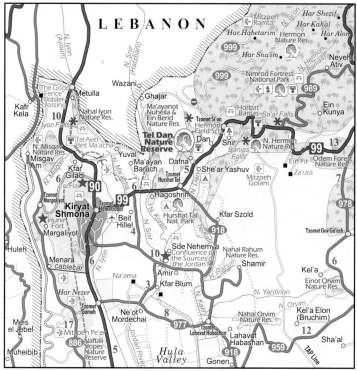

© Carta, Jerusalem

the hiker treads alternately between smoothly-paved and muddy-slippery paths and over bridges spanning rivulets, with the sound of the flowing stream accompanying every step. Many of the areas in the nature reserve are shady and the sky is hidden because of the abundance of vegetation. The foothills of the Golan and Mt. Hermon itself constitute an integral part of the reserve's landscape.

FAUNA

The flowing streams and the pools beside the current constitute an excellent environment for the development of various species of animal life. Fish swim in the crystal-clear cold water, and the deeper undercurrents are breeding grounds for trout. On the stone bed of the streams are many black-grayish snails. The calm waters serve as a breeding ground for rare amphibians such as the orange salamanders. The mature salamander has a glossy black color with orange dots; it lives in the water and along the banks. At the time of mating, they descend into the water and spawn tadpoles. Like the adult

Nahal Dan.

salamander, they have four legs and a tail, are light-gray in color and live under the water, breathing with the aid of gills. Upon reaching maturity, they lose their gills, breathe through their lungs, and acquire the colors of the adult of the species.

FLORA

The vegetation is particularly lush and exploits the full range of moisture conditions from flowing water to complete aridity. Species of vegetation are found here which do not exist in other areas of the country. Large ferns known as Long Brake (*Pteris Vittata*) grow beside the water and beside them appear the roots of willow and other trees that sustain themselves directly from the nourishing spring water in the Nahal. The reserve has a wealth of large trees from many species: oak and terebinth (Atlantic pistachio) are a continuation of the Hermon forest. A few years back a large terebinth which was about 600 years old was destroyed by fire. Other trees found here include the Oriental Plane tree (*Platanus orientalis*), common willow (*Salix acmophylla*), and Syrian ash (*Fraxinus syriaca*), all native to a water environment. Two species from the Buckthorn family may be found here: Christ's Thorn Jujube (*Ziziphus spina-Christi*) which bears edible fruit in the summer, and the Jerusalem Thorn (*Paliurus spina-christi*). Among the many climbers are some rarer varieties such as the Fragrant St. John's-wort (*Hypericum Hircinum*) that has large yellow flowers.

ARCHAEOLOGY: ANCIENT DAN

Tel Dan is located in the eastern area of the reserve. Professor Avraham Biran conducted excavations that led to one of the most written-about findings of the 1990s, the "Beit David" inscription, often referred to as

the "House of David" inscription. Remains from the Canaanite (Bronze) period and the monarchal period have been uncovered here including sections of the city wall with a well-preserved Canaanite city gate, a sacrificial altar—perhaps the altar that was used as a shrine during the period of the Israelite kings, and various inscriptions.

HISTORY

As mentioned, Dan is cited numerous times in the Bible, often in demarcating the northernmost point of ancient Israel. Its original name was Laish or Leshem. The tribe of Dan named the town after its conqueror and this appellation

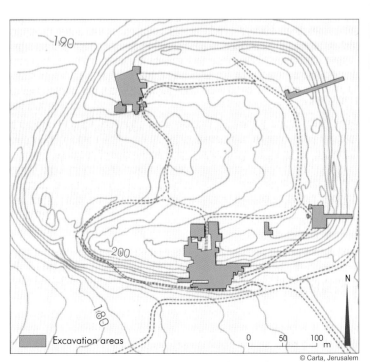

Tel Dan: plan of the mound, excavation areas, and principal remains.

remained until the 4th century CE. During the First Temple period, the area served as a ritual center for the northern tribes. After the division of the United Kingdom into Israel and Judah, Jeroboam placed a golden calf in the northern sanctuary, erected "houses in high places" (i.e., shrines), and appointed priests from outside the tribe of Levi (1 Kings 12:28–29).

SITES TO VISIT AT TEL DAN

1. The Bronze Age (Canaanite) Gate

A gate from the 18th century BCE, fully preserved with a lintel in the form of an arch. This is one of the earliest archways of its type in the world.

2. The Iron Age (Israelite) Gate

An impressive gate structure, built from three pairs of pilasters, apparently from the First Temple period.

3. The Wading Pool

A shallow bathing pool.

4. Terebinth Lookout

This observation post provides a view of the Tel Dan reserve, the Hula Valley reserve, the Naphtali hill range, and the slopes of Mt. Hermon and the Golan Heights. It is named after the terebinth (Atlantic Pistachio) which grows in this area.

5. The Flour Mill

This water-powered mill was erected 150 years ago and remained in operation until 1948. Two pairs of millstones remain at the site.

6. Lookout Post

Used by the Israel Defense Forces until the Six-Day War in 1967. There is a good view of the patrol path, the Hermon slopes, the abandoned Syrian military outpost Nuheila, and the southern Lebanese village of el-Khayam.

7. Cultic Site

Apparently, the place where King Jeroboam built a sanctuary for sacrifices following the split in the kingdom in 930 BCE.

8. Ein Leshem (Ein el-Qadi)

A cluster of springs at the base of the ancient mound. They are also called "the Tel springs."

9. "Paradise" (*Gan Eden*)

Quiet brooks, very tall True Laurel (*Laurus nobilis*) and other types of trees.

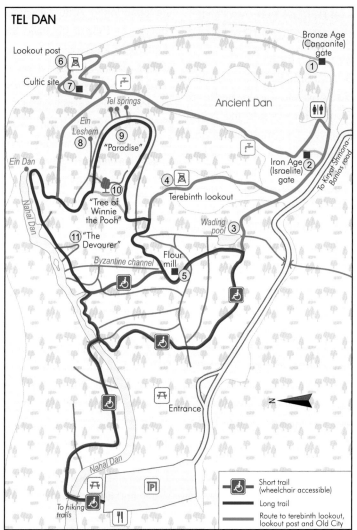

© Carta, Jerusalem

10. "Winnie-the-Pooh Tree"

A large and colorful Syrian ash, reminiscent of the tree in A. A. Milne's Winnie-the-Pooh stories.

11. "The Devourer"

A hole in the ground that absorbs a vast amount of water without leaving any mark. The rivulets beside it serve as a habitat to salamanders.

OUTSIDE THE NATURE RESERVE TRAILS

Beit Ussishkin

Beit Ussishkin (the Ussishkin House) is a museum located inside Kibbutz Dan beside the Nature Reserve. The museum informs the visitor about various aspects of the region: its landscape, nature, archaeology, history and so forth. Various activities are scheduled. The museum serves to expound on what the visitor has seen in the reserve.

Kiryat Shmona

Kiryat Shmona (*shmona* in Hebrew is "eight") is a town in the Upper Galilee panhandle named after Joseph Trumpeldor and seven of his comrades who fell while defending the neighboring settlement of Tel Hai in 1920.

The town was established in 1949 as a transit camp for Jewish immigrants on land belonging to the abandoned Arab village of Khalisa. In 1953 it obtained the status of a local council and in 1975 it officially became a town.

From the end of the 1970s, the town became the target for Katyusha rockets fired from Lebanese territory and was heavily shelled during the military events in the summer of 2006.

Golani Lookout

This is a commemorative site on the northern Golan plateau, 3 km north of the village of Kfar Szold. Before the Six-Day War it was a fortified Syrian post. During the War, it was captured by a Golani unit of the Israel Defense Forces following a fierce and prolonged battle. There is a memorial plaque with the names of the 34 soldiers who fell in the battle to take this position. From this observation point there is a panoramic view of the Hula Valley and its settlements.

Hoopoe.

Mycenaean charioteer vase from Tel Dan, Late Canaanite (Bronze) period.

Nahal Sa'ar

The Nahal begins in the slopes of Mt. Hermon, northeast of Majdal Shams. It flows south and then west until it empties into Nahal Hermon. Its western descent is windy and dotted with flour mills and several waterfalls, the highest of which is 23 m (Resisim Falls).

Beit Hillel

This settlement serves as a tourist resort. There are artists engaged in various creative activities. There is a large dairy which is open to visitors.

Waterfalls in Nahal Sa'ar.

68

NAHAL IYON (AYOUN) NATURE RESERVE

Location: on Route 90 (Kiryat Shmona–Metulla), about 1 km S of Metulla, to the E

Best season: year-round

Length of visit: ½ to 1½ hours

Tel.: 04-6951579

Fax: 04-6817050

Entrance fee

I went down...to see the fruits of the valley... (Song 6:11)

Hiking trail

Outdoor recreation

Lookout point

Picnic site

WC

Snack bar

Accessibility Rating

In addition to the three main sources of the Jordan River, there is a fourth, Nahal Iyon. Its volume is far less and it dries up several months after the rainy season. Nevertheless, its course passes through one of the more impressive landscapes in the country. Its source is outside the country's borders, in the Ayoun (Heb. Iyon) Valley in Lebanon, and its waters are not derived directly from the snow run-off of Mt. Hermon. The stream gathers force as the rains increase and reaches a peak in April. Because the Lebanese farmers divert its waters for crop irrigation, by July the streambed is completely dry. Located in a gully east of Metulla, the stream drops 100 meters over the course of a kilometer and a half, which is a very sharp decline.

WATERFALLS AND LOOKOUT POINTS

Along the length of the gully there are four waterfalls. From north to south they are: Iyon, close to the northern entrance to the Nature Reserve; the Tahana (Mill) Falls situated in the central area of the reserve; the Eshed (Cascade) Falls; and the Tanur (Oven) Falls near the southern entrance. The area is sometimes called the Tanur Reserve. The falls vary considerably in height and force. Iyon and Cascade are relatively small and less impressive than the other two waterfalls. Mill Falls is both high and wide and descends into the

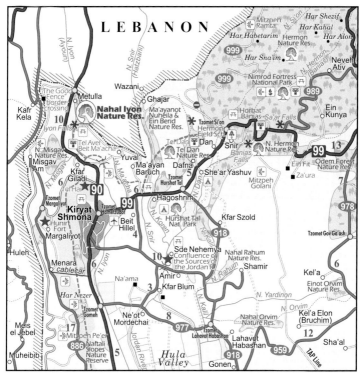

© Carta, Jerusalem

Nahal on its eastern bank. In the middle of it there is a step-shaped rock from which the water fans out. In the spring its waters are crystal clear and abundant, later in the season it is reduced to two narrow streams and eventually the streambed is completely dry. In winter, when there are flash floods in addition to the volume supplied by the mountain-fed springs, the stream becomes a torrent carrying much sediment making its waters brownish. In the past, the current activated a flour mill, the remains of which can be seen at the base of the falls and from which the falls derives its name. From this location, the water flows into a canyon with steep walls, plunges over Cascade Falls and continues to the Tanur Falls. This latter waterfall has two parallel cataracts separated by a large boulder. The waters descend with a roar into a deep crevice spraying water in all directions. The Hebrew word "*tanur*" is the translation for the Arabic name for the waterfall—el-Tabun— some say because of its oven- like shape, while others aver that it obtains its name from the

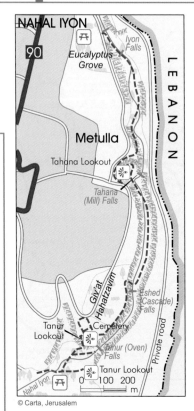

NAHAL IYON

Iyon Falls

Eucalyptus Grove

L E B A N O N

Metulla

Tahana Lookout

Tahana (Mill) Falls

Givat Hahatzavim

Cemetery

(Shed Cascade) Falls

Tanur Lookout

Tanur (Oven) Falls

Private road

Tanur Lookout

Nahal Iyon

0   100   200   m

© Carta, Jerusalem

noise accompanying the water's descent which is akin to the noise of a roaring hot oven. In either case, the name stuck. Below this waterfall, the slope of the Nahal is more gradual and the water flows gently south to the Jordan River, among the trees and oleander shrubs. Two observation points allow one to view the beauty of the Nahal and the falls: one is the Tahana (Mill) Lookout on the west bank opposite the Mill Falls; the second is Tanur Lookout, situated on a rise south of the falls. In the words of a song, what one sees from there one does not see from here, and the falls appear in a different light when viewed from each location. This landscape, as it appeared decades ago, was immortalized in a poem by the poet David Shimonowitz entitled "Siona" and it continues to impress sightseers both when its current is at full force as well as during the dry season.

THE VEGETATION

The plant landscape of this nature reserve, especially during the springtime bloom, is as impressive as its waterfall features. Every space of the ravine is covered with flowers in a rainbow of colors. Among the rarer species to be found here is the Common Snapdragon (*Antirrhinum majus*) which bears a bowery of large pink blossoms on its tall stems. This flower is found on the cliffs of the northern and western Galilee. Another rare type is the Rough-

Rough-leaved Michauxia.

leaved Michauxia (*Michauxia campanloides*), also with a tall stalk often exceeding a meter in length, and bearing large white flowers. This flower, too, may be found on the cliffs of the Galilee. Trees wrapped in varieties of climbers flourish along the bed of the Nahal.

FAUNA

Rare birds may be seen among the wildlife in this rich tree and plant environment. With luck, during the spring bird migration one can spot the Wallcreeper (*Tichodroma muraria*), so named because it clings to the sides of cliffs, in the nearby Nahal Amud,

Tanur Falls.

Arbel, and Tanur. In flight, this red and grey bird looks like a huge, colorful butterfly.

THE CEMETERY

Above the Tanur Lookout and in the direction of Cascade Falls, there is another sight that should not be missed: the Metulla cemetery. Like many of the cemeteries of the old Jewish settlements dating from the late 19th and the early 20th century, this cemetery is a storehouse of historical information. The names of the founders of Metulla, some of whose families reside in the town today, often bear interesting tombstone inscriptions.

HIKING TRAILS IN THE NATURE RESERVE

This Nature Reserve offers two pleasant hiking trails:

The Short Trail: This begins and ends at the lower parking lot. It reaches Tanur Falls and the observation point from which the Falls may be viewed.

The Long Trail: This trail begins at the upper parking lot. The trail follows the slope of the Nahal and takes about one-and-a-half hours. It passes all four waterfalls in Nahal Iyon, offering scenic vantage-points and finally reaches the cemetery. It is advisable to have transportation waiting in the lower parking lot for the return to the starting point. Otherwise, hikers will have to retrace their steps.

OUTSIDE THE NATURE RESERVE AREA

Sites to Visit in Metulla

Canada Center. This sports center was built through the

Flock in Nahal Iyon, near the Tanur Falls.

contributions of Canadian Jewry. One may spend from two hours to an entire day in this complex. There is a heated indoor pool, and an outdoor pool open from late spring to fall. Both have slides and shallow areas for children, jacuzzis, saunas and health treatments (massage). There is an artificial ice-rink for skating. In addition, there are facilities for handball and table tennis.

Iyon Falls.

The Farmer's House. This is one of the first houses built in Metulla in 1896. The house has been renovated and restored, and today is a museum giving an account of the history of the settlement from its founding to the establishment of the State in 1948.

Zami's Music Box. A museum containing special musical instruments. One can listen to Zami playing various melodies.

Menara Cliff

This is the highest cliff in Israel. It may be reached by taking a cable car from the southern end of Kiryat Shmona. At the upper station one can rent mountain bikes and coast down the steep incline. The bicycles may be left at the lower cable station in Kiryat Shmona. Alternative methods of descent are the omega rope or a hike along a labyrinthine path from the top of the cliff.

Tel Hai

Land at Tel Hai was purchased by Baron de Rothschild in 1893. In 1918, the place was settled by veteran members of the "Hashomer" [The Watchman] and the "Ro'eh" [the Shepherd]. At the end of WW I, the northern Galilee was under French jurisdiction. On the first of March 1920, armed Arab bands from the Khalisa village—now Kiryat Shmona—attacked the settlers at Tel Hai. In the ensuing clash, eight of the defenders fell, among them Joseph Trumpeldor. Following this battle, Tel Hai and the Upper Galilee salient were evacuated by its Jewish settlers. The steadfastness of these settlements during the battle influenced changes of the boundary line between the French and British mandates in Palestine. Seven months later, the Jewish settlers returned to their homes and began reconstruction.

Location: from Route 90 (Rosh Pina–Kiryat Shmona), 3 km N past Yesud Hama'ala Junction.
Best season: Spring, Fall, Winter
Length of visit: 2 hours
Tel.: 04-6937069
Fax: 04-6930706
Entrance fee

HULA NATURE RESERVE

Where the birds make their nests… (Ps 104:17)

Lookout point	Outdoor recreation	Picnic site	Sound & light show

Snack bar	Telephone	WC	Souvenir shop

Accessibility Rating

Thousands of years ago, in the Jordan Valley, which is part of the Syrian-African Rift, there was a long sea that stretched southwards from the foothills of Mt. Hermon to Hatzeva north of the Red Sea in the Arava. With climate change and reduction in the amount of rainfall, this sea, known as the "Jordan Sea," shrank and the resultant land masses divided the waters into three saline lakes: the Hula, Kinneret, and the Dead Sea, all connected by the Jordan River.

Lake Hula was small and shallow, measuring about 20 sq. kilometers in area with a maximum depth of 6 m. There was a huge swamp to the north of it whose area was also about 20 sq. km into which flowed branches of the Jordan River. An accumulation of basalt silt dammed this lake in the south, but a channel was carved through it by the forceful current of the Jordan—now a section of the Jordan Valley—to the Sea of Galilee (Lake Kinneret). The descent in this sector is approximately 200 m over a distance of 11 km.

FAUNA AND FLORA

Lake Hula and the swampy area to the north of it comprised a unique natural treasure. Here there was a mix of northern plants such as the Frog Bit (*Hydrocharis morsus-ranae*) with tropical plants such as the Paper Reed (*Cyperus papyrus*) and dozens of plant species,

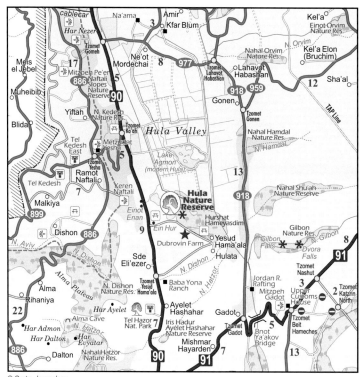

© Carta, Jerusalem

distributed over the area, taking root according to the water depth suitable for them. The waters were home to different varieties of fish and marine animals such as water turtles and snails. The Hula is on the Europe/Africa migratory route of many birds because of the rich supply of nourishment it can supply for them. Some birds are year-long residents of the Hula Reserve; others visit during the winter or summer months, and still others remain for only a few days during the migratory seasons. Among the larger visitors are the pelicans who feed on fish; small birds include warblers and the Zitting Cisticola (*Cisticola juncidis*) which nest in the reeds. Some of the plant and wildlife species were unique to the country, and found nowhere else in the world.

DRAINING THE SWAMP

The major shortcoming of the Hula was the presence of malaria carried by the Anopheles mosquito that nested in the swamp. The mosquito infected all who were bitten by it and many died from the disease. In 1934, the British Mandatory

Young pelicans in Lake Agmon.

government awarded jurisdiction over the Hula and the boggy area to its north to the national Jewish institutions. A decision was taken to drain the swampland in order to free up land for agriculture, to save the water that evaporated and hence lost to irrigation, and to use the available peat. However, the principal objective was to spray the area in order to stamp out malaria. The entire project was delayed until the early 1950s, initially by the Arab disturbances of 1936 to 1939, then by World War II, and finally because of Israel's War for Independence (1948–1949). Today, there are conflicting opinions as to whether the draining of the swamp was an ecologically correct decision. In any case, by the mid-1950s the swampland was drained and led to the disappearance of the Hula body of water.

MODERN HULA (LAKE AGMON)

Towards the end of the Hula drainage project, naturalists feared that the elimination of the lake and the swamp would lead to the extinction of flora and fauna unique to this area. They demanded that a small portion of the area be retained as a nature preserve, an unfamiliar notion in the country at that time. Their demands were only partially met. When drainage was completed, the government set aside about 1,000 acres, part of it flooded,

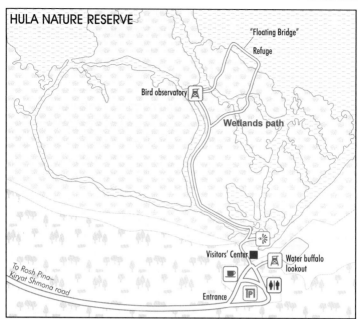

HULA NATURE RESERVE

"Floating Bridge"

Refuge

Bird observatory

Wetlands path

Visitors' Center

Water buffalo lookout

To Rosh Pina–Kiryat Shmona road

Entrance

© Carta, Jerusalem

Modern Hula — Lake Agmon wetlands.

for this purpose. In a dragged-out process lasting a number of years, the water problem was solved and the nature reserve came into existence. Today, it retains the essential form of its original constitution. Part of the area is open water, albeit a diminished representation of its former self, and part is swampland. Some of the former plant- and wildlife has vanished and cannot be recovered; other plant life continues to live and thrive in the nature reserve.

The Israel Nature Reserve Authority, which predated the Israel Nature and National Parks

Authority that manages the area today, established a visitors' center which is the starting point for an exploration of the Reserve. Within the reserve, there is a paved winding path that visitors follow which leads to a bird observatory. A herd of water buffalo was brought from the northern end of the Sea of Galilee, thus replenishing a species of wildlife that had been absent for many years. In 1994, an additional 250 acres of peat were flooded in the northern sector of the Reserve. This area was flooded in any case by winter rains because the peat-based earth continually sank beneath its preceding ground level. The flooding of the area improved the quality of the water that flows to the Sea of Galilee because all the organic material which made its way into the larger, lower lake, thereby polluting it, now sinks into the lake bed of the Hula.

Phragmites and the Paper Reed are the primary plant life in the Hula landscape and are the northernmost habitat in the world for the varieties within this species. Other numerous plant species are: reeds, Yellow Flag Iris (*Iris pseudacorus*), and water lilies (*Nuphar lutea*) which were endangered in the drainage process. As in the past, small birds nest in the reeds and bulrushes. From the path one can see turtles coming up for air and sunbathing.

Natural life in the reserve is not without its problems. For example, catfish have multiplied and grown much larger and they prey on all the small fish which provide food for the bird life on

Water lilies.

Pelicans.

Channel in the Hula Reserve.

the Reserve. Even the pelican cannot devour a large catfish and the result is a reduction in the number of water fowl which inhabit the area. Some of the birds choose the reed area—that area which was drained and was flooded in the 1990s. Nevertheless, plenty of birds may still be sighted and many natural elements from the area's past life have been preserved.

OUTSIDE THE NATURE RESERVE AREA

The Dubrovin Farm

This is the farm of the Dubrovin family which settled here in 1909. The father, Yoav Dubrovin, was a Sobotnik Christian who later converted to Judaism. The Sobotniks were Russian Christians who followed many Jewish religious observances, especially those connected to the Sabbath. Dubrovin came to the country with his entire family, bought 162 acres of land west of Yesud Hama'ala, and with his exceptional farming skills established an outstanding farm. However, malaria struck down members of the family and some of them resolved to move to Rosh Pina. Only one son, Isaac, remained on the farm. In 1968, Isaac, who was childless, transferred ownership of the farm to the Jewish National Fund (JNF).

The farm was restored and then opened to the public. The display depicts farm life at the beginning of the 20th century. The premises also contain the archives of the Yesud Hama'ala settlement, the John and Sidney ceramics studio, and a restaurant.

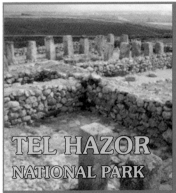

Location: Route 90 (Rosh Pina–Kiryat Shmona), opposite Kibbutz Ayelet Hashahar.
Best season: Spring, Fall, Winter
Length of visit: 1 to 3 hrs
Tel. (Tel Hazor): 04-6937290
Tel. (museum): 04-6934855
Entrance fee

TEL HAZOR
NATIONAL PARK

...for Hazor beforetime was the head of all those kingdoms. (Josh 11:10)

 Muslim site
 Antiquities
 Lookout point
 Snack bar
 WC

Accessibility Rating

Tel Hazor (the upper city) is part of a larger city which for a long period of time was *the* most important city in the northern area of the country. It is mentioned in 18th century BCE documents from Mesopotamia; among a list of cities conquered in 1478 BCE by Egypt's pharaoh, Thutmose III; in the Tell el-Amarna letters; and in the Bible. The lower city is situated to the north of the Tel, and covers an area of 200 acres; it was encircled by an earthen rampart and moat.

HISTORY

Information found in the Bible about Hazor raises some difficult questions. According to the book of Joshua, the city was conquered in the first wave of Israelite infiltration into Canaan under the leadership of Joshua. On the other hand, the book of Judges cites Hazor as an important Canaanite city in the days of the warriors Deborah and Barak, many decades after Joshua's conquest. Are archaeologists able to affirm or refute these biblical versions? Excavations on the Tel determined that the city was settled at a later date. According to Yigael Yadin, the archaeologist in charge of the excavations, the lower city was destroyed during the course of Joshua's conquest; on the other hand, the upper city dated from the time of Deborah. The archaeologist Yohanan Aharoni disagreed with this interpretation

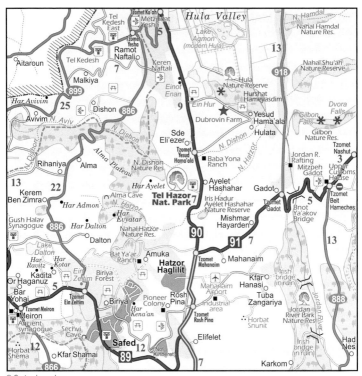

© Carta, Jerusalem

of the findings arguing that the Joshua story was not a historical account but rather a later story formulated by Israelite settlers who had infiltrated into the area. The dispute remained unsettled. In the book of Kings, King Solomon is accredited with building three cities: Megiddo, Gezer and Hazor. This gave grounds for assuming that important structures, for example the gates of the three cities, would be similar. The archaeologist R. A. S. Macalister conducted excavations at Gezer early in the 20th century at a time

when the rules of excavation did not require documentation, and areas left unexcavated were not safeguarded for future generations of archaeologists.

Macalister destroyed a large part of his dig. From the city gate, which he dated to the Hasmonean period, only a half remains. When Megiddo was excavated, and an entire gate attributed to the days of King Saul was exposed, close inspection revealed that it was identical to the remaining half of the gate at Gezer. Explorations were then conducted at Hazor where its gate was expected to

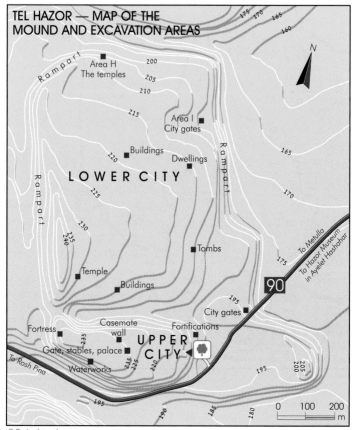

TEL HAZOR — MAP OF THE MOUND AND EXCAVATION AREAS

Area H
The temples

Area I
City gates

Buildings

Dwellings

LOWER CITY

Tombs

Temple

Buildings

City gates

Casemate wall

Fortifications

Fortress

UPPER CITY

Gate, stables, palace

Waterworks

To Rosh Pina

To Metulla

To Hazor Museum in Ayelet Hashahar

90

0   100   200   m

© Carta, Jerusalem

be, and findings revealed that this gate was indeed similar in structure and dimensions to the other two.

ARCHAEOLOGY

The excavations conducted by Yigael Yadin at Hazor indicated that the city's population ranged between 25,000 and 30,000 inhabitants—a very large settlement for these times. This certainly confirmed the biblical claim that it was "the head of all those Kingdoms" (Josh 11: 10). The city was founded and flourished in the Middle Bronze II period (18th–17th cent. BCE). This large city was destroyed suddenly by fire in the 13th century BCE and was not rebuilt. Findings from this site are on exhibit at the Hazor Museum on the east side of the bypass, within the gates of Kibbutz Ayelet Hashahar (visiting arrangements for groups only).

Excavations at Tel Hazor uncovered numerous finds from various early periods until the days of the Assyrian king, Tiglath-pileser III, who destroyed the city in the course of his conquest of

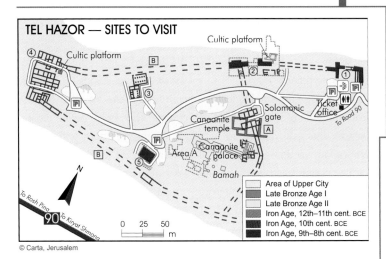

TEL HAZOR — SITES TO VISIT

© Carta, Jerusalem

the Kingdom of Israel in 732 BCE.

It is clearly impossible to excavate the entire site. In the six locations that were excavated, many important finds were exposed: the city gate, streets, colonnades, residential structures, a sanctuary, statues, various artifacts, and inscriptions. A Hebrew inscription found on one vessel reads: "To Pekah Semadar." This may be a reference to a king of Israel, Pekah son of Remaliah. Another name inscription, Machbiram, is not found in the Bible. The Tel is not a single city, but rather several cities on top of each other, and if identification is correct, there is a Canaanite city at one level, above it a composite city built by King Solomon, and King Ahab's city above this. The water system is a most impressive finding and bears some resemblance to that uncovered at Megiddo. It has a

vertical shaft, 40 m in length, with descending rock-cut steps. Unlike Megiddo, an underground tunnel from the bottom of the shaft does not extend beyond the city wall but to a water source within the city. Tel Hazor is a National Park and its excavation continues. The last word about its history has yet to be revealed.

SITES TO VISIT AT TEL HAZOR

Only the sites on the upper mound are open to the public. The sites below are listed according to archaeological periods.

The Iron Age (Israelite period, 9th–8th cent. BCE)

1. Remains of fortifications, living quarters and a granary.
2. City wall from time of Ahab.
3. "Beit Yael" — a restored residence with an olive press, a "pillared building" that served as a

public storehouse. The structure was relocated from Area A to allow for excavation work on the Canaanite palace.

4. Remains of an Israelite fortress from the time of King Ahab. In its façade is a gate decorated with embossed capitals. A gate of similar design has been found at other public buildings dating from the same period. The fortress was destroyed by Tiglath-pileser III in 732 BCE.

5. Water system built by King Ahab. A descending staircase of 80 steps led to the water source 40 m below ground level. Access was via a rock-hewn shaft.

Iron Age (10th cent. BCE)

A. A gate at the entrance to the Israelite city with six chambers, three on each side, from the time of King Solomon. Similar gates may be found at Gezer and Megiddo. Two towers, one on each side of the entrance gate, frame this part of the façade.

B. A casemate wall that continued both north and south until it reached the end of the Tel and then turned westward. Thus, it enclosed the entire western part of the upper city.

Iron Age (12th–11th cent. BCE)

A ritual platform (*bamah*) from the period of the Judges stands beside the Israelite fortress (4).

Late Bronze I period (14th–13th cent. BCE)

A Canaanite royal palace. Excavations have exposed a large courtyard with an altar at the center, two huge pillar bases, and a throne room with rooms on either side. In the palace are several inscriptions in cuneiform written on clay tablets, and stone and bronze statues.

Late Bronze II period (15th–14th cent. BCE)

A Canaanite temple discovered below the Solomonic gate.

OUTSIDE THE NATIONAL PARK AREA

Hazor Museum

The museum is located inside the entrance to Kibbutz Ayelet Hashahar. Various findings from Tel Hazor are exhibited here including reliefs of lions, Canaanite temples with ritual vessels, statues and artifacts.

Basalt lion from Tel Hazor, now at the Israel Museum, Jerusalem.

Excavation Finds from Tel Hazor

"Stelae temple" containing a row of basalt stelae and a statue of a seated figure, 13th century BCE.

Basalt statue of a seated figure — front and side views.

Nahal Hatzor Nature Reserve
Nahal Hatzor begins at the Dalton plateau and spills into the Jordan River beside Kibbutz Hulata. The central sector of the Nahal forms a canyon and along its length are recesses and caves. These were largely formed through karstic dissolution processes and the remainder was hewn by man to provide living quarters.

The canyon cliff is a nesting place for birds of prey.

This entire area is included in the Nahal Hatzor Nature Reserve.

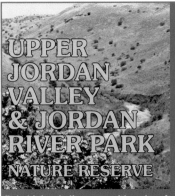

UPPER JORDAN VALLEY & JORDAN RIVER PARK
NATURE RESERVE

Location: N of the Sea of Galilee, between Bnot Ya'akov and Arik bridges; entrance from Route 888 or Route 91.

Best season: year-round

Length of visit: 2 hours

Tel. (Park): 04-6923422, 050-369217

Entrance fee to the Park

Behold, he shall come up like a lion from the swelling of Jordan... (Jer 49:19)

Outdoor recreation	Hiking trail	Lookout point	Swimming	Picnic site

Snack bar	Restaurant	WC

The trails in the nature reserve are only for hikers, and are not accessible for individuals with disabilities.

In sharp contrast to its legendary dimensions, the Jordan River is neither wide, nor deep, nor long, and according to the definition of many geographers it is a stream rather than a river. Nevertheless, for millions of people, it is a most important river, perhaps better known than the rivers in their own country. The Jordan and its banks are variegated, and one section is quite unlike the next. Between the Bnot Ya'akov Bridge and the Sea of Galilee, a distance of only 11 km, it becomes a gushing mountain stream, descending from an altitude of 70 m above sea level to 210 m below sea level, a major drop by any standard. This section is called the "Jordan Valley" (in the past it was referred to as the "mountainous Jordan") and together with its slopes constitutes a nature reserve.

For many years, this section of the river was inaccessible and unknown to the public, for lack of trails. When the borders for Palestine were established by the British Mandate, all this section of the river, together with a strip of land 300 m wide to the east of it, were included in the Mandate's jurisdiction. During Israel's War of Independence, the Syrian armed forces succeeded in capturing the territory to the east of the Jordan River, and this prevented access to it. In effect, the Syrians maintained strategic domination over the western section of the valley, part of which had been

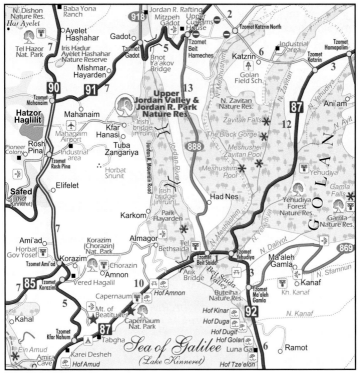

© Carta, Jerusalem

declared a demilitarized zone. Israeli inaccessibility to this area prevented the Government from beginning the National Water Carrier Project. The Project contained plans for building a dam beside the Bnot Ya'akov Bridge in order to divert water from the river.

After the Six-Day War in 1967, the entire area came under Israeli administration. For the first time, hikers discovered this wild watercourse in all its splendor: a torrential stream, especially in spring; small waterfalls skipping over black basalt rock; along its banks a thick growth of reeds, willow trees, and oleander bushes that produce abundant flowers in shocking pink. There are steep slopes on both sides of the river that yield herbs in winter, as well as the Christ's Thorn Jujube tree (*Ziziphus spinus-Christi*). This gives the eastern bank landscape the appearance of a "forest."

The bed of the river widens as it approaches the northern part of the Sea of Galilee. The lower section, closest to the lake, has been set aside as a recreation and nature area called Park Hayarden (Jordan River Park).

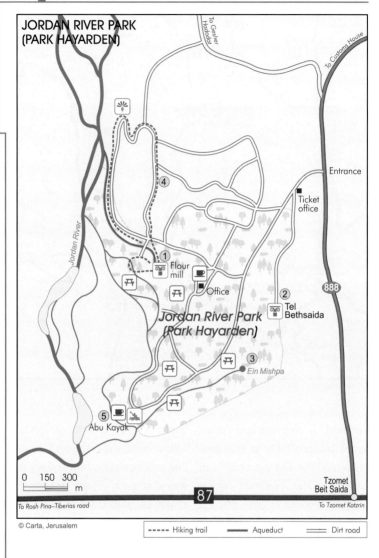

JORDAN RIVER PARK
(PARK HAYARDEN)

To Gesher Hadalot

To Customs House

Entrance

Ticket office

Jordan River

① Flour mill

Office

② Tel Bethsaida

888

Jordan River Park
(Park Hayarden)

③ Ein Mishpa

⑤ Abu Kayak

④

0 150 300
m

87

Tzomet Beit Saida

To Rosh Pina–Tiberias road

To Tzomet Katzrin

© Carta, Jerusalem

----- Hiking trail   ▬▬ Aqueduct   ═══ Dirt road

The Jewish National Fund [JNF] has made large investments in landscaping and facilities. At the bends in the river there is rich vegetation, some of it planted, as well as designated recreation sites. Remnants of flour mills driven by the water's current, with conduits leading to each one, have been preserved, and add to the historical ambiance of the landscape.

SITES TO VISIT

The JNF began developing the park in 1975. Visitors enter a recreation area of 250 acres with hiking trails, bridges that span the rivulets, expansive grassy areas and picnic tables. Overnight

Flour mill in Jordan River Park.

camping is allowed with advance notice. Archaeological sites are scattered throughout the park, including remains of settlements beginning from the period of the First Temple, and flour mills.

1. Flour mills

The voluminous water current powered more than 12 flour mills, the majority of which were of the "horizontal type." This model was used where there was a strong current; in weak-current streams, mills were constructed with flues and were known as "vertical wheel" mills. These flues concentrated the water and amplified the strength of the current. The JNF renovated several aqueducts and restored two "horizontal" water mills.

2. Bethsaida

In the days of the Second Temple, there was a fishing village on this site which took its name from the Hebrew word for "fisherman" (*dayag*). Philip, the son of Herod the Great, was appointed tetrarch of Gaulanitis (the Bashan) and made this urban center its capital. He named it Julias after the daughter of Augustus Caesar.

The town is mentioned many times in the New Testament. According to Christian tradition, three Apostles—Peter, his brother Andrew, and Philip—were born here. Jesus visited Bethsaida when he set out to preach in the Jewish villages of Galilee, and several miracles are attributed to him at this place. Bethsaida was destroyed in the great Jewish revolt against the Romans. Excavations have exposed the Old Testament city, as well as finds from the Second Temple and Hellenistic periods.

3. Ein Mishpa

This spring is southwest of Bethsaida. A rivulet that reaches the Jordan River flows from the spring source forming a beautiful pool. There are picnic tables all along the rivulet.

4. Park Hiking Trail

The Jewish National Fund built a walking trail which begins at the flour mills, traverses a rivulet of the Jordan, continues north the entire length of the water's course and returns to the water mills. There are picnic tables the length of the rivulet.

5. Abu Kayak

Kayaking and rubber boats, suitable for the entire family, are available in the Park. This facility is located in the southern section of the Jordan River Park.

OUTSIDE THE PARK AND NATURE RESERVE

Katzrin: Archaeological Park

The archaeological park is located southeast of the new town of Katzrin on a low rise which gradually slopes northward. An archaeological survey conducted by Shmarya Guttman in 1967 uncovered the remains of an ancient synagogue from the first centuries CE. These findings are in relatively good condition. The structure was built from locally-hewn stone. The gate of the synagogue is in place, as well as many architectural features of the building. Inscriptions were found, including a tombstone inscription in Hebrew which reads: "Rabbi Avon, may he ever be respected." Later surveys uncovered additional items: a

Mouth of the Jordan flowing into the Sea of Galilee.

large doorpost upon which stood a candelabrum with five branches, and a bird that appears to be a peacock. The entire complex (synagogue, living quarters, and agricultural facilities) has been restored and renovated and is open to the public.

Golan Antiquities Museum

The museum, located near the central commercial area in Katzrin, exhibits artifacts from three historical periods: prehistoric, Canaanite, and First and Second Temple. A fourth exhibit displays findings from synagogues. In addition, there is a collection of items from churches, as well as sculpture and art motifs.

Golan Winery Visitors Center

A visit to the winery includes a guided tour of the production process, a video giving background to wine production in the area and the establishment of this winery, and a tasting room accompanied by explanation of several varieties of wines and the art of tasting.

Jordan River Park.

KORAZIM (CHORAZIN) NATIONAL PARK

Location: from Route 90, turn E at Korazim Junction, toward Moshav Almagor

Best season: year-round

Length of visit: 1 to 2 hours

Tel.: 04-6934982

Entrance fee

...and the cities shall be inhabited, and the wastes shall be builded: (Ezek 36:10)

 Jewish site
 Christian site
 Antiquities
 WC
Picnic site
 Lookout point

Accessibility Rating

 1   1

 P ✔   ✗

The Korazim National Park is situated within the basalt area of the eastern Galilee, beside the road between Korazim junction and Almagor. The Park is on the grounds of ancient Chorazin and its central feature is the remains of the ancient synagogue dating from the second or third century. CE. Korazim was a Jewish city during the mishnaic and talmudic period and it is mentioned in sources as a sight of select crops to be harvested during the period of the *Omer* and sent to the Temple in Jerusalem. The tractate *Menahot* in the Babylonian Talmud contains the following reference: "The wheat of Korazim is sought as an *Omer* offering, even though [the town] is not close to Jerusalem."

Korazim also appears in the New Testament. Called Chorazin, it is just above Capernaum on the Sea of Galilee, and is one of the first places where Jesus preached his gospel. The Jewish inhabitants of this area were devoutly religious and rejected his teachings. In anger, he cursed these towns:

Woe unto thee, Chorazin! Woe unto thee, Bethsaida! For if the mighty works, which were done in you, had been done in Tyre and Sidon, they would have repented long ago in sackcloth and ashes. But I say unto you, It shall be more tolerable for Tyre and Sidon at the day of judgment, than for you. . . that it will be more tolerable for the land of Sodom in the day of judgment, than for thee.

(Mt 11:21–24; cf. Lk 10:13 ff.)

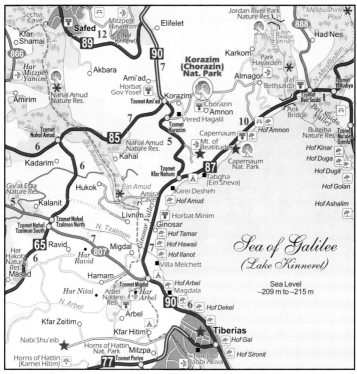

© Carta, Jerusalem

The Jewish settlement of Korazim was, indeed, destroyed in the 4th century CE. Eusebius writes about a "Galilean village that was cursed by Christ, according to the Apostles. Today, it is in ruins." Much later, the location became a Bedouin village centered around a sacred grave and was known as Karazeh.

THE SYNAGOGUE

At Korazim, there are partial remains of buildings and other facilities from the ancient city. The feature find at Korazim is the ruins of a magnificent synagogue, built entirely of black basalt stones. Anyone who has worked with basalt knows how hard this rock is and how difficult it is to work decoratively with it. Sculpting it leaves little room for repairs and patchwork; a shard shaved off in the wrong place or cut inaccurately, and the entire stone is ruined. Here one finds delicate and exact ornamentation that only the most highly skilled artists can craft. This artistry is quite evident when comparing this synagogue with the one found at Capernaum a little more than 2 km to the south.

Ancient synagogue at Chorazin.

Capernaum could also boast of a splendidly-built synagogue from the same period, but it was built of white stone brought from afar and contrasted sharply with the black basalt of Capernaum's environs. Perhaps there is room for reflection here: when the inhabitants of Korazim saw the inhabitants of Capernaum, who were more wealthy, building their luxurious synagogue with material brought from some distance, they may well have said: "We'll show you who we are, we indigent; we'll build from local stone, and we shall have something no less beautiful."

Indeed, when one sees the stones of the destroyed Korazim synagogue scattered around the site, it is possible to discern how rich and refined is the artistry that went into it. This is clearly discernible in the partial restoration of the synagogue in which some elements were restored *in situ*. The architectural style of the synagogue is similar to the other stone-built synagogues in the Galilee: its splendidly-ornamented façade faces south and it has three entrances; the main central entrance flanked by two, smaller ones on either side. Because the synagogue is built at the top of a slope and the base of its frontal wall is high, a wide flight of steps was built to ascend to the entrances. That ornamentation which has remained intact gives this synagogue an appearance of being more richly constructed than others but this might perhaps be attributed to the durability of the basalt rock construction which

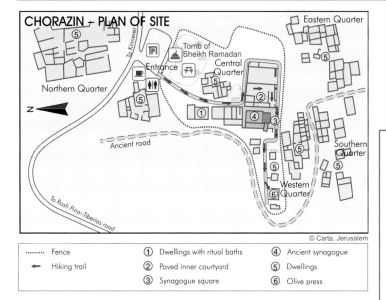

CHORAZIN – PLAN OF SITE

Eastern Quarter

Tomb of Sheikh Ramadan

Central Quarter

Entrance

Northern Quarter

Ancient road

Southern Quarter

Western Quarter

To Rosh Pina–Tiberias road

To Kinneret

© Carta, Jerusalem

········	Fence		①	Dwellings with ritual baths
←	Hiking trail		②	Paved inner courtyard
			③	Synagogue square
		④	Ancient synagogue	
		⑤	Dwellings	
		⑥	Olive press	

is less subject to erosion than the limestone found elsewhere. In the restoration work, a large triangular gable made of sandstone and meticulously decorated was erected.

Other hewn basalt remains include the so-called "Seat (Cathedra) of Moses" bearing the inscription: "Remember with favor Judan, son of Ishmael, who constructed this pillared room and the stairway, whose reward will be with the righteous." Large conches, executed with great exactitude and which rested on the friezes, were also found. Other objects of interest include statues of lions and zodiac signs. In the course of restoration work on the synagogue, other parts of the city were exposed including streets, parts of houses, and facilities such as a ritual bath and an olive press. And thus another ancient Jewish city has emerged from the ruins.

OUTSIDE THE NATIONAL PARK AREA

Rosh Pina

The name for the town of Rosh Pina is derived from the Bible: "The stone which the builders rejected has become the 'chief cornerstone' [rosh pina]" (Ps 118: 22). In its first life, this settlement, founded in 1875 on land which belonged to the Arab village of Ja'uni, was called Guy Oni. Following economic difficulties and drought, the inhabitants abandoned the settlement and returned to Safed. In 1882, an association of Jewish pioneers from Romania, joined by several families from Russia, purchased the land where the failed settlement once stood. Because the Turkish Sultan did not permit the building of new houses, the settlers resided in Arab houses in Ja'uni. After initial hardships, the settlement received the support of Baron de Rothschild. He built a silk factory, but the Baron's administrators treated the settlers as inferior, which distanced the settlers from their benefactor.

Commencing in the 1970s, artists and self-employed professionals began making their homes in Rosh Pina. With the help of Israel's Nature Preservation Society and other conservationists, old houses were restored and opened to the public at large. Among the reconstructions that are now tourist attractions are an ancient olive press from Roman times, PICA House—the administrative center for Baron de Rothschild's settlement scheme, the community center, and the first synagogue. In addition, there are art galleries, artisan studios, a music shop (Song of the Tree), restaurants and cafes.

Vered Hagalil

This is a holiday resort in the Upper Galilee which caters to those who are interested in seeing the countryside on horseback. Some residents are engaged in breeding horses. Facilities include a guest house, restaurant, and parking lot.

TIBERIAS & ENVIRONS

The following sites and attractions can be found in and around Tiberias:

Head of Medusa, from the finds discovered at Chorazin.

Hamat Tiberias National Park (Tiberias Hot Springs)

These hot springs, known in antiquity for their remedial cures, are located about 2 km south of Tiberias. The Ernest Lehman Museum at the Park's entrance exhibits the history of these springs. The mosaic floor of a 4th century synagogue is on display in an outdoor area of the Park.

The tomb of Rabbi Meir Ba'al Hanes (miracle-maker)

The tomb is inside the white-domed building situated beside the hot springs. Every year on the 14th of Iyar, there is a public celebration in memory of the saintly rabbi.

Tomb of Maimonides (the Rambam)

This tomb is situated in the lower city. Maimonides died in Egypt in 1206 and was buried in Tiberias. Beside his grave are the tombs of Rabbi Yohanan ben Zakkai, Rabbi Eliezer, and other sages. This cluster of tombs is a pilgrimage site.

Ottoman Remains

The old city walls of Tiberias have long been a landmark of this town. Some segments were built by Dhahir el-Omar in 1738, and other parts of the wall were repaired in the 19th century. The most impressive remnant is the northern fortress which has been almost completely preserved.

The Promenade

This follows the shore of the Sea of Galilee and is dotted with cafes, restaurants, hotels, and a marina. There are a number of wharfs from which to take boat cruises on the lake or to different destinations around the lake.

Decorated gable, from the synagogue at Chorazin.

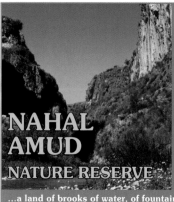

Access from N: from Rte 89, c. 1 km W of Ein Zeitim junction.

Access from S: from Rte 85 (Acre–Safed road), c. 1 km E of Nahal Amud junction.

Access from W: from Rte 866, c. 1 km S of Kfar Shamai, to the E.

Best season: October to May

Entrance fee

NAHAL AMUD
NATURE RESERVE

...a land of brooks of water, of fountains and depths... (Deut 8:7)

Hiking trail | Antiquities | Lookout point

WC | Snack bar

The routes in the nature reserve are only for walking, and are not accessible for individuals with disabilities.

The directional course of Nahal Amud differs from the majority of riverbeds in Israel. Whereas streams that descend from the country's water divide flow either to the east or to the west, Nahal Amud flows from north to south! Its name both in Arabic and Hebrew comes from the large, natural stone pillar which stands at the southern end of the Nahal's course where the Nahal exits from the canyon and changes direction before spilling into the Sea of Galilee. The Nahal begins as three small springs in the highlands between Safed and Meiron: the central and main stream is Nahal Amud, which originates in the Dalton Plateau. The western stream is Nahal Meiron, and the eastern stream is Nahal Sekhvi which is joined by Nahal Biriya north of Safed. Confluence of the three small streams takes place beside the Yakim and Po'em springs, and from here they enter the main canyon, which itself is the principal part of Nahal Amud and that of the nature reserve. The Nahal Amud Reserve is attached to the large Mount Meiron Nature Reserve. Seven kilometers south of here an additional Nahal enters from the east—Nahal Akhbera—that passes along the bottom of one of the isolated cliffs in the Galilee, Akhbera Rock (*Sela* in Hebrew). The "Israel Nature Trail," which originates in the north of the country, enters Nahal Amud at the Nahal

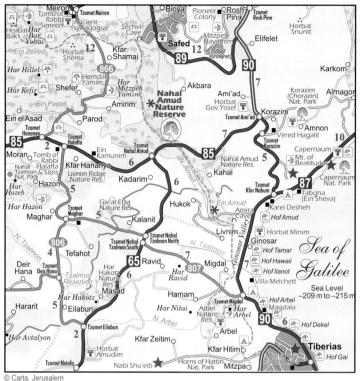

© Carta, Jerusalem

Meiron juncture, continues with it until the stone pillar, and then continues south.

Nahal Amud was designated a nature reserve on the basis of its landscape, its stream, and its vegetation. At its southern opening, not far from the pillar, there are several caves which have gained special importance in the study of human anthropology. Route 85 from Akko (Acre) to the Ami'ad junction traverses the Nahal between the upper canyons of Nahal Akhbera and upper Nahal Amud—which in Arabic are called Wadi Lamun (= Lemon) because of the number of orchards found there—and the central canyon. In the past, spring water flowed through the entire length of the canyon, irrigating the fruit trees and powering the flour mills. Today, the water is diverted for human use, and pure water no longer flows in the Nahal. The pipe that siphons water from the Sea of Galilee to the National Water Carrier crosses the Nahal in the middle of the canyon. This marks the end of the trail in the upper section of Nahal Amud. The trail now continues south, through the canyon, until it reaches the natural stone pillar.

FLORA

Vegetation in the reserve is quite varied: the Nahal crosses a very old forest of Tabor oak that in the past ranged from the foothills of Mt. Hermon to the Yarkon River. Tabor oak grow along the fringes of this grove together with Officinal Storax (*Styrax officinalis*), Juda's Tree (*Cercis siliquatrum*) and other trees and shrubs. Along those slopes which are less exposed to sun one finds the Kermes oak. These Mediterranean trees mix with Christ's Thorn Jujube (*Ziziphus spina-Christi*) which have a tropical origin. Riverbank vegetation grows along the bed of the Nahal, in particular, oleander bushes. In the spring the slopes are covered with a luxuriant floral display of shrubs and herbal plants. A noteworthy plant in this Nahal is the Two-Flowered Tulip (*Tulipa biflora*) which grows on the steep banks with reddish-white blossoms.

FAUNA

The Nahal exhibits a rich assortment of animal life. Passing through this area in 1863, the naturalist H. B. Tristram noted:

> The cliffs are perforated with caves at all heights, wholly inaccessible to man, the secure resting place of hundreds of noble griffons, some lammergeyers, lanner falcons, and several species of eagle. But no description can give an adequate idea of the myriads of rock pigeons (*Columba schimperi*). In absolute clouds they dashed

Small owl.

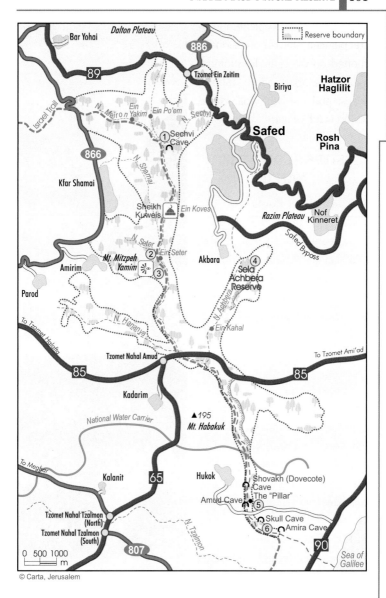

© Carta, Jerusalem

to and fro in the ravine, whirling round with a rush and a whir that could be felt like a gust of wind. It was amusing to watch them upset the dignity and equilibrium of the majestic griffon as they swept past him. The enormous bird, quietly sailing alone, was quite turned on his back by the sudden rush of wings and wind. . . . The wall-creeper exposed its red wings as it scurried up the rocks.

Tristram also saw a Syrian brown bear cross the Nahal. Today's wildlife is not as abundant, but griffons still nest here, as well as rock pigeons.

The very rare and splendid wall-creeper can still be occasionally spotted on the cliffs. In addition, there are partridges, rabbits, hares, and the odd wolf. Nahal Amud is full of life.

SITES ALONG THE NAHAL

1. The Sekhvi Pools

These pools are formed from the convergence of Nahal Sekhvi and Nahal Amud. Beside the pools stand large Oriental Plane trees (*Platanus orientalis*). Here, one can immerse oneself in the cool water and rest in the shade of the trees.

2. Nahal Seter

Nahal Seter is reached by approaching Nahal Amud from the west, from Kfar Shamai. This is a short and winding Nahal with plenty of caves, cliffs and cascades.

3. Mt. Mitzpeh Yamim

The lookout offers a breathtaking view of the Galilee, the Sea of Galilee, and the Golan Heights as far as Mt. Hermon. At the summit there are remains of an ancient Israelite fortress.

4. Akhbera Rock

A barren rock cliff with numerous caves and niches where birds of prey and griffons nest.

Nahal Amud.

5. The Pillar

The pillar, from which the Nahal gets its name, is at the southern end of the Reserve. It is a 30-m-high rock formation which is noticeable from a distance. This natural feature was once a part of the Nahal's embankment but

Amira Cave.

over time the neighboring rocks were eroded leaving this isolated and upright pillar.

6. The Caves in Nahal Amud
In the lower part of the Nahal, close to the pillar, there are caves in which impressive remains were found that illuminate the activities of prehistoric man in the area. The most significant caves are: Shovakh (dovecote), Amud (pillar), Skull, and Amira caves. Extensive excavations were carried out in the Skull and Amira caves where human remains dating from prehistoric times were found. The remains of a Neanderthal female skull of a special type were found in the Skull Cave to which the name

"Galilee man" was appended.

These findings, along with humanoid remains in caves in the Carmel range and in the Kedumim cave in the Nazareth Hills, help in the reconstruction of the development of the human species and human lineages from their source in Africa to the rest of the world via the coastal strip of the western Mediterranean Sea.

OUTSIDE THE NATURE RESERVE

SAFED—SITES TO VISIT

1. The Abuhav Synagogue
An old Torah scroll brought to Safed by Jews expelled from Spain in 1498—specifically attributed to Rabbi Isaac Abuhav,

SAFED — THE OLD CITY

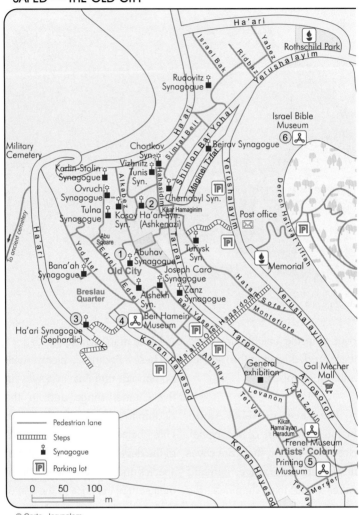

© Carta, Jerusalem

a scribe in the 15th century—is preserved here. The Jews of Safed believe that because of the presence of this Torah the southern wall of the synagogue was not destroyed in the powerful earthquake of 1837.

2. The Ashkenazi Ha'ari Synagogue

This synagogue was built in the place where it is said Rabbi Isaac Luria (Ha'ari) gathered with his pupils to welcome the Sabbath. The original structure was destroyed in the 1837 earthquake and restored

instruction from Elijah in a small alcove which is located in the eastern side of the synagogue.

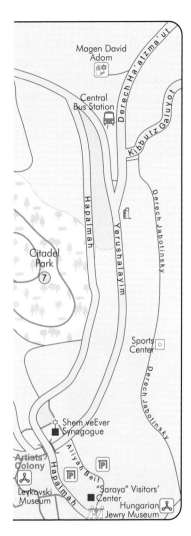

4. The Beit Hameiri Museum

This is a museum and institute for the study of Jewish settlement in Safed. It was founded by the journalist, the late Yehezkel Hameiri. It contains a large and varied collection of items pertaining to the history of Safed over the last 200 years.

5. Museum of Printing

This was built to commemorate the first Jewish printing house, established in Safed in 1576. There are collections of printed material and books arranged according to the following topics: history of printing, development of printing presses, the Hebrew alphabet and its development. A special exhibit is devoted to Sir Moses Montefiore and his wife, Judith, who were patrons of printing in the 19th century.

through the donations of the philanthropist Isaac Guetta.

3. The Sephardic Ha'ari Synagogue

This is the oldest of the synagogues in Safed and was originally called the synagogue of Elijah the Prophet. According to tradition, Ha'ari received

6. The Israel Bible Museum

This museum exhibits the drawings and sculptures of Philip Ratner, founder of the museum. His works draw upon biblical themes. The museum also contains works by the sculptor Hanoch Glitzenstein and a collection of drawings by the artists Maneh Katz,

Samuel Hirschberg, and Leopold Gottlieb.

7. The Citadel

The ruins of a fortress may be seen at the summit of the hill which is at an altitude of 834 m. The hypothesis is that there was a fortress on this location during the days of the Jewish revolt against the Romans (66–73 CE). In the 12th century, the Crusaders built a large citadel here. It was conquered by the Sultan Baybars in 1266, and towards the end of the 18th century was taken from the Ottoman Turks by the armed forces of Napoleon. It was destroyed in the 1837 earthquake and was never restored. During Israel's War of Independence it was captured by Arab forces but its re-capture by Jewish forces was the decisive phase in the military campaign for the town. Today, the grounds are a municipal public park planted with a grove of pine trees. There is a commemorative monument to those who fell in the War of Independence.

Caves in Nahal Amud.

The "pillar" (Heb. amud).

Nahal Amud.

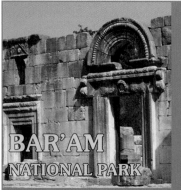

Location: on Route 899, N of Hiram Junction

Best season: Spring, Summer, Fall

Length of visit: 1–2 hours

Tel.: 04-6989301

Entrance fee

BAR'AM
NATIONAL PARK

And your ancient ruins shall be rebuilt... (Isa 58:12)

Jewish site   Antiquities

WC   Picnic site

Accessibility Rating

The synagogue at Bar'am is one of the most beautiful and impressive vestiges of a synagogue from the talmudic period. There is no historical information about this location, nor has the name of the synagogue come down to us, but the remains point to an established and well-to-do community.

This place is first mentioned in 1210 in the book "Voyage to Palestine" by Samuel bar Shimshon:

We came to the village of Bir'am; at the entrance we found the grave of rabbi Pinchas ben Ya'ir and on top of it was a large tombstone in the shape of a grindstone. Beyond this stood a very beautiful synagogue with its walls still standing; there we found an open floor with a house of learning above it.

An unknown traveler, a student of the Ramban (Nahmanides), passed by this place at the beginning of the 14th century, and he wrote in *Boundaries of the Land of Israel*:

The distance from Gush Halav to Kfar Bar'am is about 2 parasangs [about 13 km]. Inside the village there is a synagogue dedicated to rabbi Shimon bar Yochai, a very magnificent building, with large glazed stones and large, lengthy columns. I had never seen such a magnificent building.

Rabbi Moses Basola, who traveled through the country in 1523 and left us the most important book of the period, writes:

Afterward, we went to Kfar

© Carta, Jerusalem

Bar'am, and this is a large village; there [preached] Obadiah the Prophet, one of the great sages of Zion, and below it the cave. And beside this a destroyed building; only two portals remained and on the lintel of the small portal was inscribed in square letters:

"May He give peace here, and in all the places in Israel," and I was told that on another stone that had fallen was written: "Do not be astonished by snowfall in the month of Nisan (April); we saw it in the month of Sivan (June)." And they say that this was a house of prayer for Obadiah. In the upper part of the village there was a synagogue that they say was built by Rabbi Simeon Bar Yohai.

The wall and portals in front of it are still standing, and he built 24 synagogues in the Galilee.

The writer was not accurate in his quotation of the first inscription. It was found and transferred to the Louvre and it reads: "Let there be peace in this place and in all places in Israel. Yosseh Halevi ben Levi made this lintel. May his deeds be blessed. Pea[ce]." The second inscription has not been found.

Thus, there were two synagogues in Bar'am. The ruins of one, called "the little synagogue," could still be seen in the 19th century, and there even remains a drawing of the central portal with the inscription of Joseph HaLevi. It was completely destroyed and its stones were used for constructing village houses. This synagogue was attributed, as stated above, to the prophet Obadiah. Several holy gravesites were situated in close proximity to the synagogue. One is said to be that of Queen Esther; others are claimed to be the graves of Mar Zutra and of Obadiah the Prophet; another is attributed to Nahman Hatufa, a mysterious character from the 12th century, a kind of *wunderkind* who remained silent for 12 years, then made five important predictions, and either died prematurely or was kidnapped. The predictions of the child are known from Kabbalistic writings. All this information was gathered by Abraham Ya'ari in his travels throughout the Land of Israel, and may be found in *Encyclopaedia of the Land of Israel* by Ze'ev Vilna'i [Hebrew].

The most important and extensive of the remains in the National Park is the large synagogue. It is one of a number of stone synagogues built between the 2nd and 4th centuries CE and writers in the Middle Ages attributed it to Shimon Bar Yohai. Its façade, the southern wall which faces in the direction of Jerusalem, is the most preserved of all the synagogues built in this period. It stands as it was in its original position and remains unaltered except for some minor restoration work.

The superb main entrance in the central section of the wall is capped by a level lintel with an arch, entirely intact, above it. The entrance leads to the central hall.

Remains of the synagogue at Bar'am.

On each side of the entrance are two simply constructed entrances leading to the side aisles. On the right lintel there are remains of an inscription: "built by Elazar bar Yudan." A row of columns, some restored, stand in front of the synagogue. Inside the synagogue, there are partial remains of the stone floor and pedestals which separated the main hall from the aisles. The synagogue probably had a second floor.

The entire structure bears considerable resemblance to the synagogue at Capernaum. Apparently, synagogues from this period did not have a permanent platform [*bamah*] or ark for the Torah scroll. The congregants

Main entrance of the synagogue.

entered from the southern side, then turned 180 degrees to face Jerusalem, whereupon they commenced their prayers. In the Golan Heights' synagogues from the same period, the frontal façade and the entrances are on the north side. The Bar'am synagogue is one of the most luxurious of the four ancient synagogues discovered in the Upper Galilee and is evidence of the flourishing Jewish life that continued in this area for hundreds of years following the destruction of the Second Temple.

OUTSIDE THE NATIONAL PARK

The Bar'am Forest Reserve

The size of this reserve is about 250 acres. It is comprised of natural groves and an expansive stretch of Kermes oak, Officinal Storax (*Styrax officinalis*), and Boissier oak (*Quercus boissieri*). The grove was protected apparently because it was the property of the Maronite Church. In winter, about 80 varieties of mushroom grow there. There is an observation tower at the summit of Mt. Shifra (alt. 743 m). From the tower one can see the Bar'am–Aloni Forest, Mt. Meiron, Mt. Adir, Mt. Hiram, Gush Halav, and the northern Golan.

The Yitzhak Rabin parking lot on the other side of the road is a convenient starting point for a walk along the red, blue and black-marked trails of the Reserve and forest. The path traversing the forest and reserve is part of the Israel Nature Trail.

Façade of the synagogue at Bar'am.

Reconstruction of the synagogue at Bar'am.

Kibbutz Yiron—Agam-Hai ("Live Pond")

At the entrance to Kibbutz Yiron, there is a small lake formed by a spring-fed stream. Peddle boats are available and fishing is allowed. Fishing rods may be rented on location. There are also pony rides for children and visitors may pet the animals at the enclosure provided for them, feed the gazelles at appointed times, and view the llamas and alpacas.

Plant hobbyists would be well-advised to visit the Land of Israel Tree Nursery, the largest in the country. The kibbutz also boasts a new and pleasant winery, Harei Hagalil.

Nahal Hatzor Reserve and the Alma Cave

Nahal Hatzor begins at the Dalton plateau and spills into the Jordan beside Hulata. There are many karst caves in the Nahal, among them the Alma cave which has a very large entrance and numerous and sizeable internal passages containing stalactites and stalagmites. In the 1990s, naturalists found several rare bat species. Entrance to the cave is forbidden from 1 October to 1 April so as not to bother their hibernation period. Entrance to the cave is only permitted with an authorized guide, who follows the passages marked with illuminated arrows.

Location: access from Route 89 (Ma'alot-Tarshisha–Safed), S of Kibbutz Sasa.
Best season: year-round
Length of visit: 2 hours to a day
Tel.: 03-7762186
No entrance fee

There shall be a handful of corn in the earth upon the top of the mountains… (Ps 72:16)

MOUNT MEIRON
NATURE RESERVE

Lookout point

Outdoor recreation

Hiking trail

Picnic site

Accessibility rating for the tomb of Rabbi Simeon bar Yohai

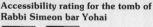

The Mount Meiron Nature Reserve is the largest reserve in the northern area of the country and covers tens of thousands of acres. The mountain has something to offer at all seasons of the year. From several perspectives, it offers the ultimate in Israeli vegetation. Most of the mountain is above 1,000 m and its summit reaches a height of 1,208 m. In a good year, the amount of rainfall reaches 1,000 mm and combined with the suitable weather, results in the luxuriant display of hundreds of plant species, from mosses and lichens to a variety of trees. There is one settlement on the mountain, the Druze village of Beit Jann, and several more are located on the lower fringes. It is likely that in the near future the entire mountain will be declared a Biospheric Reserve which takes into consideration natural assets, scenery, and needs of the local population.

THE SUMMIT TRAIL

The Greek anemone and other rare flowers grow on the summit of Mt. Meiron. This location is also a most important observation point for military reasons and thus is closed to the public. However, there is a circular path around the summit set aside for the public dotted with observation posts enabling a view of the entire countryside. Access to the parking lot near the summit is via a road at the foot of the mountain on its north side.

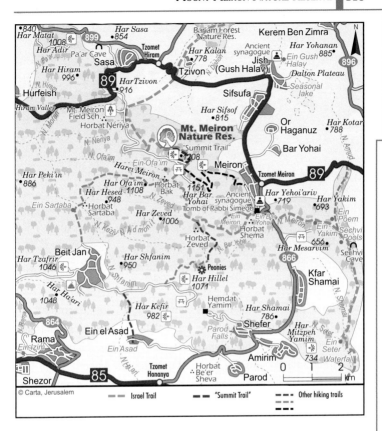

•840
Har Matat 1008
Har Adir
Har Hiram 996•
Hurfeish
899
Har Sasa •854
Tzomet Hiram
Pa'ar Cave
Sasa
Har Tzivon 916
89
N. Pa'ar
N. Hiram
Hiram Valley
Bar'am Forest Nature Res.
Har Kalan •778
Tzivon
Jish (Gush Halav)
Kerem Ben Zimra
Ancient synagogue
Har Yohanan 885•
Ein Gush Halav
Dalton Plateau
Seasonal lake
896
Mt. Meiron Field Sch.
Horbat Neriya
N. Moran
N. Neriya
N. Ofa'im
Ein-Ofa'im
Sifsufa
Har Sifsof •815
Mt. Meiron Nature Res.
"Summit Trail" 1208
Or Haganuz
Bar Yohai
Har Kotar •788
N. Amud
Har Peki'in •886
Ein Sartaba
Harei Meiron
Har Ofa'im
Har Hesed 1108 •948
Horbat Sartaba
N. Keziv
Horbat Bak
N. Zeved
Har Zeved •1006
N. Admonit
1151
Har Bar Yohai
Tomb of Rabbi Simeon
Meiron
Tzomet Meiron
Har Yehoi'ariv •719
Ein Bar Meiron
Horbat Shema
Ein Bar Yohai
N. Meiron
89
Har Yakim •693
Ein Poem
Ein Yakim
Sechvi Pools
Beit Jan
Har Tzafrir 1046
Har Ha'ari 1048
N. Shfanim
Har Shfanim •950
Horbat Zeved
Bar Yohai
Har Mesarvim 656•
866
Sechvi Cave
Kfar Shamai
N. Shemai
Peonies
Har Hillel 1071
Hemdat Yamim
Ein el Asad
Ein Asad
Har Kefir 982
N. Ha'ari
Parod Falls
Shefer
Har Shamai 786•
Har Mitzpeh Yamim
Ein Seter
Har Seter 734
Waterfall
864
Rama
Ein-zim
Shezor
85
Tzomet Hananya
Horbat Be'er Sheva
Parod
Amirim
0   1   2
km

© Carta, Jerusalem

— — — Israel Trail   ▪ ▪ ▪ "Summit Trail"   ▪▪▪ Other hiking trails

The path to the summit leads from the parking lot. Seasoned hikers can choose from several paths—from Meiron in the east, from Mt. Mitzpeh Yamim in the south, from Beit Jan in the west, or from the Israel Trail beginning at the Hiram junction. The trail passes by the field school, ascends Mt. Meiron and Mt. Bar Yohai and descends to the Meiron spring beside the tomb of Rabbi Simeon Bar Yohai.

VEGETATION

Israeli forest vegetation reaches its developmental peak on this mountain, an entanglement of Kermes oak and Terebinth, with all the trees and shrubs that accompany them, as well as the climbers that hug them, making for an impassable forest. In the higher sections of the mountain the Terebinth is joined by deciduous trees which cope with cold weather—the Boissier oak and trees from the rose family that add variety to the grove. The entire bloc of mountains that are called "Mt. Meiron" include Mt. Bar Yohai, Mt. Hillel, and Mt. Ha'ari. They form a sort of grand horseshoe which encircles

Near Ein Hazaken, a spring along the "peony path."

the upper part of Nahal Keziv and its rivulets. The brooks in the north, situated in Nahal Neriya and Nahal Ofa'im, are the most picturesque part of the grove. By virtue of the Kermes oak and several additional species, the mountain is green throughout the year, but many other trees and plants are decorated in a palette of colors reminiscent of fall foliage, blending with the perennial green. Even the Kermes oak, which appears to maintain a constant green color, for several weeks of the year exhibits an invigorating display completely different from the

Terraced vineyards.

leaves of the previous year. And what more can be said about the Pistacia, a deciduous tree whose leaves turn red as blossoms before they fall and the Judas tree (*Cercis siliquastrum*) with its pink blossoms, the Syrian Pear and the Spiny Hawthorn extending their white blossoms, and the Eastern Strawberry Tree revealing its dark red-skinned trunk. Most of the blooms, however, come not from the trees but from the shrubs and herbs snuggled in the barren spots of the forest. Here we find tiny flowers of all colors. The wave of blossoming begins in February-March and reaches a peak in May-June. In April, the Coral Peony (*Paconia mascula*) blooms on Mt. Hillel, flaunting a large and most rare flower.

The Spiny Broom (*Calycotome villosa*) blossoms in a profusion of yellow and is then succeeded by the Spanish Broom (*Spartium junceum*) which covers the by-ways. This is followed by the white-blossomed Sage-Leaved Rockrose (*Cistus salviifolius*) and the Soft-Hairy Rockrose (*Cistus incanus*) flowering in pink, and a host of small flowers. Blossoming and leafing continue into the summer when the red colors of the Pistacia, Eastern Strawberry, and Hawthorn fruit appear.

FAUNA

Species of animal life are also abundant in this Reserve. Salamanders—one of six varieties of amphibia found in the country—congregate in and

Peonies.

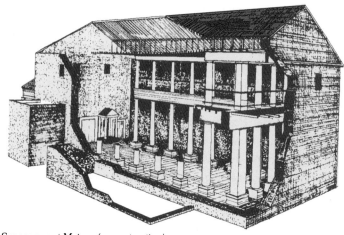

Synagogue at Meiron (reconstruction).

about the small springs and pools. In the winter, they descend into the pools and spawn tadpoles which mature by the summer and develop their adult colors. Here one also finds the green lizard and other reptiles, as well as varieties of birds nesting in the trees. The Mt. Meiron Reserve, we may conclude, contains one of the country's most profuse mixtures of nature's sights and sounds.

SITES WITHIN THE RESERVE

Horbat Bak Ruins

The sole settlement within the Reserve is the Druze village of Beit Jan. In 1836, there was an attempt to establish a Jewish settlement on this mountain. At the time, Pasha Ibrahim, son of the Egyptian ruler Mohammed Ali, was governor of the southern Syrian area. Rabbi Israel Bak and his son, Nisan, received a plot of land on Mt. Meiron from the pasha and established an agricultural farm. Unfortunately, Pasha Ibrahim was expelled from the country in 1840 and the Ottoman Sultan was not enthralled with the notion of Jewish settlement in the Galilee. The settlers had to leave and were removed to Jerusalem. The site on which they built their farm is now called Horbat Bak.

Ancient Meiron

Meiron was an important town in the mishnaic-talmudic period. It was mentioned in the list of towns of residence of the priests and the residence of the Yehoiariv family. A large synagogue from the 3rd–4th centuries CE was found here, but except for a beautiful section from the façade, fragments of a cornice, and pedestals, nothing else from the structure remained.

Meiron was the residence of Rabbi Simeon Bar Yohai, one of the great sages of the second century CE, and according to tradition, the author of the *Zohar*. His influence turned Meiron into a pilgrimage and retreat for Kabbalists and there are many holy gravesites here.

SITES OUTSIDE THE RESERVE

The Sa'ar Cave

This is a karst cave to the west of Kibbutz Sasa. In effect, it is a sinkhole that was created in the middle of an undrained valley. Rainwater penetrated the valley and spread out in deep cavities. In years when there is a heavy rainfall, the mouth of the cave fills up with sediment, the entire surrounding area is flooded, and a small lake forms in which only the tops of trees can be seen. In the area of the mouth of the cave are large trees—Kermes oak, Boissier oak and Hawthorn that are preserved thanks to Sheikh Wahib, a holy man who was apparently buried close to the mouth of the cave.

El-Buqei'a (Peki'in)

This village, most of whose residents are Druze, is located on the southwest slopes of Mt. Meiron. In addition to the majority population, there are Muslims who arrived in the 11th century and Christians who came with the Crusaders. In the vicinity of the village, there are archaeological remains pointing to the foundations of a Jewish village from the Roman-Byzantine period. Beside the village spring a very old carob tree covers the entrance to a cave. According to legend, this is the cave in which Simeon Bar Yohai and his son, Eliezer, hid from the Romans and where he wrote the book, the *Zohar*. The small Jewish community maintained a continuous presence here since the destruction of the Second Temple, and grew following the influx of residents from Safed after the earthquake in 1759. At the beginning of the 19th century there were about 90 Jewish families residing in Peki'in. In 1837 the Jewish community built a synagogue on the foundations of an older synagogue. It may be found today in the center of the village. In the early 20th century the situation of the Jewish residents began to decline. In the Arab uprisings of 1936–39, the Jews abandoned the village. When the bellicose situation subsided, one Jewish family, Zinati, returned, and its descendants still live in the village.

Location: N of Route 899 (Kvish Hatzafon), access is from Kibbutz Granot Hagalil, Kibbutz Eilon, or Moshav Ya'ara
Best season: year-round
No entrance fee
Trail for hiking enthusiasts

NAHAL BETZET
NATURE RESERVE

As the valleys are they spread forth, as gardens by the river's side... (Num 24:6)

Hiking trail

Lookout point

The routes in the nature reserve are only for hiking, and are not accessible for individuals with disabilities.

Betzet is the northernmost Nahal in the western Galilee, if one leaves out of account the tiny Nahal that descends from Kibbutz Hanita to the Mediterranean Sea. The Nahal emerges from Mt. Magor on the Lebanese border and includes within its compass the two Nahals that descend into it from the north and south, Nahal Namer and Nahal Sarach respectively. In the past, part of it, namely Karkara springs, and west of it, Eitan springs, flowed all year long, but after their waters were diverted for human use the current slowed to a trickle. Because of its landscape and virgin forest, the Nahal and its steep banks, and part of the Nahals that enter it, have been designated as the Nahal Betzet Nature Reserve. Between route 899 (the northern highway) and the road that leads to Adamit, the Nahal leaves the mountainous area and widens into a cultivated depression called Shefa Valley, which continues towards the sea.

VEGETATION

The forest in this reserve is dense, luxuriant and varied. It grows on a layer of hard limestone and stony ground and the trees take root in the clefts in the rocks. The forest takes on different appearances from season to season: at the end of the summer, prior to the first rains, it is faded; its deciduous trees, such as the Terebinth (*Pistacia Palaestina*), turn yellow or reddish, the evergreen trees lose their green sheen, the Spiny Broom bushes (*Calycotome villosa*) become dry and appear

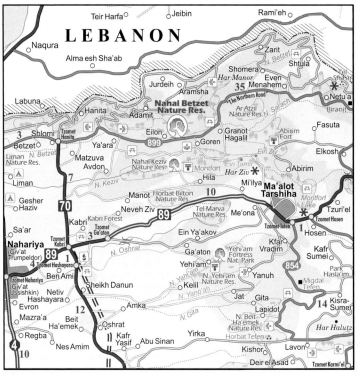

© Carta, Jerusalem

completely dead. With the first drops of the fall rains, the forest undergoes a metamorphosis. Even before the annuals begin to germinate, the Crocus (*Colchicum Decaisnei*) and the Common Narcissus (*Narcissus tazetta*) begin to populate the winter landscape.

The forest consists of the regular variety of trees such as Kermes oak, Terebinth, and Carob, but the less plentiful varieties are more interesting and give the woodland its special character. All these trees and shrubs are found in other places but not in the mix that we find here. There are many wild olive trees which serve to remind us that this is the land native to this tree and that from here they spread throughout the Mediterranean basin. Alongside the wild olive are trees and shrubs of the *Phillyrea* species, related to the olive, but which look more like the Kermes oak than an olive tree. Here and there the red-brown trunks of the Eastern Strawberry tree stand out, and even more salient are the abundant True Laurel (*Laurus nobilis*) which the Israelis today call "Dafna." This

Plane blossoms.

Oleander.

name used to be the scientific designation for a large plant that grows in the Edom Mountains in Jordan, but naturalists decided to change the names—the Edomite shrub would henceforth be called in Hebrew *dafnit*, and the True Laurel which was called "Laurel Leaves" (*alei dafna* in Hebrew) would simply be called "*dafna.*" Nor should the oleander, which contributes a pink shade to the Nahal landscape, be overlooked.

THE RIVULETS OF NAHAL BETZET

Nahal Sarach

This Nahal begins at the Lebanese border, and then passes through a deep gorge in the Reserve. Beside the Abirim settlement before it joins Nahal Betzet, there is a stalactite cave—the Sarach cave. To the west of the confluence of the Nahals are the Karkara springs where there are large Oriental Plane Trees. Since the diverting of the spring's waters into irrigation pipes, these trees have struggled to maintain themselves. From the springs, a road ascends to Kibbutz Eilon.

Nahal Namer

This Nahal also begins in the north. Its name is based on the fact that there were leopards (Hebrew singular, *namer*) in this area up to the middle of the 20th century. During the British Mandate period, there is a record of a British soldier killing a mother leopard and sparing her cub. The cub was taken to the zoo in Tel Aviv and lived there to old age. An old leopard was killed by a Bedouin shepherd in the 1960s. This was apparently the last of the Galilean leopards and thus this sub-species became extinct. Nahal Namer begins at the Bedouin village of Aramsha on the border with Lebanon, continues west along the border, and then turns southwest into a steep gorge. A winding road

Keshet Cave.

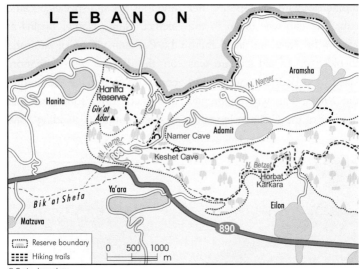

© Carta, Jerusalem

ascends along the eastern ridge of the gorge to Kibbutz Adamit and from this route one can see the many large caves on the western side of the gorge. Nahal Namer joins Nahal Betzet in the Shefa Valley.

SITES ALONG THE NAHAL TRAIL

The Sarach Cave

A karst cave with stalactites and stalagmites is situated on the north ridge of Nahal Sarach shortly before it joins Nahal Betzet. Its length is 180 m. Enter with a flashlight and proceed with caution—the walls are steep and wet. There is an iron ladder giving access to an upper chamber where there is a side exit. From October through March the cave is closed to the public because the bats are in hibernation.

Karkara Ruins

At this site there are ruins of an ancient settlement from the Byzantine period. An olive press which is in very good condition is worth the visit.

The Namer [Leopard] Cave

A breathtaking stalactite and stalagmite cave with three levels. In the lower level, the dripstone formation is still active. Entrance is with a guide only.

The Keshet Cave

This cave is located beside the road that goes up to Adamit. It is at the head of the northern cliff of Nahal Betzet and is a special geological phenomenon. The roof of the cave collapsed leaving the forward part as a sort of natural bridge at the head of the cliff. A good path leads from the

Entrance to Keshet Cave, from the south.

road to the cave. From the head of the cliff beside the cave there is a splendid view of the forested Galilee.

OUTSIDE THE RESERVE

Hanita and the Nahal Hanita Reserve

Kibbutz Hanita was founded in 1938 in the framework of the "stockade-and-tower" settlements that were erected overnight by the Zionist Yishuv. No Jewish settlements were in the area and the Jewish pioneers came under attack on the first night of their encampment. During the first year of its existence, 10 people fell in defense of the kibbutz. There is a monument to them beside the Kibbutz museum. Among the findings in the vicinity are flint tools and pottery from the Chalcolithic period, caves from the Canaanite period, a burial cave from the Roman period, remains of a church with a mosaic floor, and remains of large buildings from the end of the Byzantine period.

The dwelling of the first Hanita pioneers was built over the foundations of the church ruins and today it is a museum displaying mosaics and other findings from the area. A wing of the museum is dedicated to the "stockade-and-tower" period. In the Nahal Hanita Reserve, located to the east of the kibbutz, there is a mature grove of True Laurel, Kermes oak, and Syrian Maple (*Acer obtusifolium*). The Reserve comprises approximately 300 acres and it is located alongside Nahal Betzet.

Location: the Reserve begins at Route 89, between Elkosh junction and Tzuri'el. It includes the stream and the steep banks on both sides, and continues W for 51 km, to Ein Hardalit, S of Moshav Avdon. The park is situated in the center of the reserve.

Best season: year-round

No entrance fee

Hiking trail: medium difficulty

...wilt thou be to me like a deceitful brook, like waters that fail? (Jer 15:18)

| ✝ Christian site | 🛆 Muslim site | Antiquities | ✳ Lookout point |

| 🚶 Hiking trail | 🌲 Outdoor recreation | 🏕 Picnic site |

Accessibility rating for the Montfort observation point

♿ 2   🧍 3

P ✓   🚻 ✓

Nahal Keziv is the longest Nahal in the western Galilee. Mt. Meiron and the bloc of mountains connected to it form a sort of horseshoe which encompasses the upper streams of the Nahal that are part of the Mt. Meiron Reserve.

In the past, water coming from the Ziv spring north of Ma'alot flowed in the Nahal bed throughout the year. However, this stream, except for sections of the streambed fed by small springs, is now dry because of diversion for human needs. The most important of the springs is Ein Tamir, whose waters emerge from underneath the Montfort Castle and continue to flow for 2 to 3 km. The loss of flowing water in the Nahal has had a deleterious effect upon its landscape. In the past, thick copses grew alongside the Nahal bed. Several varieties predominated, mainly large Oriental Plane trees whose roots reached into the Nahal bed itself. Desiccation of the streambed resulted in the loss of many of these trees and the deteriorated condition of those that remained. Current growth along the Nahal is sustained by the torrents generated by heavy winter rainfall.

Access to the Nahal through the dense undergrowth is almost impossible except via several paths leading down from the north and south banks. North of the Nahal and opposite Montfort Castle is the Goren Park; at its

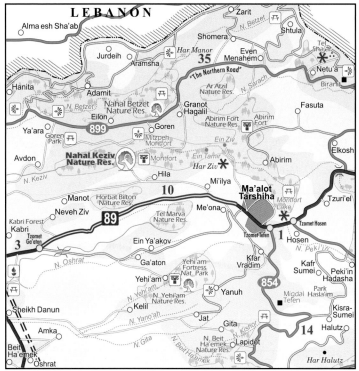

© Carta, Jerusalem

far end, above the Nahal, is an observation post which gives a nice view of the Crusader structure and parts of the Nahal.

VEGETATION

Kermes oak and Terebinth form part of the dense growth of the Nahal's slopes. Vegetation is more sparse on the northern than the southern side, a phenomenon characteristic of all the Nahals in the country. Among the distinctive sites in the Nahal is the massive flowering of the large Common Snapdragons (*Antirrhinum majus*) in a blaze of red, and the Rough-leaved Michauxia (*Michauxia Campanuloides*), a rare flower whose large, white petals are borne on tall stems. Another rare flower is the Madonna Lily (*Lilium Candidum*); Nahal Keziv is one of its last refuges. Apparently, it has been seriously depleted by Christian pilgrims who, regarding it as a religious keepsake, take the bloom or uproot it entirely. The remaining Madonna Lilies grow in rock clefts where access to them is difficult. Their very fragrant and large flowers also grow on tall stems. The forest

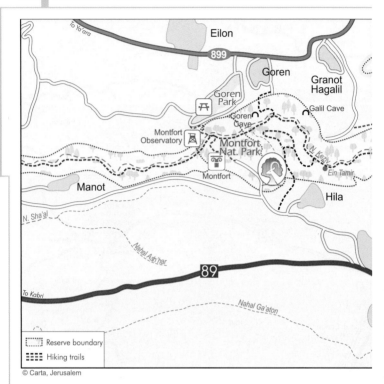

© Carta, Jerusalem

also yields trees and shrubs that leaf and bloom in a variety of colors. In spring, the different colored leaves appear and this is followed by the multicolored blossom display.

THE MONTFORT CASTLE

The citadel, meaning "mountain stronghold" in French and "mighty mountain" [*Starkenberg*] in German, was one of the important Crusader citadels in the north of the country. Along with Château du Roi (Mi'ilya) and Judin (Yehi'am), it guarded the northwest entrance to the Holy Land. It is built on a steep rocky slope on the south bank of Nahal Keziv and only a narrow stretch of land connects it to the area behind it. The citadel and the farm around it was built in the first half of the 12th century. In 1229, it was awarded to the German Order of the Teutonic Knights who christened the place Starkenberg. In 1266, the Mamluk sultan Baybars attacked the fortress in his Galilee campaign but only succeeded in capturing it after five years of siege. The Crusader warriors who surrendered were allowed passage to Acre along with their goods and their archives, which are preserved to this day in the Tyrolean region of Austria.

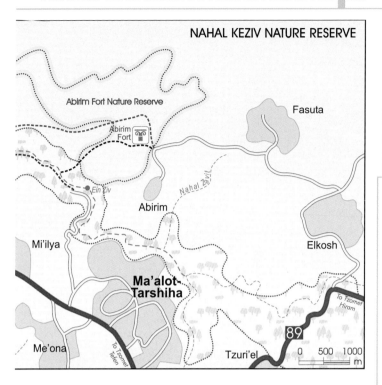

The citadel is built on a long and narrow spur protected on almost all sides by steep slopes and separated from the area to its east by a moat. The forest grew within the grounds of the fortress and what remained of it is still impressive. Remains of the council chamber and the refectory are situated above the cellars and two ornate pillars are still standing here. To the east of the refectory is a long hall and further on, the remains of a central watchtower (donjon, or keep). At the bottom of the slope, from the citadel to the Nahal, are remains of a large building that was used for producing the needs of its inhabitants, as well as remains of a flour mill powered by water. The Nahal Keziv Reserve and the Montfort castle which towers over it are among the more beautiful spots in the western Galilee landscape.

OUTSIDE THE RESERVE

Lake Montfort (also Lake Hosen)

This is an artificial body of water (c. 15 acres in area) which is situated north of route 89 (Hurfeish–Ma'alot-Tarshiha), beside the Hosen junction. It is a recreational area with lodge and sport facilities, including fishing.

Montfort—general view.

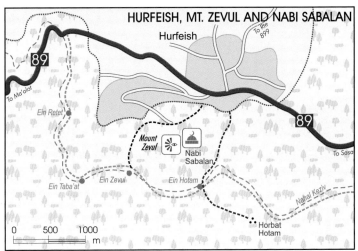

© Carta, Jerusalem

There are pedal boats and kayaks for rent. Although the quality of the water is good, swimming is not allowed for safety reasons. A promenade around the lake leads to an open-air stone sculpture exhibit. A sculpture symposium is held annually and the creations from the symposium remain on display until the following year. The sculpture from previous years may be seen in various locations in the nearby town of Ma'alot. Beside the lake there is an ice-skating rink called "Achla-Kerach" and a swimming pool which is open everyday during the summer and on weekends the rest of the year.

Abirim Fort Nature Reserve

A Crusader fort, built from hewn stone, was probably used as an agricultural facility. Access is via the road from Fasuta to Abirim.

Hurfeish, Mt. Zevul (Sabalan) and Nabi Sabalan

Hurfeish is a Druze village about 5 km west of Kibbutz Sasa. Scattered within the village are the remains of the foundations of structures, graves and pillars indicating the existence of settlement from the Roman to the Arab period.

At the western entrance to the village there is a monument commemorating the Druze soldiers who fell in Israel's military campaigns. The south of the village is part of the summit of Mt. Zevul (alt. 814 m). From these heights there is a good view of the Galilean landscape with its densely forested slopes.

At the summit of the mountain there is a cave containing a grave reputed to be that of the prophet Sabalan, who is revered by the Druze. According to

Nahal Keziv, flowing from Mi'ilya down to Ein Ziv.

legend, Sabalan, persecuted by the Muslims, fled to this cave. A miracle saved him from his pursuers. According to legend a dam formed in Nahal Keziv causing the waters to rise until they reached the height of the mouth of the niche in the cave where he was hiding and hence he was saved. Every year on September 10 the Druze make a pilgrimage to his gravesite where they ask for a blessing or make other supplications. Those whose requests were granted in the past offer a sacrifice and celebrate with a thanksgiving meal.

In the settlements of Goren, Manot, Hila and Abirim, which overlook the Reserve, there are guest houses for vacationers in the area.

Ein Tamir.

Common snapdragon.

Madonna lily.

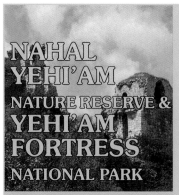

Location: S of Kibbutz Yehi'am; access from Tzomet Ga'aton, on Route 89 (Ma'alot-Tarshiha–Nahariya), going S.

Length of visit (at fortress): 1 to 2 hours

Tel.: 04-9856004
Fax.: 04-9856085
Entrance fee to Fortress

Draw thee waters for the siege, fortify thy strong holds… (Nah 3:14)

 Christian site
 Jewish site
 Muslim site
 Antiquities
 Lookout point

Outdoor recreation | Hiking trail | Restaurant for special events | Snack bar | WC

Accessibility rating for Yehi'am Fortress

NAHAL YEHI'AM

This Nahal begins south of the municipality of Ma'alot-Tarshiha. It flows in a westerly direction and beside the co-operative settlement of Amka it joins Nahal Beit Amka. In Arabic, the Nahal is called Wadi Majnuna ("the Crazy Wadi"), because of its tortuous course. Part of the Nahal is within the reserve and features cliff landscapes with steep slopes rich in vegetation. The Yehi'am Fortress is located within the Reserve.

YEHI'AM FORTRESS

This is a Crusader citadel from the 12–13th centuries. Despite the destruction caused over the years, large parts of the structure remain in their entirety and are impressive for their dimensions. The structure was part of a system of Crusader forts in the Western Galilee which included Montfort, Château du Roi (at Mi'ilya) and Casal Imbert (at Achziv). Its name was Gadin or Judin. In 1208, the stronghold was placed under the jurisdiction of the Teutonic Order which controlled the western Galilee, but in 1265 the Mamluk sultan Baybars destroyed it and it remained deserted for hundreds of years. In 1738, the Bedouin Sheikh Dhahir el Omar occupied the fortress in his conquest of the Galilee. During the peasant uprising against the Egyptian ruler, Mohammed Ali, the rebels hid here and the fortress was

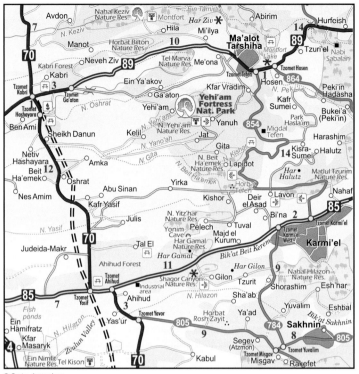

© Carta, Jerusalem

shelled by his son Ibrahim Pasha. In the disturbances of 1936–39, this fortress was a center for Arab bands and the place where they set up their judicial court. Today, the structure comprises the remains of the various periods. Nahal Yehi'am, which passes to the south of the fortress, may be seen clearly from the Yehi'am stronghold. In 1946, Jewish pioneers from the Hashomer HaTza'ir movement established a kibbutz here and gave it the name Yehi'am after Yehi'am Weitz, one of 14 Jews who fell in an explosion at the Achziv bridge during the "night of the bridges," on 17 June 1946, when 11 bridges were blown up throughout Palestine by the Hebrew Resistance movement. During the first stage of establishing the settlement, the kibbutz members resided in the fortress. Within a year, the War of Independence broke out and this settlement found itself an isolated Jewish outpost in an Arab area. A convoy sent to its defense was ambushed at the Arab village of Kabri and suffered heavy losses. Today the fortress is a national park.

NAHAL YEHI'AM NATURE RESERVE

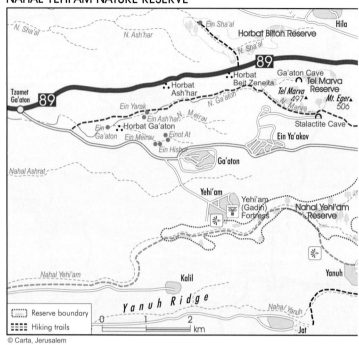

© Carta, Jerusalem

THE YEHI'AM CONVOY

At the beginning of the War of Independence, Kibbutz Yehi'am with its fifty members, forty of whom were men, found themselves under siege together with 30 others from an armored corps. On 21 January 1948, Lebanese troops under the command of Adib Shishakli attacked the kibbutz. Local combatants from the neighboring villages also took part so that the attacking force numbered about 450. Despite the numerical superiority of the enemy, the defenders managed to return fire and during the five hours of fighting finally repelled them. Four defenders were killed. The Israeli army sent a rescue contingent of 90 soldiers from the Carmeli Brigade. The unit was attacked close to the Kabri junction and lost 47 soldiers in a battle that lasted 10 hours. There is a cenotaph close to this location commemorating the soldiers who fell in this military encounter.

OUTSIDE THE RESERVE

Ma'alot-Tarshiha

This town is the result of an amalgamation between the Jewish local authority of Ma'alot and the Arab local authority

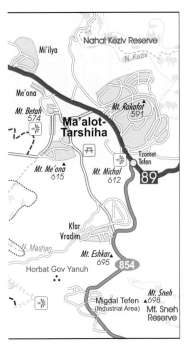

Memorial to the Yehi'am convoy.

Memorial to the Yehi'am convoy.

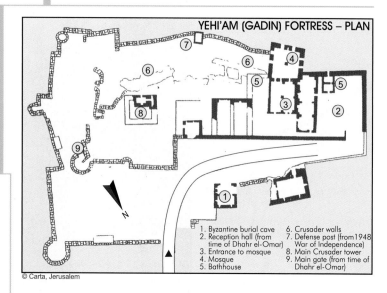

YEHI'AM (GADIN) FORTRESS – PLAN

N

1. Byzantine burial cave
2. Reception hall (from time of Dhahr el-Omar)
3. Entrance to mosque
4. Mosque
5. Bathhouse
6. Crusader walls
7. Defense post (from 1948 War of Independence)
8. Main Crusader tower
9. Main gate (from time of Dhahr el-Omar)

© Carta, Jerusalem

of Tarshiha. This is the first municipal amalgamation of a Jewish and an Arab settlement. Ma'alot was founded in 1957 as an immigrant town, and Tarshiha was a large Arab village built on the foundations of an ancient Israelite settlement. During the Crusader period fierce battles were waged between Christian and Muslim forces. During the War of Independence, Tarshiha served as a base for the Arab "Liberation Army" of Fawzi al-Kaukji until it was taken in the Ben Ami Operation that was aimed at wresting the Galilee from Arab control.

Every Saturday morning there is a colorful *shouk* (market), which is a recommended visit.

Sela'im Park Promenade

Huge boulders stand in the landscape at the turn from the village of Kisra-Sami'a to Peki'in (route 854). They were created by geological processes many eons ago. A black-marked circular path, negotiable also by handicapped persons, goes around the boulders. The path also affords a magnificent view of the Galilee highlands.

Nahal Shagur Canyon (Beit Hakerem Canyon)

The entrance to this canyon is from route 85 (Acre–Nahariya road). The Nahal drains the Beit Hakerem Valley to the west and carves out a narrow and deep canyon whose walls reach a height of 20 m. There are wrens and falcons nesting among the laurel plants and crevices of the cliffs. The trail is registered as moderately difficult; it crosses

Beit Hakerem Canyon.

over tiny rivulets amidst luxuriant Nahal vegetation. After two hours of walking alongside the shaded streambed, the path turns to the south, traverses Nahal Hilazon, and ends at the road leading to Sha'ab.

Kelil

A settlement close to the western exit of the Yehi'am reserve; its houses are widely dispersed on the hillside. Many artists live here—ceramicists, musicians and artists from various other fields.

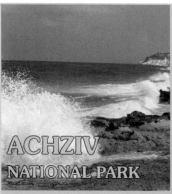

ACHZIV
NATIONAL PARK

Location: western Galilee, on Route 4, N of Nahariya.
Best season: Spring, Summer
Length of visit: 1 hour to half a day
Tel.: 04-9823263
Fax: 04-9822079
Entrance fee

...the houses of Achzib shall be a lie to the kings of Israel. (Mic 1:14)

Christian site | Muslim site | Antiquities
WC | Snack bar | Restaurant | Telephone | Souvenir shop
Beach | Showers | Parking | Outdoor recreation | Picnic site

Accessibility Rating

| ♿ 2 | 🚶 3 |
| P ✓ | 👫 ✓ | 🍴 ✓ | 🏊 ✗ |

Side by side at Achziv are a National Park on land and a Nature Reserve which spreads along the coastal waters of the Mediterranean Sea. The Reserve includes several small rock islands about one and a half kilometers from the coast: Sgavyon Island, named after the head of the Kezib (Achziv) synagogue mentioned in *Tosefta Shevi'it* (supplementary notes to the Mishnah), Achziv Island and Shuni'ot (= reefs) Achziv. Several additional islands that are in fact composed of reefs are part of the Rosh Hanikra Island Reserve located a few kilometers farther north.

FAUNA

The unique quality of the Achziv National Park is its reefs. This stretch of Israel's coast contrasts sharply with the rest of the country's shoreline which is straight, sandy, mostly void of cliffs, and has few bays or inlets. The reefs are full of pits and covered by shallow water which rise and fall with the tide and create large breaking waves when whipped by the incoming wind. This is an ideal infrastructure for a wide variety of marine animal life whose way of life accords with the ebb and flow of the churning water. Among the prevalent marine

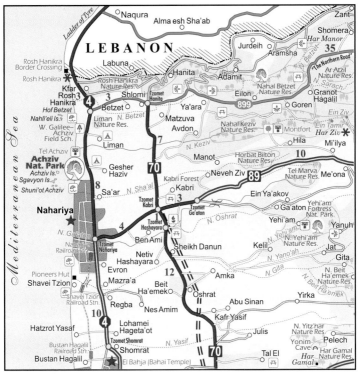

© Carta, Jerusalem

life are water lilies, sea urchins (*echinus*) and small octopi. During the summer months, female sea-turtles settle on the beaches to lay their eggs.

HISTORY

Between the reefs a small harbor was created which served the small marine vessels of antiquity. This natural feature favored the establishment of a settlement, mention of which can already be found in the Bible, in the description of the inheritance of the tribe of Asher [Joshua 19:29] and in a Sennacherib inscription from the end of the eighth century BCE. During the period of the Mishnah, the location was called Keziv, and was famous for its dye industry producing colors in pale blue and purple, manufactured from sea snails. The Crusaders built a fortress on the spot and named it Casal Imbert. In 1271, Achziv was captured by the Mamluk sultan Baybars. Until the War of Independence, there was an Arab village called ez-Ziv. Many are mesmerized by this location. Today, it is a holiday resort with sleeping accommodations and a

Coast of Achziv, looking south from Rosh Hanikra.

branch of the Club Med chain.

THE EZ-ZIV BRIDGES AND THE "NIGHT OF THE BRIDGES"

In the framework of the Yishuv's (Jewish settlement's) struggle against the British Mandate during the period before the establishment of the State of Israel in May 1948, the Hagana, the military wing of the Zionist resistance to colonial occupation, presented a plan of responses and reprisals to the National Institutions—which represented the Jewish population in Palestine—for countering British activities hostile to the Zionist enterprise. Among the operations designed to subvert British rule, the Hagana blew up 11 bridges at various locations near the projected borders for a Jewish state. At Achziv, the Hagana forces blew up the road bridge and the railway bridge that traverse the mouth of the Nahal where it empties into the sea. On 17 June 1946, a Palmah unit approached the bridges, but was discovered. The combatants were forced to carry through their plans under fire. As they got close to the railway bridge an explosive they were carrying accidentally exploded. Fourteen Hagana soldiers were killed. In memory of the fallen, the youth hostel nearby is called Monument to the Fourteen.

Achziv.

OUTSIDE THE NATIONAL PARK

Rosh Hanikra

A rock-cliff formation that rises 70 m above sea level. At its foot is the beginning of the "Ladder of Tyre." This was the starting point of the coastal road which was part of the Acre-Tyre highway and one of the most ancient and important routes in the north of the country. At the bottom of the cliff there are grottoes and tunnels formed by geological processes and the crashing of waves against the cliff. A cablecar descends to the grottoes where visitors may then enjoy the scenery and spray of this cavernous marvel. During

"Elephant's Foot" limestone formation at Rosh Hanikra.

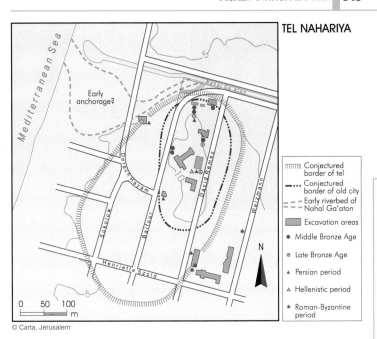

© Carta, Jerusalem

the British Mandate a tunnel was hewn through the bottom of the rock cliff for the Haifa-Beirut rail line. At the far northern point of the summit is the Israeli-Lebanese border crossing with a police station and a customs house.

Tel Nahariya

The name of the town, "Nahariya," is the Hebrew combination for "river" [nahar] and "town" ['iri'ya]. The modest "river" which cuts through the center of town is called the Ga'aton. The Arab name for the town is en-Nahar. The town was founded in 1934 by Jewish immigrants from Germany.

The tel situated within the town contains remains from various periods. It stands on a ridge of coarse sand, on the southern banks of Nahal Ga'aton. The site was inhabited in the Middle and Late Bronze (Canaanite) periods, and during the Late Persian–Early Hellenistic period. A sanctuary was excavated about 650 m north of the tel and beside it a cultic platform [bamah] where rituals to the goddess Asherah-of-the-Sea took place. A Byzantine basilica containing an ornate mosaic floor with a Greek inscription was excavated to the east of the town.

Kibbutz Gesher Haziv

The kibbutz operates artists' workshops in many fields. Visitors may observe artists at work, purchase art objects, or participate in the workshops.

146

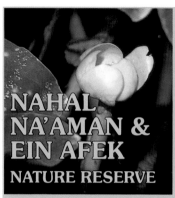

NAHAL NA'AMAN & EIN AFEK
NATURE RESERVE

Location of Reserve: from Rte 4 (Akko–Haifa), turn E at Ein Afek Junction (Rte 79), near Kiryat Bialik

Best season: year-round

Length of visit: 1–2 hours

Tel.: 04-8779992

Fax: 04-8774052

Entrance fee to Reserve

Thou didst cleave open springs and brooks... (Ps 74:15)

 Lookout point
 Antiquities
 Outdoor recreation
 Sound & light show
 Snack bar
Telephone
 WC
Picnic site

Accessibility Rating

 2 3

 P ✔ ✔ ✔

NAHAL NA'AMAN AND THE ZVULUN VALLEY

To the south of Acre there is a large bridge over Nahal Na'aman. The name "Na'aman" is relatively new and is borrowed from the Arabic. During the Hellenistic period, the Nahal was called Balos, which is perhaps a transformation of the Canaanite god, Baal. Those trying to find a Hebrew name for this place chose "Shihor Libnath" following the passage of Joshua 19:26 that describes the borders of the tribe of Asher: "and it reached to Carmel westward, and to Shihor-libnath."

Nahal Na'aman, like all the Nahals on the coast, has been harmed by sewage seeping into it. Several decades ago, the water that flowed here was uncontaminated and normal human activities took place in its waters and at its beaches. The Nahal widens considerably just before it meets the Mediterranean Sea. Going upstream towards the east, and then south, the waters begin to mix with the fish ponds of Kibbutz Ein Hamifratz and Kibbutz Kfar Masaryk. Here the water is quite saline, suitable for fish hatcheries but not for drinking or irrigation. Beyond the fish ponds there are swamps and springs, among them the nature reserves of Ein Nimfit and Karei Na'aman; south of these are Tel Afek, formerly Tell Kurdani, and the Ein Afek Reserve. The many swamps sum up Zvulun

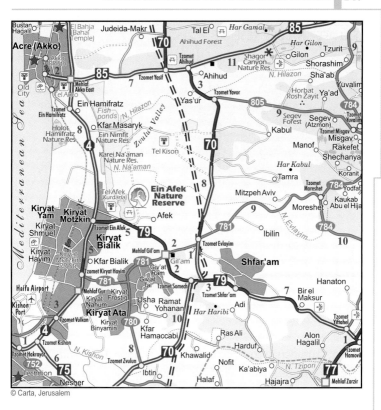

© Carta, Jerusalem

Valley's past history: this area, which today is a center of human settlement and an economic hive of activity, until the 1940s was completely desolate. The railway and the road passed through an area where there were no permanent settlements except for some Bedouin tents between the swamplands and the sand dunes. Nahal Na'aman and its swamps made this area uninhabitable and impassable; ancient byways to Acre detoured to the east to circumvent this environmental impediment. Tel Afek and its springs were important as a way station in this uninviting environment.

EIN AFEK

The name "Afek" occurs in several places in the country and generally designates important springs, such as those found at Rosh Ha'ayin. Biblical Aphek was also an important site in ancient times. There are remains from the Middle Canaanite period, that is, about 4000 BCE. It lies on the coastal road and is mentioned in the writings of the Egyptian Pharaohs and the Assyrian monarchs. In the period

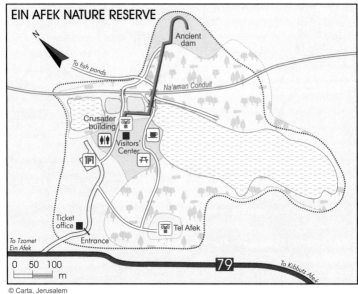

EIN AFEK NATURE RESERVE

N

To fish ponds

Ancient
dam

Na'aman Conduit

Crusader
building

Visitors'
Center

Ticket
office

Tel Afek

To Tzomet
Ein Afek

Entrance

0 50 100
m

79

To Kibbutz Afek

© Carta, Jerusalem

of the Crusaders a fort was built here, as well as water mills. The latter may be seen today in the center of the Reserve; springs, numerous plants, and animals have developed around them. The principal asset as well as the major problem of the Reserve is its water: in good years, it flows, creating streams and marshland, but in years of drought these features dwindle, even becoming completely arid and desiccated in summer, so that sources of water replenishment must be found to prevent the total extinction of the area's flora and fauna. When the Reserve is healthy, its polls and channels thrive with a variety of water plants, both native and rare, beginning with algae and duckweed, and including the common reed and Narrow-leaved Reedmace (*Typha domingensis*). For plant flowers, the glory of the Reserve is its Yellow Water-lily (*Nuphar lutea*) and above all, the Blue Water-lily (*Nymphaea caerulea*). The last-mentioned plant is native to the African continent and this is its most northern locale. Its leaves float on the surface of the water and its pale-blue flowers bloom between the leaves. This rare plant is a protected species, aided by its presence in the Reserve. In the spring the slopes of the Tel are covered with an abundance of flowers; especially noteworthy is the Crown Anemone (*Anemone coronaria*) which yields a carpet of color. Among the animals is the sea-turtle which spawns on the banks and on every rock. Bird life includes those which come to find food and those which come to make their nests.

In 1991 the reserve received seven buffaloes that were transferred from the Hula Reserve. They may be seen sometimes galumphing in the water reservoir that was built for them or chewing their cud in the vicinity of the reservoir.

Remains of human activity include a fortress, a water mill and conduits which in the past brought water from the upper springs to the mill. At the mill, the water descended several meters through a shaft directly to the grist wheel. The Ein Afek Reserve is a favorite visiting place for the local population.

Nesting grey heron.

OUTSIDE THE RESERVE

El Bahja—The Bahai Temple

The Bahai faith has two shrines in the country: their central headquarters in Haifa; the grave-site of Mirza Husayn beside Acre, close to the collective settlement of Bustan Hagalil.

Long-leaf pondweed (Potamogeton nodosus).

He is the person who spread the Bahai faith after the death of its founder, Mirza Ali. Mirza Husayn, who was accorded the title Bahá'u'lláh, was arrested by the Persian Government for this activity (which the regime regarded as an act of subversion), and in 1868 he was imprisoned under the jurisdiction of the Turkish Sultan in the large prison at Acre. Towards the end of his life he was released and lived the rest of his days in his mansion at el Bahja, close to Acre. When he died in 1892, he was buried on the grounds of his estate. The Bahai Gardens, which are exquisitely well-groomed and renowned for their beauty, are open to the public.

Reservations must be made in advance.

Kibbutz Lohamei HaGeta'ot

"Beit Lohamei HaGeta'ot" (Ghetto Fighters' House) was erected in the name of Itzhak Katznelson, writer and poet, who perished in the Holocaust; the building houses a museum for remembrance of the Holocaust and an institute [archives] for the Study of the Holocaust and Heroism. There is also a Children's Holocaust Museum at the site.

Within the kibbutz there is a section of an aqueduct built by the Turkish regime in the 19th century in order to bring water from the Kabri springs to Acre. Beside the aqueduct there is a large amphitheater where the annual ceremony for Holocaust and Heroism Remembrance Day takes place.

Aqueduct from the Kabri springs to Acre, near Kibbutz Lohamei Hageta'ot.

El Bahja, Acre.

Nesting stilt.

CAPERNAUM (KFAR NAHUM) NATIONAL PARK

Location: extends c. 3 km along NW shore of Lake Kinneret, c. 4 km SW of the mouth of the Jordan River.

Best season: year-round

Length of visit: about 2 hours

Tel.: 04-6721059

Entrance fee

...then king Solomon gave...twenty cities in the land of Galilee. (1 Kgs 9:11)

 Jewish site
 Christian site
 Antiquities
 Lookout point
 WC
 Restaurant
 Souvenir shop
Picnic site
Outdoor recreation

Accessibility Rating

 2
 3
 P ✓ ✗ ✓

This National Park covers an area that was once an ancient town on one of the routes from the land of Israel to Mesopotamia. The site does not belong to the Nature Reserves and National Parks Authority. In the 19th century, the Franciscan Order purchased this plot of land and built a monastery. In addition to the remains of a town dating from the Roman-Byzantine period, there are remains of an ancient synagogue and church. There is easy access to the shore of the Sea of Galilee where there is a wharf for boats, an activities center, and public facilities. From the shore one has a view of the entire Sea of Galilee with its central town of Tiberias and villages dotted around its coast.

From here, there is easy access to the Greek Orthodox church compound at Capernaum with its picturesque garden and tranquil atmosphere fostered by large trees, peacocks and landscaping. There is an entrance fee to the Franciscan Catholic premises where there is a restored synagogue and a display of findings and restored objects found during the excavation of the site.

The National Park under the jurisdiction of the Nature Reserves and National Parks is next to the religious compound.

THE CAPERNAUM SYNAGOGUE

The synagogue discovered in Capernaum is one of the

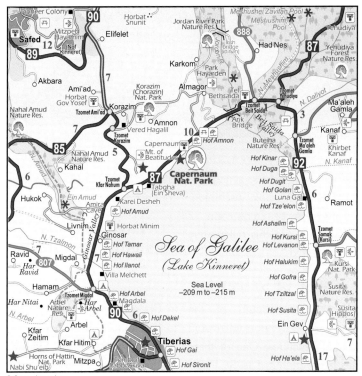

© Carta, Jerusalem

most attractive in the Galilee. It was built in the 3rd century CE, apparently on the remains of an earlier synagogue, where, according to the Christian tradition, Jesus preached. It is comprised of three units: a prayer hall 20.40 m × 18.65 m; a trapezoidal-shaped courtyard; and a plaza along the southern façade of the complex, which faces Jerusalem. The structure is built from white limestone brought from a distance and stands out against the modest basalt-stone dwellings of the village. The synagogue is exceptional for its size and ornate decorations. Among the finds are a portable ark, Jewish ritual symbols etched in stone such as a *menorah* [seven-branched candelabrum], grape vines, a grape cluster, dates, a star of David, a *shofar* [ram's horn], a model of the holy sanctuary in Jerusalem, and other symbols. On a pillar in the prayer hall is a Greek inscription which reads: "Herodus, son of Mu(ci)mus, and Justus, his son, together with their children, erected this pillar." On the base of another pillar which apparently stood in

Cornice decorated with medallions of pomegranates and other motifs, from the synagogue at Capernaum.

the courtyard of the synagogue there is an Aramaic inscription: "Helfo, son of Zaida, son of Johanan, made this pillar; may he be blessed."

HOUSE OF ST. PETER

About 30 m south of the synagogue excavators uncovered several structures. One of them has been attributed to St. Peter. According to experts, this was a meeting place of the first Christians at the end of the first century CE. In the 5th century, an octagonal church was built on this site. In 1990, a church with pillars and a glass floor was constructed above the house of St. Peter, so that one can see the

original house of St. Peter and conduct prayer services over it.

CAPERNAUM IN CHRISTIAN TRADITION

The Sea of Galilee and its coastline have an important place in Christian tradition: according to the Evangelical Gospels, Jesus of Nazareth began his activities in this area. This is where he preached, drew his apostles, and performed miracles that made his name known to many. During the mishnaic period, the area around the Sea of Galilee was densely populated by Jews and Jesus went from town to town preaching the Gospel. According to the New Testament, residents

CAPERNAUM SYNAGOGUE — PLAN AND RECONSTRUCTION

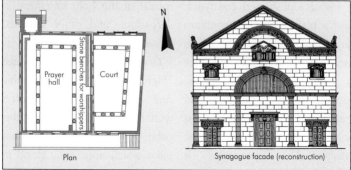

Plan

Synagogue facade (reconstruction)

© Carta, Jerusalem

of Chorazin, Capernaum, and Bethsaida rejected his teachings, and in response he predicted their destruction. When the remains of the synagogue at Capernaum were discovered, many Christians regarded this as a sign of the fulfillment of Jesus' prophecies (even though this synagogue was built many years after his death). The place is thus regarded as holy to Christians, and Catholic and Orthodox sects have built on these sites. The Franciscans have also partially renovated the synagogue.

OUTSIDE THE NATIONAL PARK

Susita

To the east of the Sea of Galilee, at the top of a steep rise above Ein Gev, are the ruins of an ancient city. The mount reaches an altitude of 345 m above the level of the Sea of Galilee. The city dates from the Hellenistic period up to the Arab conquest in the 7th century CE. Archaeological excavations have uncovered five Byzantine churches, Jewish sarcophagi, remains of a theater, pillars, and remains of two aqueducts that carried water from Nahal Samak over a distance of 25 km.

There was a Jewish settlement at Susita in the Hasmonean period. In the great revolt against the Romans, the non-Jewish residents of the city slaughtered the Jewish population. With the flight of the Jews to the Galilee following the suppression of the Bar Kokhba revolt, Jewish settlement at Susita was renewed. During this period, the city expanded westward to the shores of the Galilee and became a competitor to Tiberias on the western shores, notwithstanding the commercial ties between the two cities.

Mount of Beatitudes

According to Christian tradition, Jesus delivered his "Sermon on the Mount" from this site. There is a Franciscan monastery and guest house on the summit.

Barn owl.

Location: from Route 92 (E of Lake Kinneret), turn E at Kursi Junction to Route 789; after 50 m, follow sign to the site.

Best season: year-round

Length of visit: c. 2 hours

Tel.: 04-6731983

Entrance fee

KURSI
NATIONAL PARK

...the way of the sea, beyond the Jordan, in Galilee of the nations. (Isa 9:1)

Christian site Antiquities

WC Snack bar Picnic site

Accessibility Rating

♿ 2   🚶 3

P ✔   🚻 ✔   🍴 ✔

Jesus of Nazareth preached at a number of places along the coast of the Sea of Galilee and in its immediate vicinity and it was here that he performed some of his miracles. One of them is described in the Gospels of Matthew and Luke when he was in an area east of the Sea of Galilee, in the land of the Gadarenes. A man approached Jesus and implored that he be rid of the evil spirits possessing him. Jesus expelled the evil spirits from the man, caused them to enter into a herd of swine grazing in the field, which then rushed into the sea and drowned (Matthew 8:28–33; Mark 5:13ff.; Luke 8:26 ff.)

Christian traditions have tried to determine the location of this miracle. The well-known monk, Saba, traveled around the Sea of Galilee at the end of the 5th century, and arrived at a place called Kursia. A Muslim geographer mentions Kursi in the 13th century.

EXCAVATIONS AT KURSI

Prior to commencement of the paving of the Sea of Galilee circuit road in the northeast area, as well as a road leading up to Ma'aleh Gamla (junction of routes 92 and 869), no Christian site was known to be in the area. No sooner had work begun at the intersection of these two new roads, than ruins of the ancient settlement of Kursi were discovered. The route for the road was changed and orderly

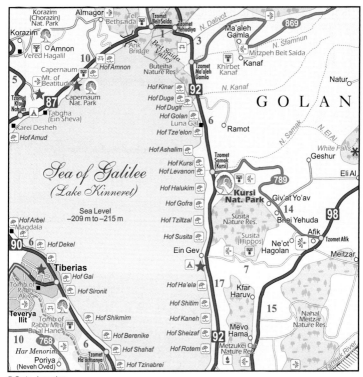

© Carta, Jerusalem

excavations began that revealed the remains of a monastery and large church dating from the 5th or 6th century. The finds were prepared as an archaeological site and declared a National Park.

The church has a mosaic floor with geometrical designs and depictions of animals. An inscription indicates that the mosaic was done in the time of Stephan[os], lover of God, head of the church and bishop (585 CE). In 741 CE, the structures were destroyed by an earthquake and Kursi was abandoned by the Christians. In the second half of the 8th century Arabs settled in the church compound and made additional changes.

OUTSIDE THE NATIONAL PARK AREA

Beit Saida Valley

This valley is about 6,260 acres in area and empties into the northeastern area of the Sea of Galilee. It is traversed by streambeds that descend from the Golan Heights and flood the valley during the period of the winter rains. It is a reserve of rivulets and lagoons containing

KURSI — PLAN OF THE BASILICA

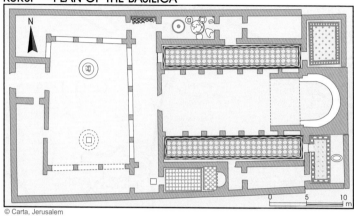

© Carta, Jerusalem

Jackal.

Kursi — stylized leaf in the mosaic floor of the basilica.

Kursi — Greek inscription in the mosaic floor of the baptistery.

an abundance of water plants including some tropical species, water fowl, fish species, and a center for migrating birds. There are two marked hiking trails in the valley: the Zaki trail and the Majrasa (Daliyot) trail. Part of the Zaki trail must be swum. Entrance to the hiking trail is from the Arik Bridge on route 87, or from the Beit Saida junction.

Golan Beach
This is a regulated beach on the northwestern shore of the Sea of Galilee. There is a water park and activities for children and adults.

Tabgha (Ein Sheva)
Tabgha (Ein Sheva) is located

Kursi — grape clusters in the mosaic floor of the basilica.

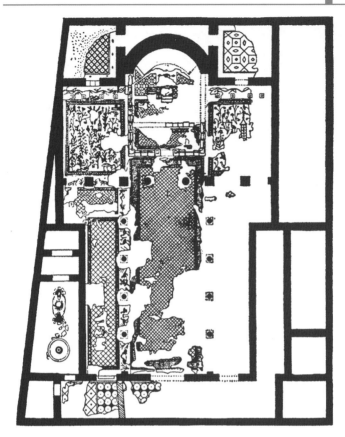

Heptapegon (Tabgha) — plan of the Church of the Multiplication of the Loaves and Fishes.

on the northwestern shore of the Sea of Galilee. There are seven springs, hence the derivation of its name both from the Hebrew (*sheva*=seven) and the Arabic. Tabgha is a corruption of the Greek "Heptapegon," meaning seven. By the shore there are several places holy to Christians.

Church of the Multiplication of the Loaves and Fishes. This church is from the Byzantine period. According to Christian tradition, Jesus distributed 5 loaves of bread and two fish to his disciples who then fed a multitude of 5,000 followers (Matthew 14:13–21; Mark 6: 30–44; John 6:1–14).

St. Peter's Church. This church was built from basalt rock in 1934. According to the tradition, the apparition of Jesus to the Apostles after the resurrection took place here (John 21:1–17).

Location: on Route 90, S entrance to Tiberias.
Best season: year-round
Length of visit: ½ to 1 hour
Tel.: 04-6725287
Entrance fee

...and bathe his flesh in running water... (Lev 15:13)

Jewish site / Antiquities

WC

Accessibility Rating

 2 3

 ✔ ✗

The settlement of Hamat beside the Tiberias hot springs preceded the founding of the town of Tiberias in 18 CE by Herod Antipas in honor of the Roman emperor, Tiberius. Thus, Hammath and Tiberias were originally separate settlements, each surrounded by a city wall. In the 11th century CE, they became one urban entity.

THE TIBERIAS HOT SPRINGS IN HAMAT

The Tiberias Hot Springs are part of a system of hot springs scattered throughout the Jordan Valley: the hot springs of Ein Gedi, of Callirhoe on the eastern shore of the Dead Sea, Hamat Gader, and others. The Jordan Valley is an unstable geological zone. This instability results from the overlapping of two plates, one from the west and one from the east of the Jordan Valley, which move horizontally towards each other. As a consequence of this geological activity, the area is susceptible to relatively frequent earthquakes. Popular beliefs have provided their own explanations for this phenomenon, and the folklorist and historian, Ze'ev Vilna'i, has supplied one of them: "King Solomon built a palace here for one of his many wives. In order to provide hot water he built an underground furnace for her and placed stokers alongside to supply it constantly with fuel. The stokers blocked their ears to protect them against the roar

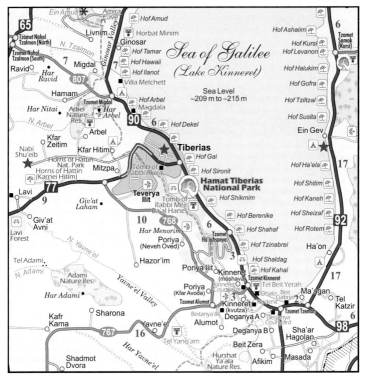

Map labels:

65 · Ein Amud · Amira · Livnim · Horbat Minim · Ginosar · Hof Amud · Hof Tamar · Sea of Galilee (Lake Kinneret) · Hof Ashalim · 6 · Tzomet Samak (Kursi) · Hof Kursi · Hof Levanon · Tzomet Nahal Tzalmon (North) · N. Tzalmon · 7 · Migdal · Hof Hawaii · Hof Ilanot · Hof Halukim · Tzomet Nahal Tzalmon (South) · Ravid · Har Ravid · 807 · Villa Melchett · Sea Level −209 m to −215 m · Hof Gofra · Hamam · Hof Arbel · Magdala · Hof Tziltzal · Hof Susita · Har Nitai · N. Arbel · Arbel Nature Res. · Har Arbel · 90 · 6 · Hof Dekel · Ein Gev · Kfar Zeitim · Nabi Shu'eib · Kfar Hitim · Arbel · Tiberias · Hof Gai · Hof Ha'ela · 17 · Horns of Hattin Nat. Park · Mitzpa · Horns of Hattin (Karnei Hitim) · Tomb of Rabbi Akiva · Hof Sironit · Hof Shitim · Lavi · 77 · Giv'at Laham · Teverya Ilit · Hamat Tiberias National Park · Hof Kaneh · 9 · Tomb of Rabbi Meir Baal Hanes · Hof Shikmim · Hof Sheizaf · 92 · Giv'at Avni · 768 · Har Menorim · 10 · 6 · Hof Berenike · Hof Shahaf · Hof Rotem · Lavi Forest · Poriya (Neveh Oved) · Tzomet Ha'achsanyot · Hazor'im · Hof Tzinabrei · Ha'on · Tel Adami · N. Yavne'el · Poriya Ilit · 3 · Hof Shaldag · 17 · N. Adami · Adami Nature Res. · Yavne'el Valley · Poriya Courtyard · Kinneret (moshava) · Hof Kahal · Tzomet Kinneret · Ma'agan · Har Adami · Poriya (Kfar Avoda) · Tzomet Alumot · Kinneret County · Tel Beit Yerah · Ohalo · Beit Gabriel · Tel Katzir · Kafr Kama · Sharona · Yavne'el · Beitanya Ilit · Kinneret (kvutza) · Deganya A · Degania Courtyard · Tzomet Tzemah · 98 · 767 · 16 · Har Yavne'el · Tel Yano'am · Alumot · Deganya B · Sha'ar Hagolan · Shadmot Dvora · Hurshat Ya'ala Nature Res. · Beit Zera · Afikim · Masada

© Carta, Jerusalem

of the fire. On this account they did not hear about the death of the king, and continue to fuel the furnace to this day, as they did in ancient days."

Since ancient times, the Tiberias hot springs have had the reputation of containing medicinal powers and, as at similar sites, a settlement had developed in its immediate vicinity. Even today, there are spa facilities on either side of the road passing the springs. Other remains from the ancient town may be found along the roadside such as the basalt door

of a sarcophagus which has the appearance of a wooden door.

THE SYNAGOGUE

The synagogue at Hamat was discovered in 1921 while paving the road from Tiberias to Tzemah. The remains standing today date from 286 to 337 CE, the period in which the Sanhedrin (Jewish high court) was still active in Tiberias. The crowning glory of the synagogue is the mosaic floor from the 4th century CE. This floor has been constructed over earlier synagogue floors. The floor now visible to the public was not the

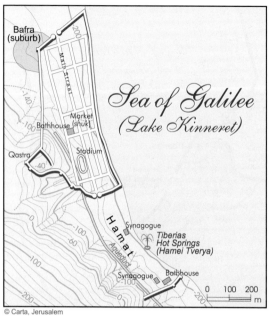

TIBERIAS
HOT SPRINGS

© Carta, Jerusalem

last floor built *in situ.* At a later date, an additional structure was erected which failed to take into consideration the ground floor, and one of the walls that was put in place destroyed a section of the mosaic floor. Nevertheless, most of the floor remained intact and retained its original beauty. The synagogue remained a house of prayer until the eighth century and provides strong evidence for the continuation of Jewish community life following the destruction of the Second Temple in 70 CE.

During the period in which the mosaic floor was crafted, Christians ruled the Holy Land and forbade the Jews to build new synagogues. As a result, Jewish artisans invested their artistic efforts in fashioning mosaic floors such as those that can be seen at Hamat Gader, Beit Alpha, Tsipori, and other locations. The elongated sides of the rectangular structure run in a north-south direction. The *bamah* is situated inside the southern façade, facing Jerusalem. Entrance is from the north.

The floor, containing several inscriptions in Aramaic and Greek, is divided into three panels. The southern panel is the sacrosanct area displaying a representation of the holy ark, on either side of which is a seven-branched candelabrum (*menorah*), standing on three legs. Beside each candelabrum

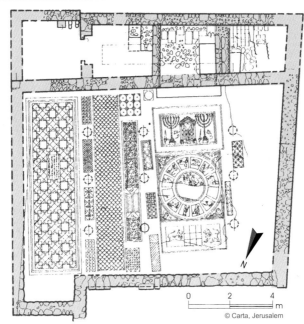

Plan of the synagogue at Hamat.

are depictions of ritual objects: a fire-pan which collects the ashes from the sacrifices on the altar of the Holy Sanctuary, ram's horn (*shofar*), palm frond (*lulav*), and citron (*etrog*). The central panel is a large square containing a detailed depiction of the zodiac; set inside the inner circle is the sun-god riding in a chariot. It is supposedly improper to find an explicitly pagan image in a synagogue, but it should be remembered that in this period idolatry had already ceased, and this illustration had solely artistic significance.

There is a large outer circle in which there are the twelve signs of the zodiac with their Hebrew names. There are several indi-cations that the mosaic was done by a non-Jewish person: the Hebrew letters of the zodiac signs are roughly created and the name of Aquarius is written in the form of a mirror; the Libra is depicted by an uncircumcised naked youth! In the corners of the panel, between the circle and square, are pictures of four maidens who symbolize the four seasons—fall, winter, spring and summer, each bearing fruit appropriate to its time of year. In the northern panel, two lions guard the entrance gate and between them are dedications. The synagogue is also called "the synagogue of Severus," who is mentioned in an inscription as its builder.

Menorah

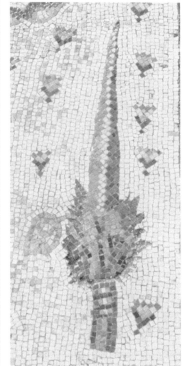

Lulav *(palm branch)*

Lion

Hamat Tiberias — details of the mosaic floor of the synagogue.

OUTSIDE THE NATIONAL PARK AREA

Arbel

Arbel was a well-known town during the period of the Mishnah and the Talmud where a priestly division from the House of Jeshua resided. Synagogue remains from the 2nd century BCE may be found here. At the crest of the ridge are the remains of an ancient fortress, built originally by the Galilean Zealots at the time of their revolt against the Romans. In 161 BCE, town residents attempted to block the forces of the Seleucid general Bacchides, but he attacked and slaughtered them. In 38 BCE residents of the town found refuge from the Herod regime in the neighboring caves. The Herodian soldiers overcame those who took flight to the caves by lowering soldiers in caskets from the heights of the Arbel cliff.

Karnei Hittim and Nabi Shue'ib

In 1187, a decisive battle took place at Karnei Hittim (the Horns of Hattin) between Crusader forces who governed the area from 1099 and the Muslim armies under the command of Saladin. The engagement took place on a blistering-hot day

Arbel cliff.

and the Crusader soldiers were encumbered by their heavy and clumsy armor in face of the light cavalry of their enemy. After a day-long battle, not one Crusader soldier remained alive on the battlefield.

In the vicinity of Karnei Hittim is Nabi Shue'ib, a place holy to the Druze because of the presence of the tomb of Jethro, father-in-law of Moses. Annually, on April 25, Druze from all over the country make a pilgrimage to this site to pray and make vows.

Kinneret Courtyard

This is a courtyard surrounded by a wall containing several buildings. Constructed in 1908, it is also known as the Galilee Farm which served as a learning center for the early Zionist and Labor Movement settlers. A pioneer-settler group gathered here in an attempt to form the first collective

THE BATTLE OF HATTIN (1187)

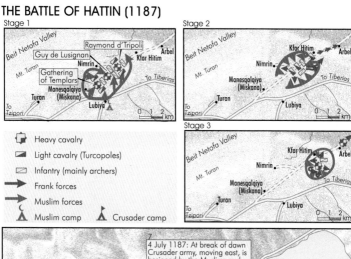

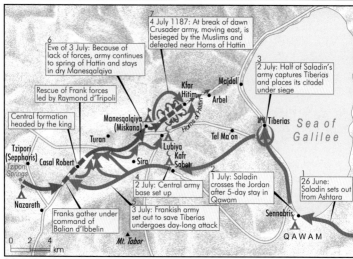

© Carta, Jerusalem

Zodiac.

community. In effect, this was the beginning of Israel's kibbutz movement and the cradle of settlement in the Kinrot Valley. Many members later became well-known in the Zionist movement: A. D. Gordon, Berl Katznelson, the poet Rachel, and others. The Kinneret Courtyard was built over the ruins of the ancient settlement of Sennabris mentioned in Josephus' writings as a fortified city in the period of the revolt against the Romans.

Beit Gabriel and the Jordan Valley Promenade

Beit Gabriel was built on the shores of the Sea of Galilee by Gita Sherover in memory of her son who died at an early age. The building is a cultural activities center. There is a restaurant and cafe with a long terrace overlooking the Sea of Galilee, a library and a movie theater. The grounds, including a lawn, are well-kept. Art exhibits and study workshops take place on the premises. The promenade, which accommodates the handicapped, begins at one end of the lawn and continues along the southern shore of the Sea of Galilee to the Christian pilgrimage site of Yardenit, where baptismal ceremonies take place.

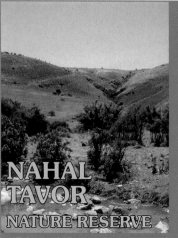

Location: E Lower Galilee, from the vicinity of Kfar Kisch to the junction of Nahal Tavor and Rte 90 (Beit She'an–Tzemah), S of Kibbutz Gesher. Entrance to the Nahal from Gazit Junct., above Rte 65 (Kfar Tavor–Afula); Rte 7276 branches off to the SE, to Kfar Kisch. The entrance to the Nahal is c. 1 km before Kfar Kisch, via a dirt road with a sign for Israel National Trail.
Best season: February to April
Hiking trail: medium difficulty
Free entrance

...Tabor and Hermon shall rejoice in thy name. (Ps 89:12)

 Outdoor recreation Hiking trail Antiquities Lookout point

The trails in the Reserve are not accessible to individuals with disabilities.

Nahal Tavor is the largest Nahal in the southwest area of the Lower Galilee. It begins at the base of Mt. Tabor and continues southeast emptying into the Jordan River. The upper part collects water only in the winter, but later on several springs emerge, and in its lower section, from Ein Shahal and beyond, there is flowing water throughout the year. The Nahal bed still reveals remains of an aqueduct and water mills. Along the length of the Nahal is a pipeline which brought crude oil from Iraq to the refinery in Haifa Bay. The section of the Nahal from Tel Rechesh to route 90 in the Jordan Valley has been set aside as a nature reserve and its deep bed forms a startling contrast to the plateau landscape on either side of it.

There are no special elements in Nahal Tavor. It descends between two plateaus, Tavor and Yisaschar, at a depth of 200–250 m below their respective heights. The sides of the Nahal are composed of basalt rock and on the northern bank there is a stratified deposit of gypsum. To the east of the Reserve, looming above the south bank of the Nahal, is the Kochav HaYarden fortress. The preservation of this reserve is justified on the basis of its springs, flora and fauna.

FLORA

The Nahal Tavor Reserve lies on an axis bridging the Mediterannean frontier with the

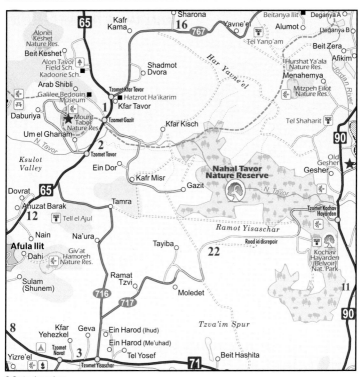

© Carta, Jerusalem

steppe land region. In the winter and spring, the rains bring about a greening of its banks and an abundance of flowers. Especially noteworthy are the Blue Lupines (*Lupinus pilosus*) appearing on the higher sections of the Nahal. In the upper areas of the south bank are cyclamens and the rare purple-colored Vartan's Iris (*Iris vartanii*). Most vegetation dries up in the summer bringing into relief the remaining perennial greens of the Judean Bird's-foot Trefoil (*Lotus collinus*) and Christ's Thorn Jujube (*Ziziphus spina-christi*). One of the special features of the Nahal is the large concentration of White Acacia (*Acacia albida*): this is a tropical tree of which there are several groupings in the country at some distance from each other: in Shimron in the Lower Galilee, in Nahal Ha'ela in the Judean Hills, and beside the town of Ashdod. The largest concentration occurs in Nahal Tavor: a significant grove with trees spread out along the slope may be seen where route 90 intersects the Nahal. The leaves of these trees fall in winter and turn green in summer.

In the Nahal bed, beside flowing

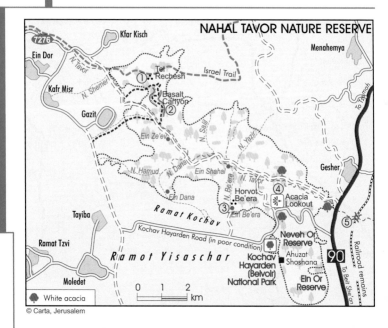

© Carta, Jerusalem

or still waters, are the riverbank plants: Tamarisks and Willows, oleander, the Lilac Chaste tree (*Vitex agnus castus*), and other water-side plants. This section of the Nahal is a gathering point for various species of animal life.

FAUNA

Nahal Tavor with plateaus on either side of its banks is the main habitat for the Israeli gazelle. The gazelle population in this area numbers in the hundreds and in some seasons has reached counts in four figures. In years of high fertility, neighboring farm land has been adversely affected. The gazelles are active during the day and are thus quite visible. In the spring mating season, females are accompanied by their fawn,

and it is not uncommon to encounter herds of young stags. Few people are indifferent to the sight of gazelles bounding about in their natural environment. These animals are not dependent upon flowing water; they can obtain the required amount to quench their thirst from plants, even from those that appear bone dry, and can live for two or three weeks without drinking. Nevertheless, from time to time they also partake of the water found in the Nahal.

The Reserve also serves as a grazing land for cattle, thereby heightening a conflict over food. Both the domestic cattle and the wild gazelles face the danger of predators in their territory: jackals and foxes found here lie in wait for the fawn, and the wolves, which appear occasionally, hunt calves and even mature cows.

The aforementioned factors engender a confrontation between the farmers and the protectors of nature. Hyraxes and hares appear occasionally, and the existence of porcupines, which are night animals, can be verified by the presence of their dens and the quills strewn about. Among the birds to be seen here are partridge, especially in the spring when they strut about with their covey of young. In the past, there were many birds of prey in the area.

ALONG THE STREAMBED

1. Tel Rechesh. When this site, in the upper sector of the Nahal, was surveyed, archaeologists found considerable remains of occupation: flint tools from the early Stone Age and periods following it, Egyptian seals, and various items from the Iron Age.

2. Basalt Canyon. A natural trail whose length is some 6 km. It begins and ends about 500 m northeast of Kibbutz Gazit. The path traverses a basalt canyon, passing by pools and small waterfalls. In the spring, the basalt slopes are covered in a delightful carpet of Blue Lupines (*Lupinus pilosus*).

3. The Be'era Ruins and Spring. This hiking trail begins at the intersection of route 90 and the road that leads to Kochav

Stream of Nahal Tavor.

Hayarden. It passes through the Ein Be'era (spring) and Horvot Be'era (ruins) and finally meets Nahal Tavor. There is a tradition that Jotham the son of Gideon, after he recited his famous allegory designed to undermine the standing of Abimelech, the city's king (Judges 9:21), hid from the men of Shechem in this area. Nahal Be'era has two springs, Ein Be'era and Ein Shahal.

4. White Acacia Observation Point. An observation point located in the midst of a concentration of white acacia trees. It is on the road descending to Nahal Tavor from Kochav Hayarden.

5. A stone bridge over the old railway tracks. On the lower portion of the Nahal there is a handsome stone bridge upon which trains once crossed from Beit She'an to Tzemah.

OUTSIDE THE NATURE RESERVE

Mt. Tabor

Mt. Tabor is situated east of Nazareth. Access to the mountain is via route 65 (Afula–Kfar Tavor). The mountain is readily visible in the form of a half-moon rising from the surrounding plain to a height of 588 m above sea level. There is a splendid view of the northern part of the

The railway bridge.

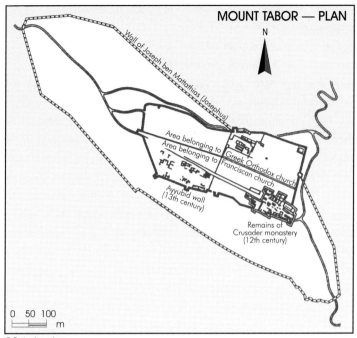

MOUNT TABOR — PLAN

N

Wall of Joseph ben Mattathias (Josephus)

Area belonging to Greek Orthodox church
Area belonging to Franciscan church

Ayyubid wall
(13th century)

Remains of
Crusader monastery
(12th century)

0 50 100
m

© Carta, Jerusalem

country from its summit. Part of the mountain is covered by the Tabor oak, which is also the scientific name for the tree. There are numerous references to the mountain in the Bible: see the description of the wars waged by Deborah and Barak (Judges 4:6), by Gideon (Judges 8:18), and the simile in the book of Jeremiah: "Surely as Tabor is among the mountains and as Carmel by the sea" (Jeremiah 46: 18). Tabor was one of the towns allotted to the Levites in the territory of Zebulun (1 Chronicles 5:62). During the Second Temple period, Josephus built a new fortress on the mountain with a 3-km-long defense wall. Remains of this fortress, which was captured by the Romans, may be seen at the summit. The settlement was renewed after the Jewish Revolt and assigned to the priestly division of the house of Aphses. In the Byzantine and Crusader periods, several monasteries were built on the summit but were destroyed by the Arabs. According to the Christian tradition, the Transfiguration of Jesus took place here in the accompaniment of several Apostles and thus the Christians call it the Mount of Transfiguration, although the specific attribution to Mt. Tabor does not occur until the 4th century. It is at this time that the tradition of Christian pilgrimage to Mount Tabor began. The pilgrims built a large monastery and fortress on the summit of the mount which were subsequently destroyed during the Arab conquest (638 CE) and then rebuilt by the Ayubbid sultan, al-Malik al-Adil in 1213. The Mamluks destroyed it in 1263 and it remained deserted until 1631, when monks of the Franciscan Order occupied the area. In 1873, this Order built a small monastery at the summit and since then there have been additions to the building.

Access to the summit may be made by taxi or by foot from the base of the mountain where there are paths on all sides.

Giv'at Hamoreh Nature Reserve

Giv'at Hamoreh is situated in the Jezreel Valley to the east of Afula at an altitude of 515 meters. The Hill of Moreh is described in the biblical account of Gideon's war against the Midianites (Judges 7:1). The Arabic name for the mount is Jebel ed Dahi, after a 7th-century Muslim saint whose tomb was built on the summit. It is also known as "Little Hermon," a nickname given to it by Christian pilgrims in the Middle Ages, drawing upon the biblical passage "Tabor and Hermon rejoice in Thy name" (Ps 89:13).

Mt. Tabor and the Franciscan monastery at its summit.

Canaanite chariot.

Ein Shahal in Nahal Tavor.

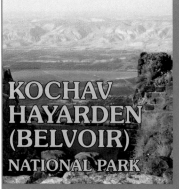

KOCHAV HAYARDEN (BELVOIR) NATIONAL PARK

Location: E Ramot Yisaschar (Issachar Ridge), from Rte 90 (Beit She'an–Tiberias); c. 15 km N of Tiberias, turn W to Rte 717.
Best season: year-round
Length of visit: 1 to 2 hours
Tel.: 04-6581766
Entrance fee

For thou art my rock and my fortress… (Ps 31:3)

 Jewish site
 Christian site
 Muslim site
 Antiquities

Accessibility Rating
 2
 3

 WC
 Snack bar
 Telephone
 Picnic site
 Lookout point

The principal attraction in the Kochav Hayarden National Park is Belvoir, a Crusader fortress, but the history of this location well antedates this period. In the Second Temple period, there was a Jewish town called Grophina or Agrippina. In the second chapter of Tractate *Rosh Hashana* from the Mishnah mention is made of the torch-raising ritual conducted on the first of every month in order to signal to every settlement in the area the beginning of a new 29- or 30-day lunar cycle:

From where would they hold aloft torches? From the Mount of Olives to Sartaba, from Sartaba to Grophina, and from Grophina to Hauran.… They did not cease waving the burning torches…to and fro, upward and downward, until the whole country appeared like a blazing fire.

This Jewish town continued to exist after the destruction of the Second Temple. The stones of its synagogue from the third or fourth century CE were reused in the Crusader fortress. Among these stones was a basalt lintel bearing a seven-branched candelabrum (*menorah*) between two holy arks.

Shortly after the Crusaders built the fortress, it was captured in 1191 by Muslim forces. This followed the effective fall of the Crusader Kingdom at the battle of Hattin in 1187. Thirty years later it was destroyed, along with other fortresses built by the Crusaders, in order to prevent their return to power.

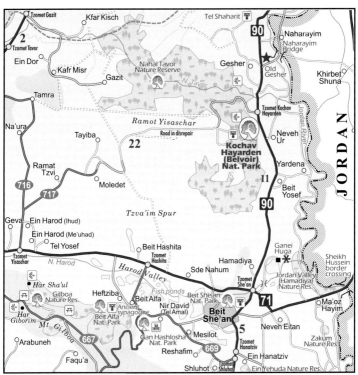

© Carta, Jerusalem

Hundreds of years later an Arab village called Kaukab al-Hawa (Star of the Winds) was built on the ruins of the fortress. The village was abandoned in 1948 on orders from the Arab armies. The order went out to all the Arab villages in the Ramot Yisaschar region to make way for the invading Iraqi armed forces advancing from the east. Military forces of the Haganah immediately took control of the area and dealt a decisive blow to the advancing Iraqi troops.

The Nature Reserves and National Parks Authority cleared the rubble that had accumulated from later construction within the fortress compound and carried out restoration work on the remains of the original fortress. Access to the fortress itself is via a path leading into the main gate from the south. There is a statuary garden beside the stronghold containing sculptures by the Israeli artist Yigal Tumarkin.

As in ancient days, this location provides a magnificent view, especially in the afternoon hours, of the Jordan Valley and the mountains beyond it to the east.

BELVOIR FORTRESS

In 1168, the Crusaders of the Hospitaller Order (Knights of St. John) built the stronghold of Belvoir (French, beautiful view). It was erected at the highest point of this mountainous plateau, at an altitude of 312 m above sea level. They called it Coquette, perhaps a corruption of the Hebrew Kochav, or perhaps a French gender term alluding to the compelling attractiveness of the structure in its natural setting. Even today, after 800 years in which the massive edifice was vandalized and laid waste, its power and magnificence are still evident. The stone blocs, partly fashioned with great care, partly left uncut, are well-measured for each section of the fortress according to the builders' design. Most of the construction blocs are hewn from basalt rock taken from the immediate vicinity, but important sections are built with limestone quarried from more distant areas. Quite a few of the stone blocs originally belonged to structures both near and far from this location. The stronghold is regarded as one of the major building accomplishments of the Crusaders.

In the center is a square courtyard. Its east side is perched on the edge of a steep slope, and on the remaining three sides it is surrounded by a wide, deep and dry moat carved from the basalt rock. The courtyard is surrounded by an outer wall with four large corner towers and a central tower built in between on each side. The towers protrude from the wall, thereby providing absolute command over any approach to the fortress. Stairways inside the four corner watchtowers descend to a narrow gate that gives access

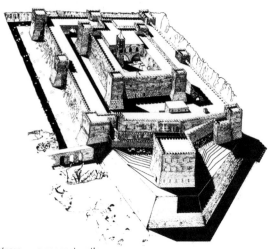

Belvoir fortress — a reconstruction.

to the bottom of the moat. On the east a large, external watchtower, of which little remains, was used to protect the main entrance. Within the open space of the main fortress there was an additional fortification. This keep, or donjon, is square in shape with towers at each corner, and could itself withstand a siege.

The only entrance to the complex was through the well-preserved gate at the southeast corner which guarded against any possible breakthrough. The fortress also had all the facilities and daily utensils needed to hold out for a long period of time.

THE OUTER FORTRESS

1. The Main Entrance Gate

There is an interesting interplay in the use of construction material for the entrance gate. Basalt rock, which is both hard and sturdy, was used in the areas susceptible to attrition whereas limestone was used in forming the arch. To the west of the wall is a wall and the remains of 3 loopholes.

2. The Outer Tower (Barbican)

This defensive structure, separate from the fortress itself, stood on the eastern side where there was no hewn moat and the fortress's protection was, in effect, the steep slope leading to the Jordan Valley some 550 m below.

3. The Inner East Gate

This is the last defensive position before one enters the fortress. When the fortress was under attack, boiling oil was poured from above onto any enemy advancing through this gate.

4. Vaults of the Outer Fortress

This is a system of roofed corridors encircling the inner fortress. The southern vault is 6–7 m wide.

BELVOIR (PLAN OF THE FORTRESS)

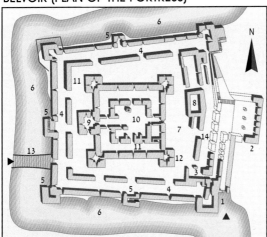

Outer Fortress
1. Main entrance gate
2. Outer tower (the barbican)
3. Inner east gate
4. Vaults of outer fortress
5. Posterns
6. Moat
7. Inner courtyard
8. Cistern and bath

Inner Fortress (The Donjon)
9. Inner west gate
10. Central courtyard
11. Vaults of inner fortress
12. Inner corner tower
13. Drawbridge and exit

© Carta, Jerusalem

The roof rested on arches where sentries stood on guard.

5. Posterns

These openings allowed besieged defenders to secretly leave the fortress. Hidden stairways led down to these exits.

6. Moat

The moat, 10 m deep and 20 m wide, was built on 3 flanks of the fortress, while on the eastern fourth side stood the barbican.

7. The Inner Courtyard

This courtyard separated the inner donjon from the outer fortification.

8. Cistern and Bathhouse

Rainwater was conducted through troughs and clay pipes into the cistern. The well was covered by a layer of thick plaster which prevented seepage. Nearby are remains of a bathhouse.

THE INNER FORTRESS (THE DONJON)

9. The Inner West Gate

The Crusaders built a complex structure consisting of two sets of gates, a gatehouse and a tower. One of the stones used in constructing the gate was taken from a nearby ancient synagogue and displayed a *menorah* relief.

10. The Central Courtyard

This square courtyard, 22×22 m, formed the central part of the fortress. Stairs in the western corner led to the donjon which served as a ceremonial hall and headquarters of the fortress commander. Remains of statues and elaborate reliefs were uncovered on the upper floor.

11. Vaults of the Inner Fortress

This area was used as living quarters, storerooms, and a refectory.

12. The Inner Corner Tower

This square tower protruding from the fortress wall contains loopholes on every side. A stone decorated with a Jewish motif was also found in its construction.

Lintel from a synagogue reused in the construction of the Belvoir fortress.

Belvoir fortress — western gate.

13. Drawbridge and Exit

The bridge comprises two parts: a permanent section built of stone, and a wooden section that could be independently raised, or burned, when there is imminent danger.

OUTSIDE THE PARK

"Old Gesher" and Naharayim

The old Gesher settlement is located close to the contemporary Kibbutz Gesher by the banks of the Jordan River where the Yarmuk River empties into it. In 1948, the kibbutz withstood an attack of the Jordanian Arab Legion, and after Israel's Declaration of Independence in May, fended off another attack from invading Iraqi forces. Following evacuation of children and non-combatants, reinforcements were brought in to the totally destroyed kibbutz and the defendants held out until the end of the War. The kibbutz museum contains exhibits which document the local war story and present a history of Jewish settlement in the region from the beginning of the 20th century. There is also an audio-visual presentation.

Near the bridge there is a large Taggart police station, a remnant of British Mandate days. In addition, there is a stone house which is the restored dining hall of the kibbutz. Opposite it, across the international border with Jordan, is the hydroelectric power station built by Pinchas Rotenberg, "the old man from Naharayim." A reconstruction of this station is open to visitors.

Location: on Route 675 (Yizre'el–Navot junctions); c. 2 km before Navot Junct., turn E to Gid'ona.
Best season: year-round
Swimming pool open only in summer
Tel.: 04-6532211
Fax.: 04-6531136
Entrance fee

MA'AYAN HAROD NATIONAL PARK

...and the Israelites pitched by a fountain which is in Jezreel. (1 Sam 29:1)

 Jewish site Muslim site Lookout point Outdoor recreation Picnic site

Accessibility Rating

  2 3

WC Snack bar Telephone Swimming Showers

  P ✓  ✓ ✓ ✓

The Arabic name for this location is Ein Jalud—in Hebrew, Ein Harod. The source of the Arabic name was apparently the story of Saul, David and Goliath, transformed in the Koran to the story of Taluth and Jaluth. The Hebrew name derives from the biblical setting for the story about Gideon and the drinking water test for selecting soldiers to fight the Midianites (Judges 7:1).

Tour guides bring their groups to the spring and relate the story of Gideon and the Midianites, and then tell the story of King Saul who encamped here with his army before battling the Philisitines. The King fell by the sword in the nearby Gilboa mountain range. In the Middle Ages, Crusaders and Muslims fought battles in the vicinity, and at a later period there were military clashes between the Mamluks and the Mongols.

SETTLEMENT IN THE JEZREEL VALLEY
(see also Megiddo National Park)

In the summer of 1921, a group of people traveled from Merhavya to the foothills of the Gilboa range. They were pioneers of the second and third immigration wave to Palestine who intended to establish a large collective settlement in the Jezreel Valley. They arrived at their destination—a spring whose waters flowed out of a cave at the foot of the Gilboa mountain range. The spring

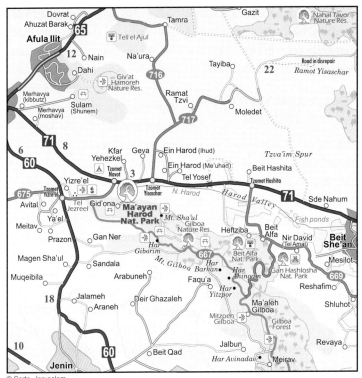

© Carta, Jerusalem

was dammed up by an aqueduct forming a large pool. Tents were pitched close to the water source. The event was commemorated in a poem by one of the party, the well-known poet Avraham Shlonsky. A line in one of his celebrated poems reads: "They recall our white tents, spreading in the vale as doves."

Nahal Harod, which emerges from the cave and wends its way eastward along the Jezreel Valley to the Jordan River, was an extensive malaria-infested swamp which eventually infected the entire group of pioneer settlers. Their kibbutz, along with neighboring settlements, invested years of labor in draining the swamps and converting them to cultivable fields and later into fish ponds. Most of the spring water was diverted for human needs, especially irrigation, and very little remained to flow along the ancient riverbed. A few years later, the first settlers, who founded Kibbutz Ein Harod beside the spring's source, moved to a permanent location in the Lower Galilee foothills but kept the name Ein Harod. A number of groups, one after the other, attempted to settle in the spring location, the last being a group of Yemenite Jews in late 1948 who named their site Gidona.

OLGA AND YEHOSHUA HANKIN

The story of settlement in the Jezreel Valley expresses itself in the string of communities that were founded in the wake of the pioneering efforts to establish Ein Harod, as well as in another very individual way. In the 1920s, Yehoshua Hankin, who had been active in land acquisition since 1890, purchased large plots in the Jezreel Valley. He became known as the "Redeemer of the Valley." Towards the end of his life, he bought a house and burial plot above the Ein Harod spring with a lovely view of the valley that was so dear to him. Although the house was built, he never lived in it. He and his wife, Olga, however, were buried in the beautifully designed gravesite. An amusing anecdote is associated with this site: after the establishment of the State, the grave was thought to be that of Rabbi Jehoshua of anonymous ancestry, and became a pilgrimage site eliciting prayer, supplication, and offerings. The house was renovated and became a museum portraying the life of the Hankin couple and the history of Jewish settlement in the region. A path leads from the spring to the museum.

THE FOUNDING OF THE NATIONAL PARK

Before the development of

Gravesite of Olga and Yehoshua Hankin.

settlements, the spring water flowed through thick Common Reeds (*Phragmites australis*), Narrow-leaved Reedmace (*Typha domingensis*), bramble and other water vegetation. Some of the water was diverted via an aqueduct and powered a flour mill. A remnant of the aqueduct may still be seen inside the National Park. In landscaping the park, the original vegetation was uprooted and an expansive grassy plot put in its place. This section of the Park includes some of the trees planted by the first settlers. The water that flows out of the cave is pure, something scarcely seen in today's rivers. It was channeled into the Nahal bed and flows into a large pond situated at the center of the Park. This is the bathing and recreation area and attracts a large number of vacationers in the summer.

OUTSIDE THE NATIONAL PARK AREA

Ma'ayan Harod National Park is located at the mouth of Nahal Harod and serves as the starting point for a number of hiking trails in this area. Above the spring is the Gilboan range with its peaks and variegated flora. This is an important hiking area, especially in the winter and spring when it is green and flowering (see Mt. Gilboa Nature Reserve). To the east, at Kibbutz Ein Harod Me'uhad, are two visitors' sites: Beit Sturman and a Museum of Art. In addition, Gan Hashlosha, with its pools and grassy areas, is nearby (see Gan Hashlosha National Park).

Corners of the Park.

Farther east is the Beit Alpha synagogue at Kibbutz Heftzi Ba (see Beit Alpha National Park).

The Beit She'an National Park is located in the town of Beit She'an. It is the largest antiquities park in the country containing an amphitheater and many impressive structures from the Roman and Byzantine periods (see Beit She'an National Park).

Tel Yizre'el (Jezreel)

To the west of the Harod Valley, beside Yizre'el, is the site of an ancient settlement. King Saul camped here before his battle with the Philistines. The biblical story of Ahab, Jezebel, Naboth and his vineyard, and the prophet Samuel took place at Jezreel (1 Kings 21 ff.). In excavations, a "winter palace," apparently belonging to the Omride dynasty, was exposed. After the fall of this dynasty, the Jezreel Valley lost its grandeur and was apparently destroyed in 772 BCE by the Assyrian king Tiglath-pileser III. A memorial to those who fell in the War of Independence in this area is west of the excavation site.

Spring's water flowing through this channel to the pool.

The pool in Ma'ayan Harod.

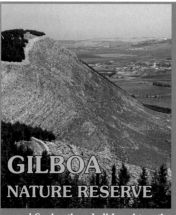

Location: S of Route 71 (Afula–Beit She'an). Route 667 crosses the Gilboa mountains from NW to SE. Parking areas and observation points all along the road.
Best season: year-round, especially January–April
Length of visit: the Gilboa route is about 25 km long. A drive along the road could include short hikes.
No admission fee

GILBOA
NATURE RESERVE

...and Saul gathered all Israel together, and they pitched in Gilboa. (1 Sam 28:4)

Outdoor recreation | Hiking trail | Lookout point | Picnic site

Accessibility Rating

Gilboa, designated as "Mount Gilboa" in the Bible, is not a single mountain but rather a mountainous ridge, appearing as a sort of bent finger or Australian boomerang, a spur of the eastern Samarian mountains going in a northwesterly direction. Despite contiguity with the Samarian mountains, it is a separate entity geographically, geologically and biologically. Mt. Barkan is a bridge between the two ranges: the southern arm joins Nahal Bezek to Mt. Barkan; the northwestern arm links Mt. Barkan to Tel Yizre'el. Because of the numerous and special features of this mountain, two areas were set aside as nature reserves: the top of the northern ridge and its slope oriented northeast, and the eastern slope of the southern spur.

HISTORY

The Gilboa is mentioned many times in the Bible: it is part of the inheritance of the tribes of Issachar and Manasseh; the wars of Deborah and Gideon took place in its shadow; Saul and his sons fell here in their battle against the Philistines, and one of the peaks is named Mt. Saul. Because the peak areas of the range lack water sources, except during the Roman period, there is no evidence of settlement. Pertaining to the Roman period, remains of settlements, agricultural installations and burial caves have been found. From the Arab conquest in

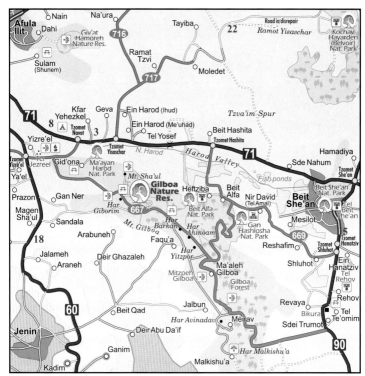

© Carta, Jerusalem

636 CE until the 1930s, the area had been completely void of occupation. Then Ein Harod, Tel Yosef, Heftzi Ba, and Beit Alpha were established on land purchased by the Jewish National Fund (JNF, or Keren Kayemet in Hebrew). These settlements were attacked by Arab bands in the disturbances of 1936–39. In May 1948, the Israeli Defense Forces captured half the range and in the Six-Day War (1967) the remainder of the range was taken. In 1958, the JNF constructed what became known as the "patrol road," giving vehicular access to the range. The JNF planted forests, set aside parking areas and observation sites, and posted signs with instructions and explanations about the area.

VEGETATION

The intersection between two different climatic regions on the Gilboa ridge accounts for the abundance and great variety of plant life in the Reserve. On the Mediterranean side there was once a frontier forest. Despite the accumulated harm caused to it by generations of human-induced incursions, a

Flowers in bloom on Mt. Gilboa.

substantial remnant remains and it is slowly renewing itself in the Reserve. Carob trees (*Ceratonia siliqua)* and the Lentisk shrub (*Pistacia lentiscus*) are scattered throughout the area, while here and there are Terebinth (*Pistacia palaestina*) and wild Almond trees, as well as Hawthorn and Buckthorn bushes. The forest groves are most luxuriant on Mt. Malkishu'a where the Kermes Oak (*Quercus calliprinos*) grows in abundance. Here, too, are many varieties of tree climbers (vines), held firmly in rocks and shrubs; the Italian Honeysuckle (*Lonicera etrusca*), Virgin's Bower (*Clematis cirrhosa*), Great Hedge-nettle (*Prasium majus*), Prickly Asparagus (*Asparagus aphyluus*), and the rare Bush Jasmine (*Jasminum fruticans*) provide evidence of the forest of olden days. Among the family of shrubs characteristically found in this transition zone between the Mediterranean and the Steppe are the Jerusalem Spurge (*Euphorbia hierosolymitana*), the African Rue (*Ruta chalepensis*), and the Pungent Sage (*Salvia dominica*). White Broom (*Retama raetam*), typically a desert plant, grows at the foot of the range.

One of the features of the Gilboa range that draws throngs of visitors is the blossoming of its flowers. Except for drought years, the mountain is decked in a rainbow of colors from the first winter rains until the period of wilting with the coming of the hot winds (*sharav*). Among the impressive displays is the wave after wave of red blooms—the Crown Anemones (*Anemone coronaria*), Palestine Pheasant's Eye (*Adonis palaestina*), Sun's-eye Tulip (*Tulipa agenensis*), buttercups, and poppies. A major drawing card is the blooming of the Gilboa Iris in the early spring. This flower, which is unique to

Israel, grows on a narrow stretch of land in the transition zone from temperate to desert climate.

The Gilboa is blessed with plant species that may not attract the attention of the average visitor but has considerable scientific and economic importance. One may find the stem species of cultivated wheat, barley, oats, carrots, radishes, and other plant types, as well as the ancestors of ornamental, incense and medicinal plants. The area is a genetic database of the utmost importance: the future of cultivated plants rests upon the maintenance of a gene base of wild plants that have developed a resistance to disease and climate changes. This is the rationale for setting aside nature reserves that are not in effect visually attractive.

ANIMAL LIFE

Animal life in the Gilboa is also plentiful and varied. Herds of deer wander about the Reserve and hyrax are found among the rocks. Fox, wildcats, hares, porcupines, and small rodents mark out their living space on the mountain range. The caves contain several bat species. In the foothills one finds swamp cats, badgers, Egyptian mongoose (*Herpestes ichneumon*), weasels, and apparently jackals and wolves, too. In the world of birds, eagles nest every summer, along with partridges, and song birds. Vultures nested here in the past.

All in all, the Gilboa range is praiseworthy for its scenery and for the long-distance vistas from its various summits.

ALONG THE GILBOA TRAIL

Nurit

This is an abandoned farm. It was initially settled by a group of immigrants from Yemen who engaged in forestry and

The Gilboa mountain range.

quarrying. Later, it was a base for Gadna youth—high school students enlisted in a mandatory pre-military training program. The name derives from the abandoned settlement of "Nuris" and from a flower by the same name—*Nurit Asia* in Hebrew (the Turban Buttercup)—which is abundant in the area.

Peaks along the Gilboa Ridge

The mounts below afford a view of the Jezreel Valley, the Harod Valley, the Galilee and the Golan.

Malkishua: 536 m   Avinadav: 440 m
Avner: 499 m   Lapidim: 434 m
Barkan: 477 m   Giborim: 350 m
Yitzpor: 475 m   Sha'ul: 302 m
Ahino'am: 451 m

Parking Areas

There are vehicle parking areas on Mt. Ahino'am, Mt. Barkan, and Mt. Sha'ul; atop Mt. Sha'ul is the Vinya Cohen Observation Post named after one of the founders of Ein Harod and an active member in the JNF.

Gilboa iris.

Mt. Barkan

The national water divide passes through the summit of Mt. Barkan at a very short distance from the Jordan River. As one descends the eastern slope, the amount of annual rainfall decreases. The northwestern arm lies in its entirety within the Mediterranean zone. The divide between the Steppe and Mediterranean regions is clearly evident to the naked eye when viewed from the summit. There is no other geographical divider of this sort in the country. Desert vegetation grows along the eastern slope of the mountain.

Summit Trail Around Mt. Barkan (a circular route)

There is a red-marked trail (3536), with signposts, which circles the summit of Mt. Barkan. During the War of Independence there was an Israeli outpost here and the bunker and communication trenches remain, undisturbed in the landscape. Farther along the trail is an ancient winepress. A hewn cleft in the rock appears to be the location where the grapes were pressed after having been trampled. Because of its unique geographical location, the summit contains plants belonging to both the Mediterranean and steppe regions along with forest planted by the JNF.

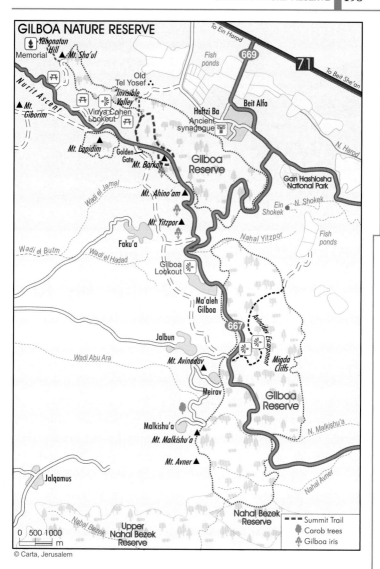

GILBOA NATURE RESERVE

| | 0 500 1000 m |

© Carta, Jerusalem

Legend:
- – – – Summit Trail
- 🌳 Carob trees
- 🌸 Gilboa iris

The Invisible Valley

The Summit Trail meets a trail (3450) that descends steeply to the Invisible Valley and to the former site of Tel Yosef. This descent is for experienced hikers. It is called the "Invisible Valley" because of its hidden location on the Gilboan slope. It was created from geological faults that carved out various layers of rock.

The descent is quite steep and navigating the slippery trail in winter is dangerous. Access to the "Invisible Valley" is also possible via a black-marked trail (3448) which begins at the "Golden Gate."

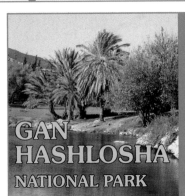

GAN HASHLOSHA NATIONAL PARK

Location: on Route 669, between Hashita and Shluhot junctions.

Best season: year-round

Length of visit: 1 hour to a day

Tel.: 04-6586219

Fax.: 04-6587822

Tel. (museum): 04-6586352

Entrance fee

As cold waters to a thirsty soul... (Prov 25:25)

Jewish site | Antiquities | Outdoor recreation | Swimming | Showers

WC | Snack bar | Restaurant | Telephone | Picnic site

Accessibility Rating

   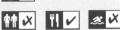

Gan Hashlosha is named after three (*shlosha* in Hebrew) members of the Haganah: Haim Sturman, Aharon Etkin, and David Mosensohn. At the height of the Arab disturbances of 1936–39, they set out for the Beit She'an Valley to find a site for the establishment of a new kibbutz. The three were killed when their car ran over a land mine in the Harod Valley; the "Park of the Three" (Gan Hashlosha) commemorates them. In its first phase, the Park consisted of a raised pool which drew upon water flowing from Nahal Amal. The elevated water created a waterfall at its exit which drove a flour mill. The pool was located in an arid environment devoid of greenery. Over the years, devoted attention to landscaping converted the pond area into a large and luxuriant park. One of the leading weeklies ranked Gan Hashlosha among the 20 most attractive parks in the world. In Israel, the Park is better known under its Arabic name Sakhne, meaning "hot spring," on account of its tepid waters.

The principal constituent of the Park is Nahal Amal which flows along its entire length. The water source emerges from a cave in the western sector of the Park and flows east towards the Jordan River. It passes through the middle of Kibbutz Nir David, one of the few settlements in Israel which has a flowing stream marking its internal

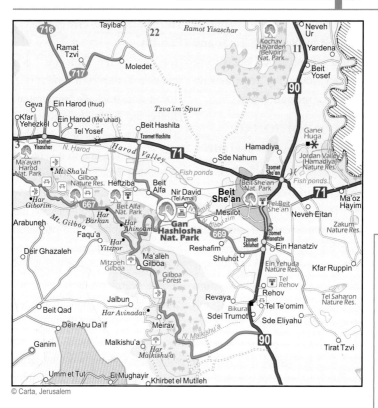

© Carta, Jerusalem

landscape. The water flowing out of the kibbutz is then diverted for agricultural purposes. In the past, the stream passed through the center of Roman-Byzantine Beth-shean (in today's Beit She'an National Park), supplying water for the entire city, its bathhouses and other installations. Several generations ago, a dam was built across the Nahal with an aqueduct leading to a mill. This formed a pool, turning a stream flowing in a narrow bed to a pond dozens of meters wide. From this initial pond, additional ponds were created. The aqueduct still exists and the mill is in working order.

The water in Nahal Amal is saline and not fit for drinking or irrigation. Hence, it was not drawn off for human use and this allowed for the creation of the Park in its expanded natural setting. After leaving the kibbutz, the stream joins other freshwater brooks, decreasing its saline content sufficiently that it may be used for crop irrigation. The salty water is not a deterrent to bathing and the thermal waters draw visitors during the winter season. If anything bothers the swimmers, it is the minnows snipping at their feet. Trees and shrubs and spacious lawns were planted around the water making it a major recreation attraction.

ADDITIONAL ATTRACTIONS WITHIN THE PARK

Museum of Regional and Mediterannean Archaeology

The museum houses a permanent collection of Mediterranean artifacts and changing exhibits with displays of findings from neighboring countries in the Mediterranean basin. There are also exhibits of findings from the archaeological excavations at Beit She'an and items from Egypt and Iran.

The "Tower-and-Stockade" Exhibit

One part of the Park has been set aside to display a replica of a "tower-and-stockade" settlement. During the Arab disturbances of 1936–39, founders of Kibbutz Nir David were the first in a series of pioneering feats to employ this overnight assembly of a new settlement. Components of the entire complex, pre-prepared for rapid construction, were brought to a nearby settlement. A double wooden-fence wall with gravel fill between was erected around a compound composed of residential huts and a watchtower. A barbed-wire fence was strung around the outer fence and at the top of the tower

Amal Pool.

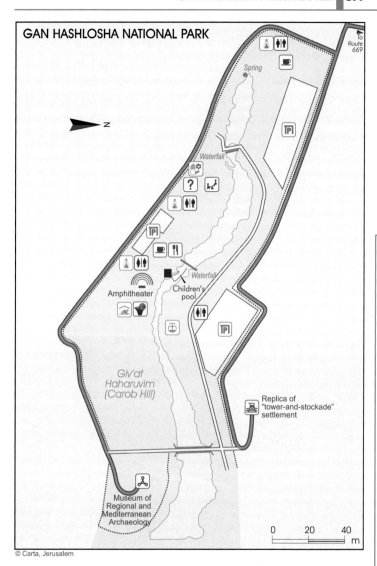

GAN HASHLOSHA NATIONAL PARK

Spring

Waterfall

Waterfall

Amphitheater

Children's pool

Giv'at Haharuvim (Carob Hill)

Replica of "tower-and-stockade" settlement

Museum of Regional and Mediterranean Archaeology

To Route 669

0   20   40
m

was a guard facility operating day and night. Fifty settlements, most of them *kibbutzim*, were established by this method and made a major contribution in shaping the present borders of the State through their ability to withstand Arab attacks during the War of Independence. All these settlements expanded in size and population; none of them today have traces of the original perimeter fence. The Tower-and-Stockade display at the Park is on a scale of 1:1 and depicts daily life in the 1930s.

OUTSIDE THE NATIONAL PARK AREA

Gan Garoo Park

Gan Garoo Park is located at Kibbutz Nir David, beside Gan Hashlosha. It is an open zoo whose animals are native to Australia—pouch animals from kangaroo to koala brought to the site from their native habitat.

Nahal Kibbutzim

The Nahal is reached via route 669. Turn into Kibbutz Reshafim, and from there, on the right, is a dirt trail to the Nahal. The stream is 3 km in length and its hourly volume is about 2.4 cubic meters. The Nahal may be easily hiked, traipsing pleasantly through water along a circular path. Waterproof sandals should be worn and children who do not know how to swim should have some form of life preserver. Characteristic water plants grow on the banks: Holy Bramble (*Rubus sanctus*), sugar cane, species of reeds, and others.

Waterfall in Gan Hashlosha.

Nest of Dead Sea Sparrow.

Location: within Kibbutz Heftziba, on Route 669, between Hashita Junction and Beit She'an.

Best season: year-round

Length of visit: c. ½ hour (Don't miss the audiovisual show on life in the ancient village and the crafting of the mosaic!)

Telefax: 04-6532004

Entrance fee

...and a pavement made for the court round about... (Ezek 40:17)

Accessibility Rating

Jewish site · Antiquities · WC · Snack bar · Souvenir shop · Picnic site

In 1928, members of Kibbutz Heftziba, snuggled against the foothills of the Gilboa range, were digging a canal to bring water to their settlement. One day, they struck a mosaic floor about one meter below ground level. At first, they ignored the finding and continued with their trenching, but one of them, Moshe Breslavsky, who afterwards became known as a humanist and historian of the Labour Movement, decided to inspect the finding. He cleaned the section that had been exposed, and much to his surprise he spotted Hebrew lettering which was part of a depiction of the Zodiacal calendar. The digging came to a halt, the archaeologist Professor E. L. Sukenik was summoned, and he immediately understood that this was part of an ancient Jewish synagogue. It must be recalled that most of the ancient synagogues known today had not yet been discovered. After Professor Sukenik completed the excavations, it became evident that this was an entire floor of a synagogue from the 6th century CE.

Historical sources do not mention a Jewish settlement at this location and there was no indication from the excavation itself of its name. Since the Arabic name of nearby ruins was Beit Ilfa, the neighboring kibbutz was called Beit Alfa, and this is also the name that was given to the newly discovered ancient

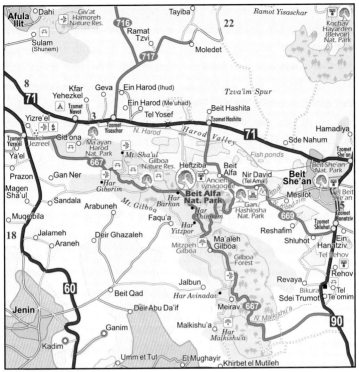

© Carta, Jerusalem

synagogue even though it is actually located on the grounds of Kibbutz Heftziba beside Beit Alfa. After the mosaic floor was restored, without a change in its existing form or content, a protective structure was built over it, and it was declared a "National Park" in its own right, belonging to the Nature and National Parks Protection Authority. Over the years, the remains of an additional 10 synagogues were discovered and excavated in this area.

The ancient synagogue was apparently destroyed in an earthquake. Part of the structure collapsed onto the floor, hiding it, and in addition covering it with debris. In effect, the rubble preserved the floor in its entirety, except for some minor damage. This is the most complete and accomplished synagogue mosaic floor uncovered to date in the country. A dedicatory inscription in Aramaic at the northern entrance indicates approximately when the mosaic floor was crafted: "In the year… [here the inscription is broken] to the Emperor Justin." The reference is apparently to Justin

I, emperor from 517 to 528. The names of the two Jewish artisans who made the mosaic are also inscribed: Marianos and his son, Hanina. These two craftsmen also made a similar floor in Beit She'an. At Beit Alfa their names are written in Hebrew–Aramaic. At Beit She'an, they are written in Greek. The local community paid for the mosaic. All this information is inscribed at the entrance to the synagogue.

During excavations carried out while the mosaic floor was being restored, remains of floors below this from earlier periods were discovered. In other words, synagogues on this spot succeeded one another, attesting to the existence of a Jewish settlement for hundreds of years after the destruction of the Second Temple.

STRUCTURE OF THE SYNAGOGUE

The original structure of the synagogue included a main hall, with an apse—where the holy ark stood—in its south wall, facing Jerusalem. The hall is divided by two rows of stone pillars into a central nave and two aisles. The women's section was on an upper story above the aisles.

The entire hall is paved with colorful mosaics. The floor of the western aisle is divided into squares of geometric patterns. In front of the door to the western aisle is a carpetlike design, whereas the mosaic in the eastern aisle is mostly unadorned.

The floor of the nave or central hall is divided into three panels, each containing a different motif. The top panel shows the holy ark with lions, birds and candelabra on either side. The central panel contains a zodiac with the monthly signs and their names in Hebrew and Aramaic. At the center of the zodiac is the sun-god Helios driving a chariot drawn by fout horses. In each

Zodiac — middle panel of the mosaic floor.

Torah ark — upper panel of the mosaic floor.

corner of the panel is an image of a woman representing one of the four seasons.

The lower panel, near the entrance, depicts the binding of Isaac. To the right is the sacrificial altar from which rise the flames of a fire and to the left is a bearded Abraham, a halo about his head, holding his little child in one hand and a long knife in the other. The names "Isaac" and "Abraham" are inscribed above the respective figures. The palm of a hand appears as if from a cloud, symbolizing the angel of God, and the inscription reads: "Lay not" from God's words to Abraham "Lay not thy hand upon the lad" (Genesis 22:12).

Beside Abraham is a ram tied to a tree, standing on two legs as if hanging because the space is too narrow for his front legs. Behind it is written: "And here is a ram."

All the panels are surrounded on four sides by a string of ornamented figures: on the west side are rhomboids containing fruit; in the south, rhomboids with birds, fish, a cluster of grapes and a pomegranate tree; on the east are grapevines with birds, animals and the figure of a man; in the north, on either side of the entrance, a lion and a bull, acting as entry guards with their eyes directed toward the congregation departing from the synagogue.

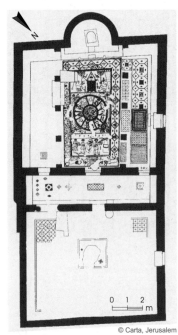

© Carta, Jerusalem

Plan of the Beit Alfa synagogue.

Bulbuls.

Sacrifice of Isaac — lower panel of the mosaic floor.

OUTSIDE THE NATIONAL PARK

Ein Moda

East of Beit Alfa along route 669, and past Kibbutz Reshafim, there is an easily traversed path on the right which leads to the Gilboa mountain range. The hiker arrives at a eucalyptus grove and spring. Ein Moda is the fourth largest spring in the valley. Its clear and fresh waters flow to a pool that is less than a meter in depth.

Location: within city of Beit She'an.

Best season: spring, fall, winter

Length of visit: 2 to 4 hours

Tel.: 04-6587189

Fax: 04-6581899

Entrance fee

BEIT SHE'AN NATIONAL PARK

And by the borders of the Manassites, Beth-shean and her towns... (1 Chr 7:29)

Jewish site   Antiquities

WC   Telephone   Lookout point

Accessibility Rating

The ancient city of Beth-shean was located at the site of the tel which is within the town's limits today. It lies on the bank of Nahal Harod and was a key entrance point on the main route which traverses the Jezreel Valley from east to west. The settlement was destroyed and rebuilt many times throughout history. Excavations have uncovered 20 levels of occupation. Elements of these cities have been restored and others are in the process of being restored.

The Roman-Byzantine city, which comprises the main part of this National Park, is one of the largest and most important archaeological sites in the country. The Park embraces only a part of the historical Beth-shean, the life story of which spans more than four thousand years. It is one of the few ancient cities in the world whose history is revealed both by the remnants unearthed today and through chronicles and other writings denoting its existence.

HISTORY

Beth-shean is mentioned as "Beit Shara" in an Egyptian inscription from the 2nd millennium BCE and already then, as well as one thousand years later, it was an Egyptian outpost. Splendid Egyptian tombstones from the city are on display at the Rockefeller Museum in Jerusalem. The Philistines brought the body of King Saul and his sons to

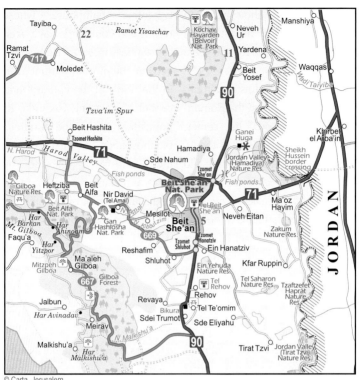

© Carta, Jerusalem

Beth-shean following their defeat on Mount Gilboa. The city was later conquered by David and remained under Israelite control. It was destroyed in 732 BCE when the Assyrian king Tiglath-pileser III conquered the north of the country.

During the Hellenistic period, a new town was established called Nysa Scythopolis: Nysa, after the nymph who nursed the god of wine, Bacchus (Dionysus), and, according to legend, was buried here; and Scythopolis, after the Scythians who were mercenaries in the service of the Hellenistic army. The city name persisted for a thousand years and then was dropped, never to be used again.

The town's population changed several times: the Hasmoneans conquered it in the 2nd century BCE; its gentile residents were exiled and it became a Jewish town. After its conquest by the Romans in 63 CE, the town again became mainly gentile with a Jewish minority. The Jewish inhabitants were massacred during the Great Revolt against the Romans. The three synagogues excavated here and the large inscription found at Tel Rehov point to the continuation of a Jewish presence for hundreds of years after the revolt.

The city reached its maximum size and glory during the Roman-Byzantine period. Its center, which is the National Park today, is in an unlikely location—in effect, inside a land depression. This area was selected because of the stream that flowed through it—today's Nahal Amal. Its waters could be channeled to all the important buildings in the town such as the amphitheater and its services, the decorative fountain or nymphaeum, the pools and both bathhouses, namely, the Roman and the larger

Byzantine bathhouse whose rooms and courtyards have been substantially restored. Beth-shean became the most important town in the north of the country, and capital of Palestina Secunda. Its population was in the hundreds of thousands, at first pagans, then Christians, followed by Jews and Samaritans. The wide boulevards, exquisite buildings, and statues stand out even in its destruction.

After the Arab conquest early in the 7th century, the city declined in size and its end came with the great earthquake of 749 which completely demolished it. The city was buried beneath its own rubble and disappeared from

BEIT SHE'AN — PLAN

1. Theater
2. Western bathhouse
3. Palladium Road
4. Sigma Plaza
5. Byzantine agora
6. Roman shrine
7. Northern street
8. Nymphaeum
9. Tel Beth-shean
10. Eastern bathhouse
11. Sylvanus street
12. "Truncated" bridge
13. Workshop
14. Amphitheater and Crusader fortress

N

0   25   50
m

© Carta, Jerusalem

Roman theater.

sight. The ancient city was only re-exposed when excavations began, first in the 1950s on the Roman amphitheater, and then under Yigael Yadin in 1983. Although much has been uncovered, much still remains hidden.

During the Early Arab period, following the earthquake, the town was rebuilt. The name Scythopolis was discarded and the ancient name Beisan, which was preserved by the Jews, as testified by an inscription at Tel Rehov, was reinstated. In the 14th century, the Jewish traveler and geographer, Eshtori HaParhi, visited this area, and wrote his important study of the Land of Israel.

During both the Ottoman and British Mandatory period, Beit She'an was a large Arab village. It was captured by the IDF in the War of Independence and rebuilt as a Jewish town, partly over the ancient Roman-Byzantine site.

NATIONAL PARK SITES

1. The Theater

The theater was built in the late 2nd–early 3rd century CE and could accommodate 7,000 spectators. It consists of three tiers, a large stage platform, and an ornate *scaenae frons* (façade formed by the backdrop of the stage). The upper level has completely disappeared. The middle level protruded from the ground and most of its stones have been stolen. The bottom tier, which was buried beneath rubble, was exposed in the excavations and is a complete structure which, with minor renovations, has been turned into a contemporary venue for shows and concerts.

Access to the theater was through eight arched passage-ways located along the western and eastern walls. These openings may also have been intended to serve as ventilation tunnels in an area noted for its sultry climate. The wall behind the stage platform was very striking. It was embellished by alternating black and red granite columns decorated with capitals and statues.

2. The Western Bathhouse

The bathhouse was built at the end of the 4th century CE on ancient foundations. It covered an expanse of 1.7 acres consisting of 8 halls with domed roofs and arches. The complex of halls included rooms at luke-warm temperature (*tepidarium*) and rooms at high temperature (*caldarium*). They were heated by a *hypocauston*, a furnace with pipes that sent hot air along the floors and walls of the rooms. The structure was surrounded on three sides by broad porticoes that opened into an additional set of rooms and vestibules. Decorative pools and fountains were built at the end of the porticoes.

3. Palladium Road

This street, 150 m long, is lined by columns. It was built originally in the Roman period, and re-built in the 4th century. It is paved with basalt rock and beneath it is a drainage channel. Along the northwest side is a roofed portico with a mosaic floor, which was built by Palladius, the district governor. The road is lined with shops. In the 6th century, the portico sidewalk was paved with marble slabs.

Mosaic of the goddess Tyche.

4. Sigma Plaza

In the center of the colonnade is a plaza from the Byzantine period. There is an inscription designating it by this name and the semicircular open space is in the form of the Greek letter sigma. Rooms form a circle around the plaza and are fronted by a portico. Several of the rooms have ornate mosaic designs, including one of Tyche (Fortune), patron goddess of the city.

5. Byzantine Agora

This plaza in the heart of the city served as a commercial center. In the Umayyad period, a large facility for ceramic production was set up here.

6. Roman Shrine

This structure was built at the intersection of the main streets during the Roman period and was destroyed in the Byzantine period. The design of the shrine is not known in its entirety, although it is clear that its main plan was circular. A staircase led from street level to the shrine. It is possible that the shrine was dedicated to Dionysus.

7. The Northern Street

This was a colonnaded street which began at the Roman shrine and continued to the tel, the city's acropolis.

8. Nymphaeum

This structure has an ornate façade that contained a public fountain, dating from the 2nd century CE. It was renovated in the 4th century.

9. Tel Beth-shean

Twenty strata were uncovered, dating from the Neolithic/Chalcolithic (5th–4th millennia BCE) to the Middle Ages. Among the most important finds: five Canaanite temples built one above the other, a public building and dwellings, the governor's residence, and

The "truncated" bridge.

basalt tombstones with ancient Egyptian inscriptions.

10. The Eastern Bathhouse

This public facility was built in the Roman period and renovated during the Byzantine period.

11. Sylvanus Street

This Roman street, monumental in appearance, was lined with columns and paved with basalt stone. In the 6th century a new road was built over the Sylvanus street. In the Early Arab period, under the rule of the Caliph Hisham, shops were built along both sides of the porticoed street.

12. The Truncated Bridge and City Gate

A street crossed Nahal Harod via a three-vaulted bridge (the "truncated" bridge), which continued to the northeast city gate.

13. Workshop

A pottery workshop from the Umayyad period was uncovered east of the amphitheater.

14. The Amphitheater and the Crusader Fortress

In the 2nd century, a hippodrome for horse races was built on a plateau outside the confines of

Mosaic floor of the synagogue.

the city. Two centuries later an amphitheater was built on this site. It seated 6,000 spectators; today, only three tiers remain. During the Middle Ages, the bench stones were ripped up and used to build the nearby Crusader fortress.

OUTSIDE THE NATIONAL PARK

Beit Sturman

Located at Kibbutz Ein Harod, this museum contains an extensive display of flora and fauna as well as a history of regional settlement in the area.

Ganei Huga

Close to Nahal Harod, beside the Ein Huga spring, is a large water park. It was established in 1994. The spring supplies 600 cubic meters of water per annum and its rate of flow is steady throughout the year.

Access to the park is via route 90 on the Beit She'an–Tzemah highway. At the She'an junction, take route 71 in the direction towards the Sheikh Hussein border crossing, then take the road north to Ganei Huga.

There are 3 large bathng pools and more than 14 acres of lawn, picnic tables, a snack bar, and a stage platform for entertainment and public events.

Kibbutz Ein Harod (Ihud)

Mishkan LeOmanut (House of Art). On the grounds of the kibbutz an "art corner" developed into an art museum named after kibbutz member and painter, Haim Atar. It is the largest museum on the premises of a Labor Movement kibbutz and contains 14 exhibition halls and a statue garden.

There are on-going temporary exhibits devoted mainly to Israeli artists. The museum awards a biennial prize for photography.

Mosaic of a zebra.

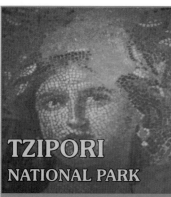

Location: on a hill N of Route 79 (Nazareth–Shfar'am).

Best season: year-round

Length of visit: 1–4 hours

Tel.: 04-6568272

Fax.: 04-6568273

Entrance fee

TZIPORI
NATIONAL PARK

And I will restore thy judges as at the first, and thy counsellors as at the beginning... (Isa 1:26)

 Jewish site
 Christian site
 Antiquities
 Lookout point

 WC
Snack bar
Picnic site
Souvenir shop

Accessibility Rating

HISTORY

Tzipori (ancient Sepphoris) is not mentioned in the Bible but receives continuous mention in Jewish and other literature beginning in the period of Alexander Yannai (103–76 BCE). It lies near the junction of two main roads, and at the foot of the hillock on which it is located is a succession of springs, the Tzipori springs, which were important for the settlement both in times of peace and war.

In 63 BCE the Romans conquered the country and Sepphoris became the center of Jewish Galilee and the seat of the small Sanhedrin. In 47 BCE Herod was appointed governor of the Galilee, and during his tenure Sepphoris was made the capital of the district of Galilee. Its residents did not participate in the revolt against the Romans in 66 CE and thus the city was spared destruction. During the reign of Hadrian, the name of the city was changed to Diocaesarea ("the city of Zeus and of the emperor").

In the mishnaic and talmudic periods, Sepphoris was an important Jewish center, even though its population was a mixture of Jews and gentiles. Many well-known sages lived here, among them Rabbi Judah Hanasi, chief redactor of the Mishnah. The seat of the Sanhedrin was also here until it was moved to Tiberias. The town possessed a degree of autonomy and had many synagogues and

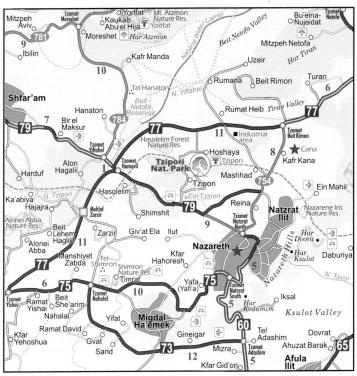

© Carta, Jerusalem

public institutions; according to the Talmud there were 18 synagogues and houses of study (*beth midrash*). The Talmud interpreted the name Tzipori as "perched like a bird on the summit of the mountains."

The Jewish settlement was maintained for hundreds of years, despite internal pressures from the Christian population. After the Arab conquest, Tzipori declined in importance; the Jewish sector, mentioned as late as the 10th century in documents from the Cairo Genizah, died out. The Crusaders built a fortress here over Byzantine ruins, as well as a church. Both structures can still be seen today.

The Crusader forces assembled at the Tzipori spring before the decisive battle at Hattin in 1187 that decided the fate of their Kingdom. Later, the Arab village of Safuriyeh was established here, and in the 18th century the Arab governor of Galilee, Dhahir el Amr, refortified the site. During the Arab disturbances of 1936–39 and during the War of Independence, this village was a center of activities against the Jewish Yishuv. It was conquered

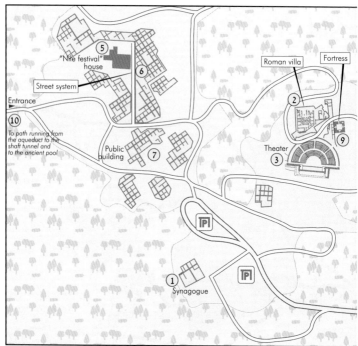

© Carta, Jerusalem

in the War of Independence in "Operation Dekel," and the Jewish agricultural settlement of Tzipori arose in its place. The area occupied by the ancient city was declared a National Park.

SITES TO VISIT

The excavations conducted and still continuing at Tzipori have uncovered a treasure of structures and findings. Some have been preserved and restored, and much, including what is still to be exposed, is awaiting its turn at restoration. The national park also includes the reservoir and other water installations located 1½ km east of the ancient site.

Mosaic depicting the "festival of Dionysus," in the Roman villa.

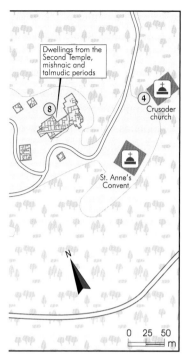

Dwellings from the Second Temple, mishnaic and talmudic periods

8

4
Crusader church

St. Anne's Convent

N

0 25 50
m

1. The Synagogue

According to sources, there were many synagogues in Tzipori. One of them is situated in the northeast section of the excavations and is considered one of the most important and impressive synagogues found to date in the country. It is long and narrow, does not face toward Jerusalem, and does not contain separate sections for men and women. Its mosaic floor, divided into 7 panels, dates from the 5th century. The pictures in each panel are characteristic of those found in other synagogues of this period: a zodiac with the signs of the calendar year and the four seasons; the sun-god at the center, seated on a chariot drawn by 4 horses; the visit of the angels to Abraham and Sarah; the binding of Isaac; the anointing of Aaron; and other familiar motifs. The mosaic depictions with their accompanying inscriptions in Hebrew, Aramaic and Greek make a major contribution to our understanding of the epoch.

2. The Roman Villa

At the top of the hill, close to the theater, archaeologists discovered a large house, dating from the beginning of the 3rd century CE. It apparently does not belong to a Jewish family. The residential rooms of the villa are paved with colorful, well-preserved mosaics located in the northern section of the structure.

The floor of the dining room is notable for its detail of the holiday celebration for the god of wine, Bacchus/Dionysus. The mosaic was crafted with great refinement and among its components is the visage of a beautiful woman who has acquired the name "the Mona Lisa of the Galilee."

3. The Theater

The Roman theater was built in the 1st century CE and apparently staged public spectacles until the Byzantine period. It was 70 m in diameter and had room for 4,000 spectators. There were 5 entrances, all interlinked by an encircling corridor. Behind the stage was an ornamented *scaenae frons* that served as a decorative backdrop to the actors' performances.

Many of the stone seats were either looted or found scattered throughout the area.

4. The Crusader Church

According to legend, the church was erected on the site of the house of Anne and Joachim, the parents of the Virgin Mary. The church currently exhibits a collection of precious stones found in the Tzipori excavations.

5. "Nile Festival" House

This building is located on the east side of the *cardo* (a main street). At its western entrance, on the sidewalk beside the *cardo*, is a mosaic floor on which are inscribed the names of the artists who made the mosaic. In one of the rooms of the building's west wing is a mosaic that depicts the Nile festival in Egypt, a large and complex work with graphic descriptions and pictures of plants and animals.

6. The System of Streets

A network of intersecting streets was uncovered in a residential area on the western side of the city. The streets were paved with hard limestone. Both sides of the streets had porticoes with mosaic floors. Small shops lined the length of the streets. Some of the structures contained ritual baths, but in the Byzantine period additional structures were built above them.

Mosaic in the "Nile festival" house.

7. Public Building

This structure was in use from the 1st to 4th centuries CE, and within it, apparently, was the market place (*agora*). It has a central courtyard surrounded by pillars, and rooms with colorful mosaic floors depicting geometric designs and animals.

8. Dwellings from the Second Temple, Mishnaic and Talmudic Periods

The residential area is situated on the western side of the hill. Between the houses were ritual baths (*mikvot*) indicating that this was a Jewish settlement.

"Mona Lisa of the Galilee" — mosaic in the Roman villa.

9. The Fortress

The fortress is located on the summit of the hill and gives a view of the surrounding area. It was built during the Crusader period. Today it serves as a small museum exhibiting a selection of the excavated findings.

10. Ancient Reservoir

This reservoir is located 1½ km east of the city of Tzipori. Water was supplied via two aqueducts drawing from the springs beside the villages of Mash-had and er-Reina. At a certain point the two aqueducts become one, but close to the city they split again. The northern aqueduct leads to a pool and the southern aqueduct to an underground reservoir. The water supply for this area depended upon the collection of rainfall and its delivery through conduits to underground wells hewn below every house.

An additional source of water was the Ein Tzipori spring about 2.4 km south of the old city.

OUTSIDE THE NATIONAL PARK

Tel Yodfat

Access to this tel is from route 784 between the Misgav and Yiftahel junctions.

The ancient Jewish city of Yodfat was the principal bastion of the Zealots in the Great Revolt against the Romans. The objective of Vespasian was to conquer the Galilee first, and then turn his attention to taking Judea and Jerusalem. Josephus was sent to Galilee to fortify a number of towns and to reinforce the main mountain passes. One of the places that he fortified and

The Crusader fortress in Tzipori.

prepared for battle was Yodfat, which in effect was naturally fortified. The siege of Yodfat began on the 3rd of Iyar 67 CE and lasted for 47 days. The first attempt of the Romans to build an earthen rampart into the city failed because the defendants raised the walls. The Romans then built a dike around the city in order to cut off access to water and incoming supplies and thereby starve its inhabitants. The city finally fell but Josephus and 40 inhabitants escaped and hid in a nearby cave. The city's remaining 40,000, except for 1,200 who were taken prisoner, were slaughtered by the Romans.

Mt. Atzmon

A dirt trail leads from the new town of Yodfat to Mt. Atzmon, 547 m above sea level. The view from the summit is one of the most beautiful in the northern part of the country. The panorama extends from Mt. Hermon and the Golan Heights to the heart of Samaria, from the coast of Rosh Hanikra to the coast of the Carmel range. Extending from the foothills of the mountain looking south is the picturesque Beit Netofa Valley. Because of the vistas afforded by this mountain, the Arabs have given it the name Daydaba, a Persian word meaning guardian or observer. The mountain is composed mostly of dolomite rock. At the peak, there are impressive blocs of rock. On the southeast slope, above Nahal Yodfat, there is a dense grove of Kermes oak (*Quercus calliprinos*) and Terebinth (*Pistacia palaestina*).

Warbler.

Location: SW of Kiryat Tiv'on, near the house of Alexander Zeid.

Best season: year-round

Length of visit: 1–2 hours

Tel.: 04-9831643

Fax.: 04-9531551

Entrance fee

BEIT SHE'ARIM NATIONAL PARK

Whose graves are set in the sides of the pit... (Ezek 32:23)

 Jewish site
 Antiquities
 Lookout point

 WC
 Snack bar
Telephone
Picnic site

Accessibility Rating

 1   2

 P ✔   ✔   ✔

Beit She'arim is cited in written sources as an important Jewish center and thus its approximate location was known to be in the foothills of the Lower Galilee in the northern part of the Jezreel Valley. Following the destruction of the Second Temple, the Jerusalem-based Sanhedrin (Jewish high court) went into exile going from place to place. One of its stations, in c. 170 CE, was Beit She'arim: it had been at Shfar'am, moved to Beit She'arim, and then was established at Tzipori (Sepphoris). There were several renowned sages, one of them being Yohanan Ben Nuri. Rabbi Judah Hanasi, whose permanent residence was in Tzipori, would come to Beit She'arim from time to time and it was here that he arranged for his burial. His sons followed suit and this resulted in Beit She'arim becoming a location where people chose to be buried, not only for Jews living in the country, but also Jews living abroad who wished to be laid to rest beside these holy sages. The settlement was completely destroyed in 352 CE, during the revolt against Gallus Caesar, and its exact location was unknown for many years. In 1872, a British archaeological survey expedition discovered two tombs at the site but no further notice was taken of these findings. In 1936, a Jewish collective settlement (*moshav*) founded 8 km from this historical site was named Beit She'arim.

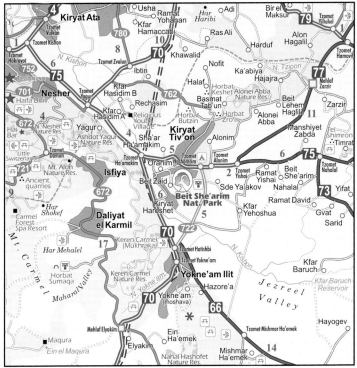

© Carta, Jerusalem

Alexander Zeid, a guard and JNF forest ranger, began to uncover settlement remains at this site during the 1930s. Orderly excavations began under the direction of Benjamin Mazar who found 26 burial caves.

Tree and lawn landscaping now graces the site adding a touch of pastoral reverence to the catacombs.

THE PRINCIPAL SITES AT BEIT SHE'ARIM

1. Synagogue and Olive Press

The synagogue was a large structure built in the 2nd century CE and destroyed two centuries later. Its prayer hall, which had 3 doorways, faced Jerusalem. Two rows of columns separated the main hall from the aisles. The building apparently had two stories. Close to the synagogue are remnants of an olive oil press. A large public building stood on the summit of the tel.

2. Bench Structure

This structure is in the shape of an open rectangle with benches along its 3 walls. It was used by those who came to pray for the dead buried here.

THE NECROPOLIS

The principal attraction at the Beit She'arim National Park is its catacombs. More than 20 burial caves were hewn into the sides of the hill. Some of them contain an elaborate network of interconnected passages with more than 20 halls including a room that could hold a large number of sarcophagi. According to the burial custom of the time, the deceased was interred in the ground; a year after burial, the bones were assembled and placed in a coffin or sarcophagus which was then placed in a niche in the family or communal cave. Belongings of the deceased were also placed in the coffin, along with items of remembrance from relatives. Some of the coffins were made from stone and covered with a heavy lid, but this did not prevent grave robbers from opening the sarcophagi or breaching it in some other way to get at the treasures within.

Some sarcophagi, especially those brought from afar, were made of lead. Coffins came from places throughout the country and the Diaspora. The burial chambers contained numerous inscriptions, in Hebrew, Aramaic, Greek, and Palmyran (a Persian dialect of Aramaic), enabling identification of the place of origin of the deceased. Among the interred are natives from Palmyra, Babylonia, Asia Minor, and Himyar (Yemen) in the Arabian Peninsula. The inscriptions are interesting both for their variety and, on occasion,

ANCIENT BEIT SHE'ARIM

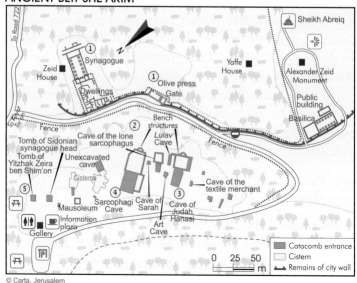

© Carta, Jerusalem

their inventive content: "He was fearless, Simon; there is no man who defeats death"; "I, Hiscius, lie here with my wife. He who dares to open the slab of this casket will not enter into everlasting life"; "Whoever changes the location of this tomb, God who gives life to the dead will judge him."

Many of the inscriptions, of course, simply give the name and place of origin of the interred such as "belonging to Jeshua who resided in the village of Arav"; "Judan, son of Levi"; "Germanus, son of Isaac the Palmyran."

The images and the reliefs on the sarcophagi and inside the burial caves contain a rich assortment of art from the period including representations of holy arks and candelabra, motifs that are common in synagogues; stone doors imitating the wooden door of a house; a boat with sails; lions, eagles and wolves; and geometrical designs.

3. Cave of Judah Hanasi

The cave has three parts: a courtyard, the cave, and an upper structure. The entrance is impressive—3 vaulted gates with a main door and two smaller doors on either side. The names of the Rabbi's sons are inscribed in Hebrew and Greek on the cave walls: Rabban Gamaliel, Rabbi Shimon, and Rabbi Hanina.

4. Cave of the Sarcophagi

Excavators recovered 135 sarcophagi from this cave which is 75 m in length and has many branches. Some of

Facade of the so-called Sarcophagi Cave.

the sarcophagi are elaborately ornamented, mainly with motifs from the animal world. There are also numerous inscriptions of names of rabbis.

5. The Cave of Yitzhak Zeira ben Shim'on

The front of the cave has an imposing stone door. Steps lead to a courtyard. To the left there is a chamber with a razed roof. Looking inside the elevated area one can see four rectangular slabs to place the deceased.

OUTSIDE THE NATIONAL PARK

Alonei Abba and Beit Lehem Haglilit

Alonei Abba, a moshav north of the town of Kiryat Tiv'on, was once a Templar village. The Templar sect had its origins in Germany in the 17th century. One of the objectives of sect leaders was to establish a spiritual center in the Holy Land on the grounds that they believed themselves to be the

Lintel relief.

Sarcophagus.

proper heirs to settle the land of Israel. According to their beliefs, the Jews had "betrayed" Jesus and this forfeited their right to the Land of Israel. A pioneering group arrived in 1868 and established settlements in Jaffa, Sharona, Haifa and Jerusalem. In the early 20th century, their descendants founded three additional agricultural collective settlements: Wilhelma (Bnei Atarot), Bethlehem of Galilee (Beit Lehem Haglilit) and Waldheim (Alonei Abba). The houses built at Alonei Abba are still standing, some of them now renovated and used as residences. There is a beautiful church with a high, pointed steeple in the center of the settlement.

In Beit Lehem Haglilit, too, most of the original houses are still standing and have been restored in order to preserve their initial design.

During WWII, the British expelled the Templars from Palestine because of their open support of the Nazi regime in Germany.

The Alonei Abba Nature Reserve

The nature reserve covers about 225 acres between Beit Lehem Haglilit and Kibbutz Alonim. A forest of Tabor oak makes up most of the nature reserve. A good trail leads through the reserve to the Bedouin village of Kabiya. From the edge of the forest, there is an observation post with a view of the Lower Galilee and the Nahal Tzipori valley.

Menorah relief.

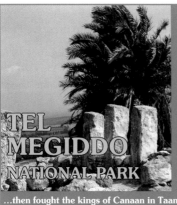

Location: on Route 66 (Yokne'am–Megiddo Junction).
Best season: year-round
Length of visit: about 2 hours
Tel.: 03-7762186
Entrance fee

...then fought the kings of Canaan in Taanach by the waters of Megiddo... (Judg 5:19)

 Jewish site
 Christian site
 Antiquities
 Lookout point
 Outdoor recreation

WC · Snack bar · Restaurant · Telephone · Picnic site

Accessibility Rating

Tel Megiddo is situated on the northern side of the opening to Nahal Iron, on the eastern border of the Jezreel (Yizre'el) Valley. Archaeological excavations have uncovered one of the most ancient cities in the country. According to the Christian tradition, this will be the site of the Apocalypse where, at the end of days, all the kings of the world will fight the ultimate battle. It is reflected in the Book of Ezekiel (chapter 39) in the Old Testament, in the war of Gog and Magog, and in the Revelation of St. John in the New Testament (Rev 16: 12 ff.). This place is called *Har Megiddon* in Hebrew and is known as Armageddon (the Mount of Megiddo) in English.

It comes as no surprise that this place should be the scene of military battles throughout the ages; its strategic location on the road leading inland via the Jezreel Valley from the coastal road (the *Via Maris*) is clear to the naked eye.

The pre-Hebraic name has not been preserved. In Arabic it is called Tell el Mutesellim, the Governor's Mound.

ARCHAEOLOGY

The first person to suggest that Tell el Mutesellim was the site of Megiddo was the 14th century Jewish geographer, Eshtori HaParhi. In 1903, excavations conducted by the German Society for Oriental Exploration under the direction of Gottlieb

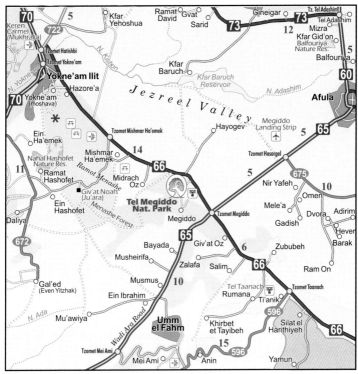

© Carta, Jerusalem

Schumacher established the identification as definite. The principal examination of the site was conducted between 1925 and 1939 by the Oriental Institute of the University of Chicago, with financial support from the Rockefeller Foundation. The digging was carried out by hand, women carrying baskets of gravel and dumping them at the edge of the tel. This pile is still visible in the northeastern area of the site. Seeds from dates eaten by the diggers and left scattered over the site took root and date trees grow on the tel to this day.

The excavations, which reached bedrock, exposed 20 strata of occupation, and if one adds a number of intermediate strata, 25 cities ranging from 4000 BCE to 400 BCE.

Today, the entire tel has been declared a National Park. The small items found on the site, some of them quite unique, have been placed in the Rockefeller Museum in Jerusalem. A seal with a skillfully crafted lion and the inscription "Belonging to Shema, servant of Jeroboam" was sent to the museum in Istanbul, and got lost there. At the

Tel Megiddo, viewed from the east.

entrance to the site is a museum which presents the history of the various cities uncovered, as well as a model of the site which can assist the visitor in identifying the various strata and their history. Among the many items visible to the untrained eye are seals, gates, remains of the fortresses and stables, and an oval sacrificial

Model of Megiddo.

TEL MEGIDDO

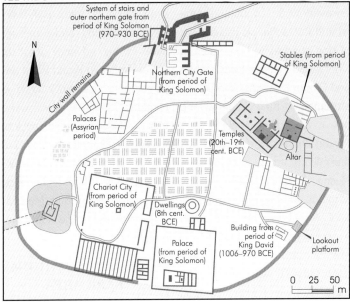

System of stairs and
outer northern gate from
period of King Solomon
(970–930 BCE)

N

City wall remains

Stables (from period
of King Solomon)

Northern City Gate
(from period of
King Solomon)

Palaces
(Assyrian
period)

Temples
(20th–19th
cent. BCE)

Altar

Chariot City
(from period of
King Solomon)

Dwellings
(8th cent.
BCE)

Building from
period of
King David
(1006–970 BCE)

Lookout
platform

Palace
(from period of
King Solomon)

0   25   50
m

© Carta, Jerusalem

altar (high place). The water system is particularly impressive. It allowed defenders of the city to obtain water from a spring on the western side of the tel without leaving the fortified area. A deep shaft, with a staircase system, descends to a horizontal tunnel that leads to the spring. The tel has not yet revealed all its secrets.

HISTORY

Megiddo is mentioned by name in an Egyptian inscription from the 15th century BCE. In 1479, the Pharaoh Thutmose III launched a military campaign against the Canaanite rulers who had rebelled against the Egyptian regime and had formed a coalition under the leadership of the King of Kadesh. Megiddo was the key rebel city on the main north-south route. On the walls of the temple at No-amon, that is, Karnak, there is an impressive description of this campaign, which includes a debate regarding the direction from which it would be best to attack Megiddo, and a list of the booty taken.

Several hundred years later, after two more Canaanite cities had come and gone, one of them perhaps mentioned in the Song of Deborah (Judges 5:19), King Solomon built one of his three key military cities here; the other two were Gezer and Hazor (1 Kings 9 ff.) The excavated gates of all three cities are very similar. Excavations are continuing at the tel and the archaeologists are not of one mind as to how much of what found in the palaces, stables and water systems should be attributed to King Solomon and how much to King Ahab.

King Josiah, who tried to halt the military advance of Pharaoh Necho II into Assyria at the Megiddo Pass, fell here in battle, and Megiddo never resumed its past greatness. During the Mishnaic period, a Jewish village, Kefar Othna'i, was close by. The Sixth Roman Legion camped there and the village became known as Legio Maximiliano-polis, a name from which the Arab village, el Lejjun, is derived. General Allenby broke through here in his advance into the Jezreel Valley in World War I and gained the nickname "Lord of Megiddo." Lejjun was evacuated in the wake of the failed attack by the Arab military leader Fawzi al-Kaukji against Mishmar Ha'emek in the War of Independence. After the war, Kibbutz Megiddo was founded on the south side of the tel.

OUTSIDE THE NATIONAL PARK AREA

Giv'at Noah (Ju'ara)

This is a height on the Manasseh

Megiddo — city gate.

Plain beside Kibbutz Ein Ha-shofet. The hill is named after a kibbutz member who was killed in a plane crash. The Arabic name of the place is Ju'ara. An old structure, used by the founders of the kibbutz in its first days, sits atop the hill. Later, it was used as a training base for the Haganah and the Palmah. Following the War of Independence, it became a military training base for the Golani Brigade and then the Gadna. In 1982, the building was turned into a museum containing exhibits of the area's history.

On both sides of the road linking Ein Hashofet with Mishmar Ha'emek are recreation areas.

Jezreel (Yizre'el) Valley

This is the largest of Israel's valleys stretching from the Galilee range in the north to the Samarian highlands in the south. Yizre'el means "God will sow" and derives from the fact that this area is excellent for the growing of cereal crops. Almost the entire valley is surrounded by mountains: Tabor, Giv'at Hamoreh, the spurs descending from the Galilee, the Gilboa range, and Mount Carmel. The valley floor is enriched by alluvial soil erosion from the surrounding heights. Criss-crossed by main road arteries, the Jezreel Valley has been the site of military

Megiddo — high place.

battles throughout the ages.

Deborah and Barak, son of Abinoam, defeated the Canaanites in this Valley, thus establishing contiguity between the southern and central tribes of Israel. King Solomon built towns and fortresses in the Valley, such as Megiddo, but in the days of the divided Kingdom, it was the border for the Kingdom of Israel. In 733 BCE, it was conquered by Tiglath-pileser III and annexed as an Assyrian province, but remained deserted for many generations. After the destruction of the Second Temple, the Valley became an important Jewish center, but was again overrun in the Arab conquest of the 7th century CE. When Jewish settlement was renewed toward the end of the 19th century, the entire Valley was deserted and partly covered by swamp with barely a trace of permanent habitation. In 1911, Yehoshua Hankin purchased a tract of land in the Valley following which the settlements of Merhavia and Tel Adashim were established. After WWI, the Jewish National Fund (JNF) purchased large land areas and in 1921 Ein Harod in the east and Nahalal in the west were founded. Since then the Valley has developed and flourished, the swamps have been drained, roads paved, and new settlements established one after the other.

Ivory box decorated with sphinxes and lions.

Corn poppies.

Chrysanthemums.

Location: on Route 4 (Tel Aviv–Haifa), 8 km N of Fureidis Junction.

Best season: year-round

Length of visit: 1 hour

Tel.: 04-9841750

Fax.: 04-9843144

Entrance fee

NAHAL ME'AROT NATURE RESERVE

And they shall go into the holes of the rocks, and into the caves of the earth… (Isa 2:19)

 Outdoor recreation
 Lookout point
 Sound & light show

Accessibility Rating

 2
 3

 WC
 Restaurant
Souvenir shop
Picnic site

 P ✓
 ✓
 ✓

The caves of prehistoric man on the Carmel range, as well as those in Nahal Amud and Mt. Kedumim beside Nazareth, share an important place in any book on the history of mankind and all research into the origins of the human species. Why is this the case? According to currently accepted scientific estimations, the origins of all hominids from the earliest type, that date back 4 or 5 million years, up to the *Homo sapiens*, are in Africa. The human species originated and spread from the southern and eastern area of the African continent to the rest of the world. Their only passage northward to Europe and Asia was through the narrow strip of land between the Mediterranean Sea and the eastern deserts—that is, through the area which became the Land of Israel. Indeed, remains from the first migrations of prehistoric man have been found at Ovadia in the Kinarot Valley and near the Bnot Ya'akov Bridge; in the above-mentioned caves, remains from a later epoch— Neanderthal man and *Homo sapiens*—have been found.

The Carmel caves were already mentioned in the 19th century writings of scholars, but scientific excavations only began in the 1920s and continued off and on until today. There are several sites along the western ridge of the Carmel in which important remains of prehistoric man have been discovered: Kebara Cave, Nahal Oren,

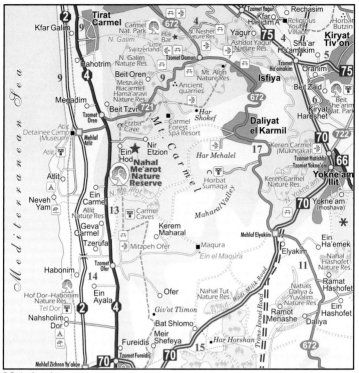

© Carta, Jerusalem

and Nahal Sfunim. However, the most impressive finds were exposed in the four caves at the Nahal Me'arot site (from south to north): Cave of the Oven (Tabun Cave), Cave of the Camel (el Jamal Cave), Cave of the Valley (el Wad Cave), and Cave of the Kid (Skhul Cave). At the Cave of the Valley, which is about 70 m long, visitors may watch a sound-and-light show of the way of life of prehistoric man. This series of caves is part of the Nahal Me'arot Nature Reserve. Their special importance resides in the fact that they do not represent one specific era of prehistoric man: they were used, with periodic intervals, as habitations for various waves of settlement beginning in the earliest stone age (Lower Paleolithic—about 200,000 years ago) until the Natufian culture of the proto-Neolithic period (about 10,000 years ago).

Even before cave excavations began, surface observance of geological formations showed ancient connections between the Mediterranean Sea and the land mass: the sea level then was much higher than it is today; the western cliff of the Carmel was a

Nahal Me'arot — model of a prehistoric family in the Jamal (Camel) Cave.

coastal reef and evidence of this is clearly seen from the fossils on the cliff's face. They appear in the shape of fossil shells called *rudistacea*, a species which is now extinct. When the sea receded, caves were formed in the face of the cliff and later humans used them as living quarters.

Findings from these cave excavations have supplied us with many details about the people who lived in them, their way of life, their food, and their forms of burial. Indirectly, they have shed light on the flora and fauna of the Carmel during these periods: cave dwellers ate the meat of animals they hunted throwing the bones towards the back of the cave. The large quantity of bones allows for a reconstruction of the forms of animal life. Thus, we know that about 40,000 years ago alongside

the Bubal hartebeest (*Alcelaphus buselaphus*) found today in East Africa, three types of deer lived on the Carmel: the Carmel or roe deer (*Capreolus capreolus*); the red-haired deer (*Cervus elaphus*); and the fallow deer (*Dama dama mesopotamica*). In the chain of nature, these animals were prey for lions, bears and spotted hyenas (*Hyaena crocuta*) which have since disappeared. Other animals, herbivorous, include wild cattle, and a species of furry rhinoceros. In the swamps in the foothills of the Carmel were river crocodiles and hippopotamus.

With regard to hominids, one late 20th century find of major scientific importance should be noted. At the time, it was supposed that Neanderthal man preceded *Homo sapiens*, and that Neanderthal man became extinct or was exterminated, and was replaced in the human link by *Homo sapiens*. Then it was discovered that Neanderthal man and *Homo sapiens* shared the same living quarters in the Carmel caves. The bones of Neanderthal man dated from about 60,000 years ago, while the remains of the *Homo sapiens* were even older!

The findings in the Cave of the Oven cover all the early periods. Their listing from the earliest to the latest may not mean much to the lay person, but to those engaged in the history of mankind they provide very significant time markers:

Acheulean: 500,000–200,000 BCE
Yabrudian: 150,000–100,000 BCE
Mousterian: 100,000–40,000 BCE
Aurignacian: 40,000–12,000 BCE
Natufian: 12,000–9,000 BCE

In accordance with today's accepted custom, archaeologicial explorations do not dig up the entire strata on a site, but rather are restricted to a portion of it, leaving the remainder to the next generation of archaeologists. In the Jamal Cave, there is a simulated depiction of a pre-historic family, and at el Wad Cave, which is the deepest cave, visitors may enter several dozen meters and watch a sound-and-light presentation. Natufian era remains may be seen at the mouth of the cave, as well as a reconstruction of a burial from this period. It is not surprising, then, that these caves have an important role in all studies about prehistoric man and his migratory paths.

ADDITIONAL TRAILS IN THE RESERVE

All the trails begin from the parking lot at the entrance to Nahal Me'arot.

The Geological Trail

The trail goes north and climbs

Bee orchid.

Owl.

a cliff along the northern bank of Nahal Me'arot. Along the way, one can see many fossils, evidence that in the past the water level was higher and that this area was part of the sea. At the summit, there is a magnificent view of the Carmel coast. The hike takes about an hour.

The Botanical Trail

This is a circular trail with blue markers. The path goes east, following the southern bank of the Nahal. Along it are various types of vegetation indigenous to the Carmel and different types of terrain. Duration of the hike is about 2½ hours.

© Carta, Jerusalem

Horbat Haglon

This trail has red markers. It goes north and then turns to the east until it reaches the Haglon ruins. Among the findings at this site are a hayloft, wine presses, and ancient burial caves from the Roman-Byzantine period. From this spot there is an excellent view of the western coastal plain. The trail ends at the Ein Hod artist's village.

This hiking trail takes about 3 hours. Hikers must coordinate their trek with the Moked Teva (Nature Hotline) office in Haifa, since the route passes through an IDF firing range.

The Ofer Observation Point

This green-marked trail is a section of the trans-Israel Nature Trail. It advances in a southerly direction and at the end is a forest ranger observation post. The entire area is covered in virgin Mediterranean forest: oak, carob and terebinth. There is a view of the Carmel range and the coastal plain.

This trail takes about an hour. Return to the parking lot by the same path or by another path marked with black signs that change to red, and returns to the parking lot via the blue-marked botanical trail.

Entrance to the Cave of the Oven (Tabun Cave).

CARMEL NATIONAL PARK & CARMEL WILDLIFE PRESERVE (HAI BAR)

Location: Park bounded by Rte 4 (on the W), Rte 70 (S), and Rte 75 (E).

Best season: year-round

Length of visit: unrestricted (overnight camping is permitted only in coordination with the Israel Nature and National Parks Authority)

Tel. (Park): 04-9841750, 04-8231452

Fax: 04-8322287

Tel. (Reserve): 04-9841750/2

Fax: 04-9843144

The hart, and the roebuck, and the fallow deer, and the wild goat... (Deut 14:5)

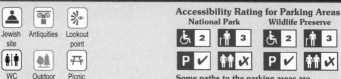

Jewish site | Antiquities | Lookout point

WC | Outdoor recreation | Picnic site

Accessibility Rating for Parking Areas

National Park	Wildlife Preserve
♿ 2 🚹 3	♿ 2 🚹 3
P ✔ 🚻 ✗	P ✔ 🚻 ✗

Some paths to the parking areas are accessible for individuals with disabilities.

This is the largest national park in the north of the country and has a special importance: it constitutes the green vista for the city of Haifa, serving as a recreation and vacation center for hundreds of thousands of people who live in the nearby settlements, as well as for those who come from farther afield. The process leading to the final opening of the park, which covers more than 20,000 acres, was complicated and entangled in a web of difficulties. In contrast to the majority of parks, which are much smaller and for the most part are located on state-owned land, large tracts of the Carmel Park were the property of private land owners. In the 1930s, the Zionist institutions encouraged many Jews to buy land on the Carmel and to build single-unit dwellings in neighborhood clusters. Part of the land had already been parceled into lots along with construction plans when WW II broke out; following the War, the struggle to establish the State and the early years of state-building further delayed construction in this area. The Society for the Protection of Nature, and the Nature and Parks Authority founded later, regarded the Carmel with its scenery, vegetation, and vistas unblemished by construction —in effect, untainted wilderness bounded by urban settlement— as a national treasure worthy

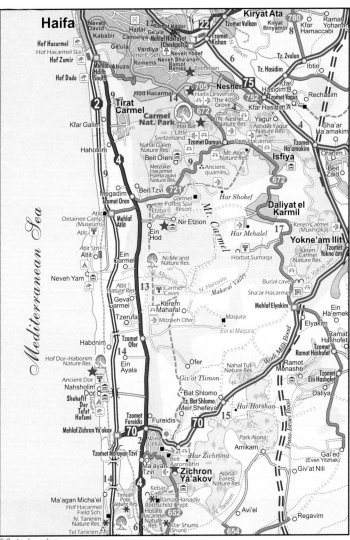

© Carta, Jerusalem

of preservation for the public good and for future generations to enjoy. They managed to convince the Israeli Government to undertake an exceptional step, namely, to freeze all building plans in this area and allocate a very large budget and alternative plots of land as compensation for the Carmel land owners. In 1971, the Carmel was declared a National Park containing nature reserves. It constitutes a sort of ring encompassing areas of the villages of Isfiya and Daliyat el Karmil, which were not included in the area of the National Park.

VEGETATION

A combination of soil, climate

and historical factors created a landscape of rich Mediterranean vegetation on the Carmel, including all the typical component species of a forest—from plants that are not flower-bearing such as mosses and fungi to large trees and the vines which climb around them. Dense forest grows on the northeast slope, and on the summit of the mountain are virgin forests of Jerusalem pine. In the barren areas, the ground is covered with a carpet of blooming annuals, bulbous flowers such as tulips, Madonna Lily (*Lilium candidum*), and flowery shrubs.

PRINCIPAL SITES ON THE CARMEL

The National Park, with its variety of scenery, comprises a single unit, but it contains many defined areas of special ambiance and interest. In addition, antiquity sites are scattered throughout the Park.

Nahal Me'arot

See the previous entry, Nahal Me'arot Nature Reserve.

Nahal Galim

This Nahal descends from the center of the Carmel to the Mediterranean Sea, is rich in forest vegetation, and renews itself after any forest fire.

Nahal Kelah ("Little Switzerland")

This is one of the most striking Nahals on the Carmel. Its cliff-side has been nicknamed Little Switzerland, a name first assigned by Haifa hikers who thought it resembled Swiss scenery. Within the Nature Reserve, parking areas have been set aside for visitors; marked hiking trails depart from these parking lots and the area has designated bird observation posts.

Pomegranates.

The Nahal cliffs are covered with Mediterranean forest made up of groups of Kermes oak and terebinth. A host of vines (climbers), ferns and mosses grow around and about the trunks of these trees, as well as plants that flourish in the humidity such as the Judas Tree (*Cercis siliquastrum*) and the Sweet Bay (*Laurus nobilis*). The cliff faces are filled with the flowering Madonna Lily (*Lilium candidum*), the Maquis Squill (*Scilla cilicica*), and the Rampion Bellflower (*Campanula rapunculus*), and among them live the hyrax, a small rabbit-sized animal.

Stone Quarries

Ancient stone quarries from the Byzantine period apparently supplied building material for nearby settlements. Later, secondary use was made of these quarries for wine and olive production and burial in hewn caves.

Ha'arbaim (the Forty) Grove

This grove, about a half kilometer south of the University of Haifa, has more than 80 Kermes oaks that are remarkable for their size. Local residents considered these immense trees holy and treated them with special care.

Ofer Lookout

See previous entry.

Sha'ar HaCarmel Car-park

This is situated just north of the Elyakim interchange. It contains interesting burial caves.

Ein Hod

Ein Hod is an artists' village southeast of the Atlit turn-off. Its houses were built over earlier ruins while maintaining their original ambiance. There

Blackbird.

Carrion-hooded crow (fledgling).

are workshops and galleries displaying local artwork, ceramic and mosaic craft shops, and an institute for lithography. There are also study courses in the plastic arts. Of historical interest is the Janco-Dada Museum, documenting the artistic career of Marcel Janco, one of the village's founders and a member of Dada—a significant movement in modern art.

Nesher Campground and Recreational Area

These recreational grounds are situated on a winding road which ascends from Nesher to the Carmel forests.

Keren Carmel (Mukhraka)

This is the southern summit of Mount Carmel which reaches an elevation of 482 m above sea level. It is about 2 km north-west of Yokne'am. A Carmelite monastery is perched atop the peak and in its courtyard is a statue of Elijah fighting the prophets of Baal (see 1 Kings 18: 18 ff.) The Arabs call this place el Mukhraka ("place of burning") in memory of the fire that descended from the heavens and devoured the sacrifice. From the summit one can see the Jezreel Valley, the Zebulun Valley and the Manasseh Plateau. The nature reserve Keren Carmel is immediately below the summit.

The Carmel Wildlife Preserve

The idea behind the Wildlife Preserve ("Hai Bar") was to revive the wild animal population native to the area, many of which had been near extinction as a result of hunting at the beginning of the 20th century. This entailed a three-stage process: encouraging growth of the animal population by penning them in a temporary enclosure; acclimatizing wildlife within large enclosures akin to their natural setting prior to their release; releasing the animals into their natural habitat.

The Carmel Preserve rears wild sheep, wild goats, the Persian fallow deer, Carmel stag, and the Israeli gazelle. Acclimatization cages have also been erected which face the cliffs of Nahal Kelah where there are eagles, owls, and other birds of prey. In the parking lot opposite Haifa University there is an information post and from it begins a green-marked trail, known as the Botanical Trail. This leads to the Wildlife Preserve, where a guided tour (fee charge) is offered.

Trails Crossing the Carmel

The routes crossing the Carmel ridge, whether they are roads or forest paths, lead to different places. Several of the main ones are: route 672 which crosses the length of the Carmel along the top of its ridge, or close to it, from Haifa University in the north to Elyakim junction in the south. One can see the Mediterranean Sea along the southern section and in the northern section Acre Bay and north to Rosh Hanikra. The road passes through the towns of Isfiya and Daliyat el Karmil and cuts through sections of forest. Various side roads branch off from this main route, among them the road to Keren Carmel with its Carmelite monastery (see above). The road from the town of Nesher to the top of the Carmel ascends a winding eastern spur with especially sharp turns in the forested area. Along this road, from the bottom to the top, the forest changes species: Carob (*Ceratonia siliqua*) and Lentish (*Pistacia lentiscus*), groves of Oak and Pistachio, and Pine forest. The forest-ranger path branches off from this road and continues 15 km SE to Keren Carmel. This is a splendid scenic

Haganah Hill.

route displaying the diversified vistas of the Carmel landscape.

Route 721 from the Damun intersection on route 672 until the Oren intersection at route 4 passes through forested areas. After Beit Oren it enters Nahal Oren, traversing ancient stone quarries and then continues along the winding bed of Nahal Oren. On either side grow wild olive trees in addition to the regular forest trees.

OUTSIDE THE NATIONAL PARK

Daliyat el Karmil and Isfiya

Two Druze villages are nestled in the heart of the Carmel forests. Many visitors stop here to enjoy a light bite or a meal at the inexpensive restaurants, or browse in the many souvenir and colorful folk craft shops.

Ramat Hanadiv Memorial Park

Ramat Hanadiv consists of a 1,250-acre nature park containing a 17-acre Memorial Garden Park.

The crypt of Baron Edmond (Benjamin) de Rothschild and his wife, the Baroness Adelaide (Ada), are located here and form the central point for the well-manicured Memorial Park which is divided into various gardens: the Cascade Garden, the Rose Garden, the Fragrance Garden, and the Palm Garden. The Nature Park has several hiking trails. The entire complex is open to the public.

Shuni in Jabotinsky Park

This archaeological-historical site is located in the southern Carmel range about 1 km north of Binyamina. Some identify it with Kefar Shami, a site mentioned in the Talmud. There are structural remains of baths and water conduits dating from the Roman period. From two springs in the area, the Romans brought the water of Nahal Taninim via an aqueduct to Caesarea. Remains of a Roman theater may be seen at an Arab farm house standing on the site. The farm was

Daliyat el Karmil — Beit Yad Lebanim (memorial for the fallen in Israel's wars).

purchased by Rothschild's Jewish Colonization Association (ICA) in 1913 and served as the initial residential quarters for the settlers in Binyanima, who called their settlement Giv'at Binyamin after the philanthopist Rothschild. In the framework of the "stockade and tower" settlements of 1939, a group of pioneers from the Betar movement founded Tel Tzur on a height between Shuni and Ramat Hanadiv. This isolated location was ideal as a military training center for the Jewish underground, Etzel (Irgun), and many missions were dispatched from here. In 1945, British Mandate forces burst into Shuni, captured 20 Etzel members and sentenced them to long prison terms.

Mt. Carmel landscape, above Kibbutz Yagur.

HOF DOR – HABONIM NATURE RESERVE

Location: from Rte 4 only. N of Fureidis Junction, entrance to Kibbutz Nahsholim, and then to Moshav Habonim.

Habonim and Dor are recognized beaches with lifeguards, and entrance fees

Best season: touring—year-round; swimming—summer

Length of visit (in Reserve): about 2 hours

Free entrance to the Reserve

...and in the borders of Dor on the west. (Josh 11:2)

Muslim site   Antiquities   Lookout point

WC   Snack bar

Accessibility Rating for Dor Beach

| ♿ 1 | 🚶 1 | Changing room ✓ | Down to sea ✗ |
| P ✗ | 🚻 ✗ | ≈ ✗ | 🍴 ✓ |

The path between the beaches of Dor and Habonim is not accessible for individuals with disabilities.

The Israeli coastline is straight for the most part except for the major indentation of Haifa Bay. In a few places, the sea meets ridges of calcareous sandstone (*kurkar*) creating small inlets and spits. In ancient times, when marine craft were relatively small, these coves afforded a safe haven; sometimes, even harbors were constructed and towns sprung up as minor emporiums. Several of these ancient port areas have been declared coastal or marine nature reserves by virtue of their special features: the small coves, the underwater rock formations, and the undulated beaches which serve as a habitat for creatures of many sub-species. These areas provide a variety seascapes, and a number of them are recreation and bathing beaches.

The Dor-Habonim beach is one of these nature reserves. Its boundaries include 4 km of coastline and a 2-km extension westward into the sea.

HISTORY AND ARCHAEOLOGY

In addition to the coast and the islets, which constitute the principal part of the nature reserve, there are significant archaeological and historical sites in close proximity to the shore. Because of its harbor, Dor was an important town in ancient times. In the middle of the 2nd millennium BCE, the Sea Peoples arrived on its shores after being driven away from the

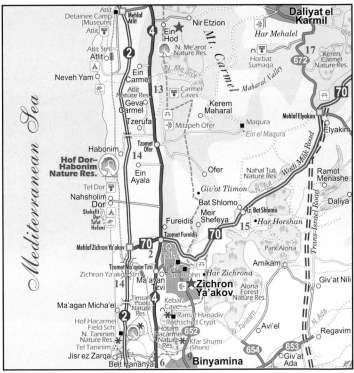

© Carta, Jerusalem

coasts of Greece and its islands. One of them, called the Tjeker or Sicels, dominated this coastal area. They are known through Egyptian inscriptions, and from the Bible which relates that the Israelites did not conquer Dor and its inhabitants until the days of King Solomon. The harbor functioned in one state or another for thousands of years. In the late 19th century Baron de Rothschild considered building a modern harbor at this location. A glass factory was built on land behind the harbor and today its main building,

situated on property of Kibbutz Nahsholim, is a museum. Many ships sank opposite the cliffs of Dor and important finds have been, and still are, salvaged from them. At Moshav Habonim to the north of the Reserve are remains of a Crusader fortress from the 12th century called Kafarlet (or Capharlet). The Crusader name was preserved in the Arabic name for the site, Kafr Lam, the name of the Arab village established here until its evacuation in the War of Independence. Moshav Habonim was built over its ruins in 1949. The fortress was not

Habonim coast.

restored and only its gates and circular corner towers remain.

HABONIM COAST

Coastal cliffs and inlets characterize the entire length of the Reserve. Only at both extremities has the topography been utilized for public bathing: Habonim beach and Dor beach. Each one has its distinctive features. Habonim beach is in effect a bay created by the sea breaking down the coarse sandstone wall, creating a sandy seabed and shallow-water basin. The sandstone heights of the bay are dotted with sea daffodils (*Pancratium maritimum*), much sea fennel (*Crithmum maritimum*) and other plants that have the strength to cope with the maritime winds and salty spray.

What sets this beach aside from the rest of the beaches along the coast are the abundance of seashells of the Livia variety which were once plentiful but now are almost completely absent except for this location.

THE COAST OF DOR

The Dor coastal area has even more to offer the visitor. Here the sandy shoreline ridge produced several peninsulas or several land protusions into the sea creating sandy inlets suitable for bathing. The calcareous sandstone ridge, which is almost entirely submerged in the sea, created several islets. They are, in effect, precipices that appear above the water. Each islet has been honored with a name. From north to south they are: Shehafit,

Dor coast.

after the gulls that nest here; Dor, named after the ancient Canaanite city (Joshua 11:2); Tafat (Taphath), after a daughter of King Solomon whose husband, Ben-abinadab, was governor of this district (1 Kings 4:11); and Hofami, after small plovers that hop about on the shoreline. These islets are important for their bird population and have been declared off-limits to human visitation. The seabed, made up of numerous cliff formations carved out by the impact of tides and currents on the calcareous sandstone, is an excellent environment for the rich development of forms of marine animal life that can adjust to the ebb and flow of the tides.

HIKING TRAILS ALONG THE COAST

The Dor-Habonim Reserve has marked trails and observation posts along its coastline.

The Short Trail

This trail begins at a parking lot at the northern end of the Reserve:

1. An **observation point** overlooking Shell Bay.

2. A **coarse sandstone hill** with a view of the Carmel range and the seacoast.

3. The **blue cave** created by sea waves that crumbled and ate away the sandstone rock. Along this coastal strip the sea formed tiny inlets and crevices of various interesting shapes and drew clams into them.

4. **Blocs of rock** that contain a large amount of clam shells

and coarse sandstone trapped in the rock by limestone (calcium carbonate). Inside the rock, the larvae have extended bodies and they build their homes as limestone encasements around themselves.

On reaching this location, the hiker returns to the parking lot.

An Intermediate Level Hiking Trail—A Continuation of the Short Trail

5. **Small Sandy Bay**. The source of this sand is in the mountains of central Africa. In the processes of erosion, the bedrock was broken up and finely granulated by the currents of the Nile as it flowed towards the Mediterranean Sea. From the mouth of the Nile, currents brought the sand to the eastern coast of the Mediterranean. Since the construction of the Aswan Dam, this sand has sunk in Nasser Lake and no longer reaches this region.

6. At this station one may see the process of natural erosion of the calcareous stone. Calcareous stone is lime-filled sandstone formed through sand being trapped in limestone and then subjected to dissolution by rainfall; the clam shells on the beach are the source of this calcareous material. The ...areous rock preserves the

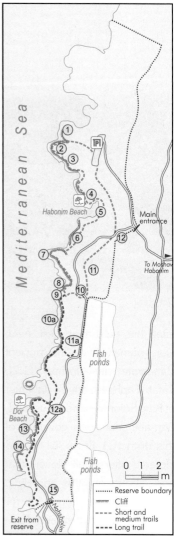

© Carta, Jerusalem

stratified shape of the dunes.

7. At this station, there is a small, flat islet which appears just above the surface of the water. This was once an elevated calcareous rock formation that eroded. On the line of sight between the coast and the islet are animals and plants that,

through special physiological adaptation, sustain themselves under the particular conditions of humid to arid climate shifts and crashing waves caused by stormy seas.

8. An observation point on top of a calcareous ridge.

9. Remains of an ancient calcareous quarry. The digging tools were wet pieces of wood which carved and penetrated the sandstone. The wood expanded and this resulted in the splitting apart and shift of location of entire blocs of stone. From this location, either return to the parking lot via 3 additional observation posts or continue south along the trail.

10. A hill which in winter and spring is filled with wild flowers such as Crown Anemone (*Anemonie coronaria*), White Broom (*Retama raetam*), varieties of orchids, and others.

11. A **water well** hewn out of calcareous rock.

12. **The trough**. A gulley between two parallel sandstone ridges. The trough is flooded every winter when calcareous rock acting as a dam prevents the water from reaching the sea. This water formation attracts many types of sea birds.

The Long Trail

From station no. 9 there is a path leading south which reaches Kibbutz Nahsholim. It passes over an area which permits acquaintance with wild plants that grow on rocky coastal terrain; the vegetation changes according to the distance from the shore (10a); an internal calcareous height with seasonal blooms in the winter and spring (11a); a trough (see 12) and a view of the southern section of the reserve with Tel

Herring gull.

Dor at the very end (12a); a large and ancient coarse sandstone quarry (13); "pool of Cleopatra" (14) that was initially hewn by man and continued to expand through natural erosion of the sandstone through action of the waves; south of the Cleopatra pool is the accumulated detritus of clams which was used to feed birds and to strengthen cement mixtures for construction (15).

OUTSIDE THE NATURE RESERVE

The Glass Factory at Kibbutz Nahsholim

In 1891, Baron de Rothschild established a glass factory for the manufacture of wine bottles to be used at his winery in Zichron Ya'akov. After a few years, production ceased and the factory remained derelict. In 1980, renovations commenced on this building and today it is the Center for Nautical and Regional Archaeology. There is also an exhibit of the history of the glass factory, findings from the Tel Dor excavations, and military equipment salvaged from a wreck following Napoleon's withdrawal from Acre in 1799.

Zichron Ya'akov

This town is named after James (Jacob) de Rothschild, father of the Baron, Edmond de Rothschild. The Baron sought to strengthen the economy of this area by building a winery and planting vineyards.

During WWI, Zichron Ya'akov was a center of resistance against the ruling Ottoman regime. A group using the acronym NILI, led by Aaron Aaronsohn and his sister Sarah, provided intelligence information to the British.

ysucker in nest feeding her young.

Sites to Visit in Zichron Ya'akov

Beit Aaronsohn

This is a botanical museum housing the collection of the botanist, Aaron Aaronsohn, which he gathered on his travels throughout the country. There is also a library, archives, and documentation of the Nili underground organization and the Aaronsohn family. Sarah Aaronson committed suicide in this house after she was tortured by Turkish soldiers who had come to arrest her. There is an entrance fee.

Rehov Hameyasdim

The first pioneer farmers of the settlement lived on this street.

The Old Cemetery

In effect, the "history" of the old settlement is interred here: Sarah Aaronsohn, David Remez (who would become Transport Minister in the first Israeli Government), and Hillel Yaffe (doctor in the pioneer settlement).

Beit Daniel

This house was built in 1910 by Nita and Michael Lange. It was initially called the Carmel Courtyard. After they passed away, Lillian Friedlander, Nita's sister, inherited the house and changed its name to "Beit Daniel," after her son who was a gifted pianist. Various cultural activities, especially musical concerts, take place here.

ZICHRON YA'AKOV

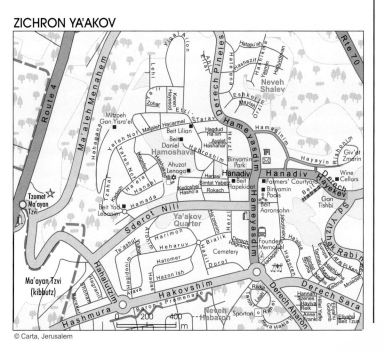

© Carta, Jerusalem

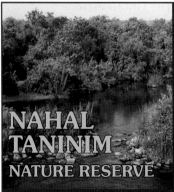

Location: S of Kibbutz Ma'agan Micha'el, where the stream empties into the sea.
Best season: year-round
Length of visit: 2 hours
Entrance fee

NAHAL TANINIM
NATURE RESERVE

...thou brakest the heads of the dragons (*taninim*) in the waters. (Ps 74:13)

Antiquities Lookout point

Accessibility Rating

Nahal Taninim begins in Ramot Menashe several kilometers southwest of Kibbutz Mishmar Ha'emek. The bed of the Nahal passes to the north of Kibbutz Gil'ad (Even Yitzhak), continues alongside the settlements of Amikam and Avi'el, and at this point it ceases to be dry; it gathers rivulets and tiny springs, although the latter hardly yield flowing water. More water joins the Nahal bed in its western sector—Shuni springs from the north and Nahal Ada in the south. North of Binyamina, it makes a large arc, turning to the north in the direction of Timsah pool, then west to the Taninim bridge south of Kibbutz Ma'agan Micha'el, and finally south where it empties into the sea.

The Nahal's importance resides in its water supply. Its springs supplied water in ancient times to Roman Caesarea when the city was at its zenith. At least two aqueducts conducted water from springs above the Nahal. A large section of the aqueduct is visible along the shoreline north of Caesarea. A section of the low-level aqueduct may be seen to the east of route no. 2, opposite the village of Jisr ez Zarqa. West of here the aqueduct passes through a sandstone ridge via a tunnel. This tunnel was blocked for generations, but after it was cleared, it became passable.

The Nahal waters were used not only for drinking and irrigation, but also for flour mills. A large dam and a series of

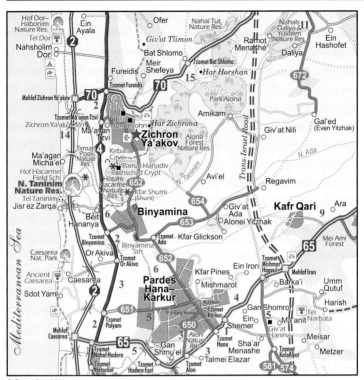

© Carta, Jerusalem

slides were built across its width. The water that flowed down the slides moved the grindstones of the mills. The dam and the slides may still be seen today. Following the construction of the dam, water accumulated behind it. With the addition of the Timsah and other springs, a large swampy area, named Kebara, was created that extended to the Carmel foothills. This became an environmental hazard, a site for malaria-bearing mosquitoes as well as an impediment to travel. The swamp was drained in the 1920s.

Nahal Taninim is the last relatively unpolluted stream on the coastal plain. Even though it is contaminated by waste material flowing in its upper section, particularly from Nahal Ada, this problem is solvable. The Nahal empties into the sea, threading its way through the fish ponds of Ma'agan Micha'el where there is abundant and varied bird life.

CROCODILES IN THE LAND OF ISRAEL

What is the source of the name Nahal Taninim (crocodiles, in

Hebrew)? Did crocodiles ever live here, or in the Land of Israel at all? Well, in fact, they did, and not only in prehistoric times. A crocodile population inhabited this area over a long period of time until the 19th century. The Arab name "Timsakh" (*timsakh* means crocodile) given to one of the pools close by the Nahal is one piece of evidence for this. The Nahal is called Nahr ez Zarqa in Arabic—the "Blue River"—for its crystal-clear waters. The name Nahal Taninim (Stream of Crocodiles) is thus not arbitrary, but rather has a historical base. In Roman times a town named Krokodilopolis stood by the estuary of the Nahal. It is mentioned in Pliny's writings which date from the first century CE, indicating that this location was an early habitat for these creatures. In the 12th century, a Christian pilgrim described the Nahal in the following words: "And in the river there are frightful crocodiles, and they hate human beings more than any other animal." These crocodiles were perhaps remnants of a much earlier population in the land, and Nahal Taninim was not their only habitat, but perhaps it was their last one. Arab folklore contributes its own version for this phenomenon: two brothers ruled over Caesarea, and one of them wished to do away with his brother who habitually bathed in the Nahal as a therapeutic cure for his leprosy. The scheming brother brought crocodiles from

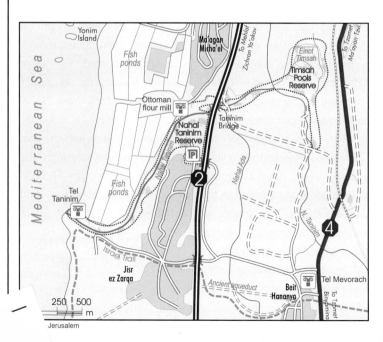

Egypt in order that they would devour his sibling, and indeed, they did so. The crocodile population grew and since that time they have lived in this Nahal. When did the last crocodile pass from the scene? In 1877, a female was caught on the bank of the Nahal.

Crocodiles lived in other places in the country. Until the end of the 19th century they could be found in Nahal Kishon. The last crocodile in the country was stuffed and may be found in the collection of the naturalist Father Schmitz in Jerusalem.

dam, a low-level aqueduct, a low aqueduct, and a stone quarry. Aqueducts channeled water from springs above the Nahal to Caesarea. A large part of the high-level aqueduct is built on arches and still may be seen along the beaches north of Caesarea. A portion of the low-level aqueduct is visible east of route 2 opposite the village of Jisr ez Zarqa. To the west of here, the aqueduct was tunneled through a sandstone ridge. As mentioned, for many generations, the aqueduct tunnel was blocked but has now been cleared for passage.

ARCHAEOLOGICAL SITES

Roman Period
Burial caves, Nahal Taninim

Byzantine Period
Six flour mills powered by water flowing from the dam.

Nahal Taninim — tunnel and wall of the dam.

Ottoman Period

Remains of a ceramic pipe factory that was used to drain the Kebara swamp at the beginning of the 20th century.

OUTSIDE THE NATURE RESERVE

The Kebara Cave

This is a karst cave about 1 km east of Kibbutz Ma'agan Micha'el. An almost complete skeleton of a prehistoric man of the Neanderthal type was discovered here. It is estimated that he roamed the earth about 60,000 years ago.

Timsah Pools Nature Reserve

This is the remaining element of the Kebara swamp, drained between 1925 and 1934 by the Palestine Jewish Colonization Association (PICA), which had purchased the land in 1922. The Reserve contains about 3,000 freshwater springs. Drainage was accomplished through the employment of ceramic conduits which channeled the water from the pool and springs to the sea. At the center of the Reserve is a natural clear-water pool with remnants of plants that grew here before the draining of the swamp, as well as a wide variety of animal life—mammals, water fowl, fish, water turtles, molluscs, crustaceans, and insects. A documented account of the draining of the swamp is on permanent

...a swamp, usually dry in this part of Nahal Taninim.

exhibit at the Carmel Coast Field School.

Yonim (Dove) Island

At a certain distance from the coast there is a tiny island, the Island of Doves (*yonim*, in Hebrew), which is a nesting place for water fowl, in particular, seagulls. Access to the island is forbidden in order not to disturb the nesting birds.

Nahal Taninim.

Heterotheca.

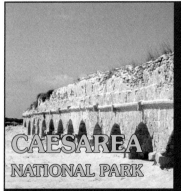

Location: close to the Coastal Road (Route 2), N of Or Akiva, next to Caesarea and Sdot Yam.

Best season: year-round

Tel.: 04-6361358

Fax: 04-6262056

Entrance fee

...to the desolate wastes, and to the cities that are forsaken... (Ezek 36:4)

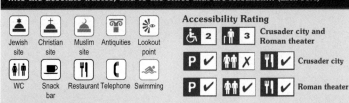

Jewish site · Christian site · Muslim site · Antiquities · Lookout point

WC · Snack bar · Restaurant · Telephone · Swimming

Accessibility Rating

♿ 2 — 🚶 3 — Crusader city and Roman theater

P ✔ — 🚻 ✘ — 🍴 ✔ — Crusader city

P ✔ — 🚻 ✔ — 🍴 ✔ — Roman theater

The ruins of Caesarea, throughout their long history, extend over a wide area and contain a cache of structures and antiquities from various periods, and the findings have not been exhausted. For many years, limestone, marble slabs, and pillars were taken from here to Jaffa and Acre where they were used in construction. A pillar supply depot, Khan el Umdan, in Acre, has dozens of columns that originate from Caesarea.

The central part of the National Park is the Crusader town, whose walls, gates and the moat that surrounds it, is well-preserved. The city, throughout its long existence, extended over a much greater area.

Systematic excavations began in 1932 and still, today, much is hidden beneath the earth and sand. Most of the city south of the Crusader town has been excavated and has exposed a splendid hippodrome built by Herod. The northern and eastern areas of the city await the archaeologist's digging tools. In addition to what now is visible at the site, and this is considerable, many items have been exposed – structures, mosaic floors, statues, and various utensils.

The Israel Nature and National Parks Protection Authority, the proprietors of the Park, is developing and preserving it. It is one of the most impressive sites in the country.

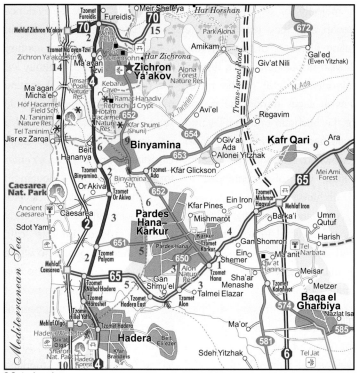

© Carta, Jerusalem

HISTORY

Caesarea is a large ancient site whose history extends over two thousand years. It was founded by King Herod in the year 20 BCE but it was not the first settlement on this site. It was preceded by a Phoenician port town called Straton's Tower. The name is Greek for Migdal Shorshon, found in rabbinic texts. It was conquered by the Hasmonean ruler, Alexander Yannai. The city built by Herod was completely new, and the harbor he constructed was an especially noteworthy endeavor. He named the city Caesarea after his benefactor, the Roman emperor, Caesar Augustus. The town had a mixed population of Jews and pagans and there was much tension between them. In 66 CE, a dispute over the building of a synagogue resulted in the massacre of many Jews, and this was the principal factor that led to the great Jewish revolt against the Romans.

Under the Romans, Caesarea became the capital of Syria Palaestina. The city grew and developed rapidly. Even though a majority of its citizens were pagan and they comprised the ruling elements of the city, the Jewish population was a distinct minority. Several of the major Jewish sages during the period of the Mishnah and the Talmud lived and taught here. The most renowned among them, Rabbi Akiba, was also sentenced to death here.

After the Hadrianic decrees lapsed, several famous *tannaim* and *amoraim* Jewish scholars lived in Caesarea, and they made many legal rulings (*halakhot*). The remains of one of their synagogues has been found in the ruins of the ancient city, as well as the remnants of a list of towns in the Galilee where the priests serving at the Temple in Jerusalem were transferred following the destruction of the Temple. There is evidence of a Samaritan community in Caesarea from the 3rd century CE. In 548 CE, this community led the revolt against the Byzantine regime, which was violently suppressed. Caesarea was also an important base for early Christianity and became a center for this religious movement from the 3rd century. Several well-known fathers of the early Church resided in this city, among them Origen, who wrote extensive commentaries on the Bible, and Eusebius, compiler of the *Onomasticon*, a gazetteer of place names in Palestine.

Caesarea was the last city to fall to the Arabs in 640 CE, marking the end of Byzantine rule in the Holy Land. The Crusaders conquered the city in 1099 and it remained an important site until

The harbor

the end of the Crusader Kingdom of Jerusalem. The Mamluks took the city from the Crusaders in 1265 and inflicted maximum destruction upon it, as well as upon the rest of the coastal cities, in order to eliminate all physical infrastructure that would facilitate a possible return of the Christian warriors. Caesarea lay in ruins for hundreds of years until Bosnian Muslims settled there in 1884 and remained until the Israeli War of Independence. The ruins of Caesarea were declared a national park.

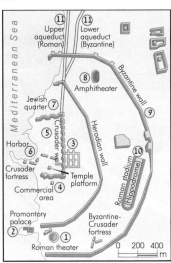

© Carta, Jerusalem

SITES IN THE NATIONAL PARK

1. The Roman Theater

This is the earliest theater excavated in the country. Built by Herod, it is situated in the southern area of the Crusader city. During the Roman period it was renovated and altered a number of times. It has seating capacity for 4,000 people.

Behind the stage floor stood an ornately designed backdrop wall (*scaenae frons*). It was built of pillars three stories high. The orchestra, the place designated for the chorus, was placed in front of the *scaenae frons* and its floor was overlaid with decorative plaster in the style of imitation marble. A statue of the goddess Artemis of Ephesus and several

other statues of cloaked women, oil lamps, and votive bowls were among the findings at this site.

Today, the renovated and reconstructed theater hosts major artistic performances for large audiences.

2. The Promontory Palace

This is a palace and pool from the Roman-Byzantine period. This location affords a direct view of the Crusader city jutting into the sea.

3. Byzantine Square and Street

Two exquisite statues, devoid of heads, that once stood at the side of the gate to the main street in Byzantine Caesarea, are among the sculptures on display here. For years, these statues gave symbolic expression to the beauty of the city.

Caesarea — the reconstructed Roman theater.

4. Commercial Area

A large part of this area was built over cellars with roof vaults that apparently served as storerooms.

5. The Crusader City

The Crusader city was the smallest in the long history of Caesarea, approximating 30 acres. It was enclosed by a wall. The western wall is almost completely destroyed and remnants can be seen close to the sea shore. The eastern wall is about 650 m long, and the north and south walls about 275 m in length. These defensive works are composed of an exterior wall, moat, and glacis (an outer sloping embankment). There are 3 gates along the length of the outer perimeter walls and a number of access paths to the moat. Nine towers, 10 to 17 m long, extend from the wall.

6. The Harbor

The harbor built by Herod is considered one of the most modern of its time. It included an outer basin with a breakwater, an inner basin, partly dredged, and a constructed wharf. Behind the harbor were vaulted warehouses. Above these vaults Herod built a temple to Caesar Augustus in Rome.

In the 4th century CE, the port sank 5 m below sea level. The Crusaders built a quay, constructed of Roman columns in secondary use. Today, the port area is a fishing harbor built after the establishment of the State.

7. Synagogue and Jewish Quarter

North of the Crusader town, capitol columns were found bearing the relief of a seven-branched menorah. In addition, a mosaic floor with a sacred text and pieces of a marble chancel with a list of the priestly "duty watch" were found. It appears that this was the location of the Jewish quarter during the Byzantine period.

8. Amphitheater

The amphitheater dates from the 2nd century CE and served as an arena for gladiator and animal sport.

Caesarea—entrance to the Crusader remains.

Caesarea—the moat.

9. Byzantine Wall

This wall is more than 2.5 km in length. It encircled the Byzantine city at its zenith.

10. Hippodrome

A race track for horses and chariots, situated immediately to the south of the ancient city, was built in the 2nd century CE. It is about 460 m long and about 90 m wide. There is seating for approximately 3,000 spectators. In the center of the hippodrome, a sliver remains from a porphyry obelisk whose original height was 27 m and comprised three sections of hewn granite.

11. Aqueducts

The water supply system for the city was one of the most sophisticated in the country. Water was channeled to the city from two sources: from springs on the southern slopes of the Carmel range via an aqueduct carried on arches (the so-called high-level aqueduct), and from a dam built on Nahal Taninim by a low-level aqueduct. The high-level aqueduct passed through a hewn tunnel whose average gradient was only 0.2 promille.

OUTSIDE THE NATIONAL PARK

Ralli Museum

This is a private museum located in Caesarea. The upper floor exhibits works of Salvador Dali and the lower floor has works of art from around the world.

Sdot Yam—Archaeological Museum

On exhibit here are findings from excavations at Caesarea relating to all its historical periods: Roman, Byzantine, Muslim and Crusader, as well as objects found in the Caesarean synagogue.

Ein Shemer—The "Old Courtyard"

Ein Shemer is a kibbutz 3 km southwest of Iron junction. It has a museum on early Zionist settlement in the country and contains displays of the way of life in the earliest days of the kibbutz in pictures and written descriptions. In addition, there are granaries designed in the style common at the beginning of the 20th century and these exhibits are accompanied by a history of wheat and bread.

Caesarea—headless red granite statue (of Emperor Hadrian?) in the city square.

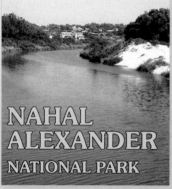

NAHAL ALEXANDER NATIONAL PARK

Location: from Route 2 (Hadera–Netanya), turn off at the Beit Yanai interchange towards Michmoret.

Best season: for swimming—summer; for nature tours—winter

Tel.: 09-8666230

Entrance fee

...I will cause them to walk by the rivers of waters... (Jer 31:9)

Jewish site | Outdoor recreation | Picnic site | Beach | Showers

WC | Snack bar | Restaurant | Telephone

Accessibility Rating

Beach: ♿ 1 | 🧍 1

P ✓ | 👫 ✗

🍴 ✗ | 🏊 ✗

Soft-shelled Turtle Reserve: ♿ 2 | 🧍 3

P ✓ | 👫 ✗

What is the source of "Alexander" in the name of this Nahal? It would be convenient to assume that it was named after the Hasmonean king, Alexander Yannai, who conquered the coastal area, especially since the contemporary settlement of Beit Yanai is named after him. However, the truth is otherwise. The Nahal is called Iskanderun in Arabic, apparently after an important folklore figure in Arab literature, and the name Nahal Alexander is derived from this source. The main streambed of the Nahal originates in the Samarian Hills and it commences near the village of Kur. It passes by the settlement of Tzur Natan, turns north, and traverses the village of Qalansuwa; this village has often been flooded by the stream bursting its banks. Beside Be'erotayim it joins Nahal Te'enim which comes from the hills west of Nablus. The largest and most important tributary of the Nahal, Nahal Shechem, descends from the major water divide between the two mountains overlooking Nablus, Mt. Gerizim and Mt. Ebal. It is not yet a flowing stream here, but it is clear that it evacuates the city's sewage westward. On its way to the sea it passes by Tulkarm adding to the waste material. This Nahal joins the main Nahal west of Gan Yoshiya in the Hefer Valley. Here, the main problems of Nahal Alexander begin. All the waste material of Hefer Valley and the

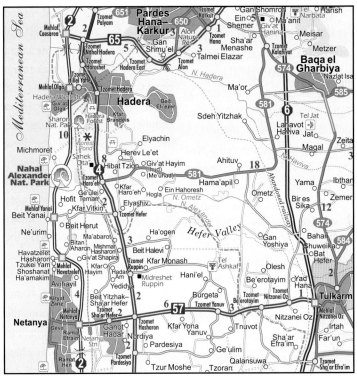

© Carta, Jerusalem

city of Netanya are channeled into the streambed. Despite all the efforts and decisions, the Nahal is still not clean.

Several features shared by the coastal streams are quite apparent in the case of this Nahal and its estuary at the Mediterranean Sea: the movement of sand in the sea from the southeast blocks up the mouth of the Nahal in the summer preventing its water from reaching the sea. The shifting sands, which the waves toss up on the shore, reach an impasse on the southeast bank of the Nahal, whereas on the north bank sedentary sands develop.

The Nahal and its shoreline hold great promise as a vacation and recreation area: boating, fishing, and various beach activities. On its northern side, it is adjacent to the Sharon National Park and a link between the two would create a new activities center in the heart of the Sharon region and prevent continuous urban sprawl between the major cities of Netanya and Hadera.

THE SOFT-SHELLED TURTLE AND THE GREY MULLET FISH IN NAHAL ALEXANDER

Among the animal life found in Nahal Alexander, the soft-shelled turtle holds especial interest. It is the largest of the reptiles that has lived in the country (except for the crocodile, which was rendered extinct in the middle of the 19th century). The turtle is large and smooth and does not have a rigid, hard protective shell; rather, its outer skin is supple. It may attain a length of 60 cm. The turtle lives in water but breathes air from the atmosphere, and thus occasionally lifts its snout and nostrils above the water in order to breathe. From time to time, it climbs up on the embankment in the manner of swamp turtles.

Pollution of the Nahal raised fears for the survival ability of these turtles, but they managed to adapt to the deteriorating conditions. When the slaughter house of Kfar Vitkin began to channel its waste products into the Nahal, the turtles ate these nutrients and began to flourish. Every year there are many nests where the females lay their eggs and dozens of young turtles emerge from them, adding to the population of the Nahal.

In the winter, a process takes place in the estuary of the Nahal which is common among the coastal riverbeds emptying into the sea: the stormy sea whips up large waves which break up the sandy barriers at the mouth of the streams, drawing the fresh water flow into the salt water of

Soft-shelled turtle.

the Mediterranean. This provides passage for the Grey Mullet, a sea fish, which goes a short distance upstream to lay its eggs in fresh water. The minnow fish of the Grey Mullet emerge from the eggs. The Grey Mullet has a high market demand, but because of its spawning habits, there is no possibility of cultivating this fish breed in ponds. As a result, on stormy nights, fishermen come to the mouths of these streams to catch the minnow Mullet and thus severely deplete the Mullet population.

ATTEMPTS TO PRESERVE NAHAL ALEXANDER

In 1994, the Israel Council for the Protection of Streams, under the authority of the Jewish National Fund (JNF), decided to attend to the problem of waste material spilling into Nahal Alexander. In 1995, a detailed plan was put forward to channel clean and purified water into the Nahal. A number of reservoirs that were built along its course are holding the sources of pollution in check and the water is undergoing purification. Part of the water is then diverted for irrigation in the Hefer Valley, and part is directed into Nahal Alexander, which is slowly becoming ecologically viable. The stream is lined with picnic tables and a 2.8-km-long trail which begins at a eucalyptus grove close to route 4 and ends at the Turtle Bridge beside Kfar Vitkin. The path is parallel to the trans-Israel Trail.

Heterotheca.

OUTSIDE THE NATIONAL PARK

Hadera

In 1890, Yehoshua Hankin bought the land on which Hadera now stands from the Lebanese national Salim el-Khuri. The first settlers suffered from swamp malaria and many died from the disease. In 1895, with assistance from Baron de Rothschild, eucalyptus trees were planted in order to drain the swamp. The attempt failed and the area was eventually drained by members of the local settlement (*moshava*).

SITES TO VISIT IN HADERA

The Arab Khan

This is a reconstructed building used as residential quarters by the early pioneers of Hadera. One section of the building has been turned into a museum recounting the history of the foundation of Hadera. A wide variety of cultural and educational activities takes place here.

The Hadera Forest

The eucalyptus trees planted by the first settlers are now an area set aside as "the Hadera forest."

The Founders' Park

This is a public park with a monument at its center symbolizing the eucalyptus tree and dedicated to the Arab khan. The names of the settlement's founders are inscribed in relief on the eucalyptus.

Boats docked on Nahal Alexander, in the days when the stream was still clean.

Beit Olga Hankin

The house that Yehoshua Hankin built for his wife, Olga, is situated on a height of land overlooking the sea, west of route 2. Today, it is a museum of local history.

The Hadera Swampland Reserve

This area contains what has been left of the once extensive marsh and bog that plagued the early pioneer settlers. The Reserve contains a still-water pool rich with rare aquatic plants. River-bank plants grow all around the pond and beside it is a tamarisk grove. The area is a nesting ground for thousands of water fowl.

Cattle egret.

Night-jar.

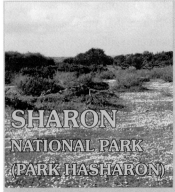

Location: entrance through the Hadera West railroad station (on the Olga interchange–Hadera junction road).

Best season: spring, winter

Length of visit: 1 hour to a day

Park is open 24 hours

No admission fee

And Sharon shall be a flow of flocks... (Isa 65:10)

Picnic site

Outdoor recreation

Sharon National Park is located between Giv'at Olga in the north, Hofit and Beit Yanai in the south, route 4 and Hadera on its eastern edge, and the seacoast on its west. Its landscape is quite unlike any other place in the country: an expanse of grassland which remains green for half the year, flowers blooming in spring, and a park forest of Carob and Tabor oak. These oak trees are remnants of an immense forest which stretched from the foothills of Mt. Hermon in the north to Nahal Ayalon in the south, and widely-spaced trees or clumps of trees have remained up to this day. Among the large bushes mention should be made of the Lentisk (*Pistacia lentiscus*) and the Ephedra, which climbs around the bushes and creates large, green meadows. In winter and spring herbal plants cover the area in a variety of colors— the Chamomile in white and yellow and the pretty Maresia (*Maresia pulchella*) in pink, among others.

Several landscape units, each quite different form the other, are situated within the boundaries of the Park. The central one consists of herbal plants, trees and shrubs, but in addition, the following are notable: vestiges of the Hadera swamp and the Forest Pond.

SITES TO VISIT

Forest Pond

Until the end of the 19th century, there were large areas of swampland in the vicinity of Hadera (the town derives

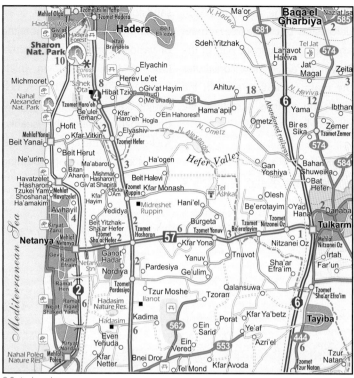

© Carta, Jerusalem

its name from the Arabic word *khadra*, meaning "green," in reference to the wild weeds that covered these marshes in the dry summer months). The swamps were not cultivable, blocked the travel route along the coast, and were a source of malaria. Settlers in Hadera drained the swamps but the disease-carrying mosquito took a heavy toll in lives. Today, only a small portion of the swamp remains. Through restoration efforts, the original landscape, and the native plant and animal life, have once again become a viable although much reduced natural habitat.

Several sections of this restored swampland are within the National Park. The largest and most important is the Forest Pond, a body of water which once covered a large part of this area. Water fowl arrive here in the winter to nest, following past patterns of migration.

Hadera Forest—Park Forest

During the 19th century, eucalyptus trees were planted over a large area on the assumption that their roots would absorb the water from the marsh.

Since then, the area has been deforested, but some trees remain and form a significant part of the National Park. It now constitutes the main recreation area in the Park and various activities take place here.

Hof Gedor Reserve

Waves strike against the coarse sandstone rock along the coast creating an undulating shoreline of various contours and depths. One of the well-known inlets is called "Chinese Bay." A rich variety of sea-life forms have developed among the seabed rocks close to the shore. Sections of this coast have good bathing beaches.

Gedor coast

Forest Pond.

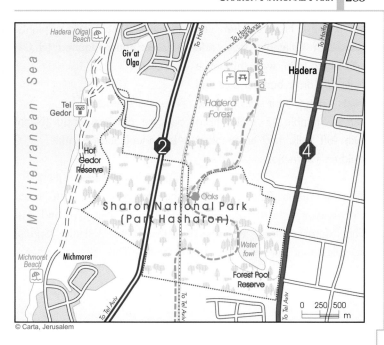

© Carta, Jerusalem

The Sand Dunes

Only 125 acres remain of the extensive sandy beaches that graced the shores of the Sharon Plain. Plant life native to a desert environment grows here but it exploits the conditions granted by the coastal sand dunes. These ecological conditions, along with Nahal Alexander which is close by in the south, make this area an ideal setting for a wide variety of human activities. It also has the advantage of being near high-density population centers such as the cities of Hadera and Netanya, and the settlements in the Hefer Valley, as well as being relatively close to Haifa and Tel Aviv. Moreover, it serves as an areal divider between Hadera and Netanya and thus prevents the undesirable development of a megalopolis.

Even though plans to establish this national park had existed for many years, it was not possible to realize them because part of the land was owned privately. And there were other obstacles. Only after a concerted length of time was it possible to turn this land into a national park.

OUTSIDE THE NATIONAL PARK

Sahek Ota (Play Along)

South of the Sharon National Park, in the industrial area of the Hefer Valley, there is a children's amusement park, the oldest and one of the largest in the country. Here children can play with inflatable toys, ride an electric train, walk through a labyrinth, drive bumper cars and boats, engage their skills in video games, tumble in tanks filled with soft balls, and enjoy other children's attractions.

Moshav Talmei El'azar— Carnivorous Plant Nursery

This farm offers afternoon activities that specialize in the growing of carnivorous plants. Advance notice required: tel. 04-637-3473.

Nahal Alexander

See the previous entry (Nahal Alexander National Park).

Nahal Poleg Reserve

The entrance is from route 2 south of Netanya and just north of the Wingate [Sports] Institute. This nature reserve

Sand dunes.

spreads over about 130 acres along both banks of Nahal Poleg and is located on both sides of the coastal highway. Its eastern section, "Poleg Gate," covers the artificial mouth of Nahal Poleg until it reaches the sea, while its western section includes hills of sedentary sand and the entrance of the Nahal into the sea. There is a concentration of rare flowers such as the Sea Daffodil (*Pancratium maritimum*), which blooms from August through October; the Coastal Iris (*Iris atropurpurea*), blossoming in February and March; the Hyacinth Squill (*Scilla hyacinthoides*) flowering February through April, a variety of orchids, and other flowers.

Joint pine in bloom.

The Reserve also has some antiquity sites, the most prominent of which is Tel Poleg where there are remains of a fortified settlement inhabited from Canaanite through to Roman times. A parking area, snack bar, lake and boating are situated in the south of the Reserve.

Pretty Maresia (Maresia pulchella).

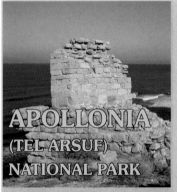

Location: Coastal Highway (Rte 2), N of Herzliya Pitu'ah, via the Nof Yam neighborhood.

Best season: year-round

Length of visit: 1¼ hours

Tel.: 09-9550929

Entrance fee

Dogs allowed only on leashes

...Assemble yourselves, and let us go into the defenced cities. (Jer 4:5)

Christian site

Muslim site

WC

Antiquities   Lookout point

Accessibility Rating

Apollonia (Tel Arsuf) is built atop a coarse sandstone ridge bordering the seacoast and extending north from Herzliya. Waves crashing against this ridge, which is on average about 30 m above sea level, are slowly eroding the sandstone. Inhabitants lived on this mound 2,500 years ago, and several cities sprang up on the edge of the cliff, one above the other. Today, Apollonia is on a list of 100 endangered sites in the world in need of archaeological preservation.

HISTORY

The Phoenicians founded the first city on Tel Arsuf during a period when they controlled much of the eastern coast of the Mediterranean. They dedicated it to Reshef, the Canaanite god of fire. Settlement on the tel was resumed by the Hellenes, who equated the god Reshef with the god Apollo, and called their city Apollonia.

Alexander Yannai, the Hasmonean leader, conquered the city in 80 BCE and included it in his kingdom. The city had a mixed population of Jews and pagans who were in frequent conflict with one another. Eventually, it became a Gentile city. During the period of Arab rule, the city was known as Arsuf, a variant of the Canaanite name Reshef. The Crusaders had difficulties in conquering it, and when they finally overran the city in 1101, they renamed

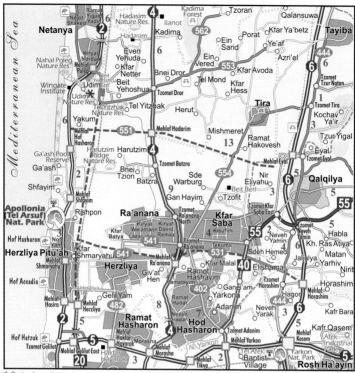

© Carta, Jerusalem

it Arsur and made it the capital of the entire region. When the Crusader kingdom fell at the battle of Hattin in 1187, the city came under Muslim rule for 4 years. In 1191, during the third Crusade, a major military engagement took place here known as the Battle of Arsur: to the north of the city there was a forest of Tabor oak and the military clash took place there. The Crusader leader was Richard the Lion-Heart. The Crusaders emerged victorious and re-established part of their kingdom in the coastal area of the Holy Land, without Jerusalem. The city became part of the domain of the House of Ibelin, at which time its walls and fortress were strengthened in 1241; its remains constitute an important part of the National Park. This fortress lasted for only 25 years, and was captured in 1265 by the Mamluk sultan Baybars, following a tough battle. He instituted a policy of destruction, leveling all the coastal cities of the Crusaders so that these locations could not serve as harbors for a new crusade. The battle lasted 40 days during which the Mamluk forces

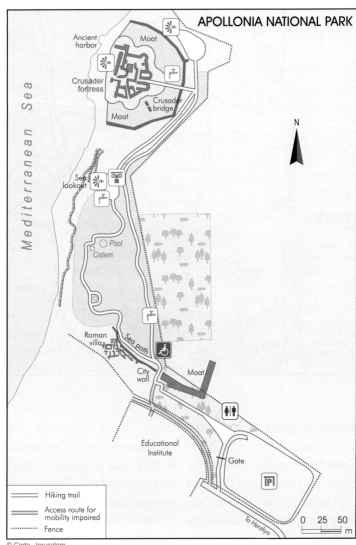

APOLLONIA NATIONAL PARK

Ancient harbor

Moat

Crusader fortress

Crusader bridge

Moat

Mediterranean Sea

N

Sea lookout

Pool

Cistern

Roman villa

Sea path

City wall

Moat

Educational Institute

Gate

To Herzliya

Hiking trail

Access route for mobility impaired

Fence

0 25 50 m

© Carta, Jerusalem

filled the moat with logs, brought war machines up to it, and then launched stones and shot arrows. The Mamluks, who were stronger and well-organized, overcame the Crusaders, forced them to destroy and put to the torch their own fortresses, and then took them prisoner.

EXCAVATIONS AT APOLLONIA AND THE ESTABLISHMENT OF THE NATIONAL PARK

Until a few years ago, the area of Apollonia was in ruins and neglected. The unfortunate proximity of a military installation prevented clearing of the ruins.

Only recently has any worthy archaeological excavation taken place, and following these explorations the National Park was established in the western section of the city by the coast. There is hope that in time the eastern section will also be excavated. This area is where the civilian population was concentrated. In its days of glory, the fortress was built just north of this sector, above the harbor. A steep wall protected the fortress on the west, but this wall was the factor that led to the further erosion of the site. The waves from the Mediterranean battered the wall and destroyed large parts of it, including the harbor at the foot of the wall. Apollonia National Park constitutes a long stretch of the coastline and the fortress is at its northern terminus. Along the way one encounters remains from earlier periods. The Crusader moat, which is apparent immediately on entry to the site from the south, and remains of the wall beside it give an idea of the size of the city at its zenith. Within and around the fortress excavators found 2,200 slingstones, most of them in the area of the inner gate. The portion of the wall dates from the time of Muslim rule over the city. From this vantage point, remains of a Roman villa may be seen.

FLORA

Apollonia sits upon a coarse sandstone ridge (*kurkar*) covered with vegetation characteristic of this type of terrain: these are shrubs and plants that can

Remains of the Roman villa.

APOLLONIA — PLAN OF THE CRUSADER FORTRESS

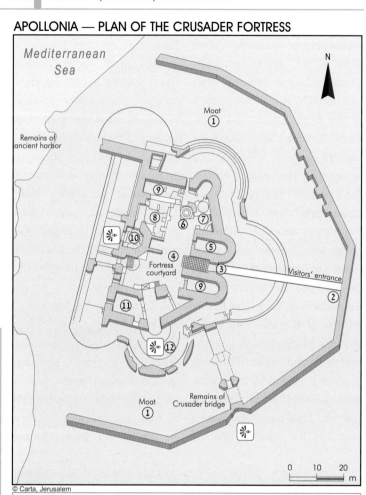

Mediterranean Sea

N

Moat ①

Remains of ancient harbor

⑨

⑧ ⑥ ⑦

⑩

④ Fortress courtyard

⑤

③ Visitors' entrance ②

⑨

⑪

⑫

Moat ①

Remains of Crusader bridge

0 10 20 m

© Carta, Jerusalem

① Moat	④ Fortress courtyard	⑦ Mill installation	⑩ Donjon lookout
② Entrance to fortress	⑤ North hall	⑧ Kitchen	⑪ Burnt room
③ Inner gate entrance to fortress	⑥ Storage installation	⑨ Dining hall	⑫ Lookout over outer fortifications system

withstand the strong winds and spray of the sea. One can find here Shrubby Saltbush (*Atriplex halimus*), Lavender (*oleifolium Miller*), Prickly Drop-seed Grass (*Sporobolus virginicus*) and Evening Primrose (*Oenothera drummondii*). There is no trace of the Tabor oak forest where the battle of Arsur had taken place.

THE CRUSADER FORTRESS

The Crusader fortress, which dominates the city and the seacoast, constitutes the key feature of the Park. It has been excavated and reconstructed. The fortress is typical for its period. It is surrounded by a deep moat and at its center is a fortified tower which was a second line of defense if the enemy succeeded in penetrating the outer defenses of the fortress.

The fortified tower also gives a fine view of the entire area, both the land structures, the sea and the remains of the port.

THE SITES WITHIN THE CRUSADER FORTRESS

1. The Moat
The moat is 30 m wide and 14 m deep. Entrance to the fortress was via a bridge.

2. Entrance to the Fortress

3. Inner Entrance Gate
The gate was two stories high flanked by a semicircular tower on both sides.

Palestinian iris.

4. The Courtyard
The courtyard, which was 28 × 10 m, allowed access both to the second story and to the subterranean chambers. Rooms were located around its perimeter and the fortified tower was located on its western side.

5. The North Hall
This is a hall and a semicircular tower. The walls were made of white plaster and reached a height of 4 m.

6. The Storage Facility
This was a round structure with a diameter of 3.3 m. It was apparently used to store grains and other food products.

7. Mill Installation
This installation was 3.4 m in diameter and was used to grind grain into flour.

8. Kitchen
The remains of 5 cooking stoves were found on one side of the kitchen. On the other side were two plastered cisterns and a water channel.

9. Dining Hall
The room was used by the fortress soldiers. Many ceramic dishes were found here, and among them were ornamented, glazed-pottery bowls in the style of the period.

View from Apollonia of the Mediterranean Sea.

10. The Donjon Observation Point

This is an octagonal structure that rises to a height of 10 m. At the top one can see the Crusader harbor with its two submerged towers beneath the sea. On a clear day, Jaffa is visible to the south and Caesarea may be seen to the north.

11. The "Burnt Room"

Evidence of scorched walls set alight when the Mamluk forces burnt the entire fortress is clearly visible in this room.

12. Lookout Over Outer Fortifications System

From here there is a view of the moat and the head of the bridge that led to the exterior gate.

OUTSIDE THE NATIONAL PARK

Shfayim

This kibbutz was founded in 1935. The source of its name is drawn from the biblical verse "I will open rivers in *high places* (= *shfayim* in Hebrew)" (Isaiah 41:18). In the years before the establishment of the State, this was a base for the Palmah and a disembarkation point for the "illegal immigrants," survivors of the European concentration camps, who were dodging the British blockade off the coast of Palestine.

On the grounds of the Kibbutz: a water park with water games, a wave-making pool, water slides, rubber tube rides, children's world and amusement installations for infants, a motor car park with various types of karting vehicles, dirt road vehicles, bumper craft, and trampolines.

Park Yakum

This park is located beside Nahal Poleg and is open on a seasonal basis. There are pedal boats, tractor-with-cart rides, and rappelling down cliffs. In addition, there is a creative activities corner for children, game installations and other amusements.

The Ga'ash Pool Reserve

This Reserve is situated to the northeast of Kibbutz Ga'ash. The pool is awash with flowers, some of them rare, as well as water fowl which flock here during most of the year. The pool contains rare amphibians—Triton, a rat-like hamster (*Cricetulus triton*) and the Common Spadefoot (*Pelobates fuscus*).

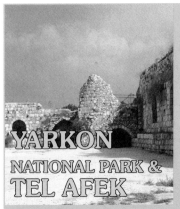

YARKON NATIONAL PARK & TEL AFEK

Entrance to Yarkon Park: from Rte 5 (Kesem–Morasha interchanges), next to Yarkonim interchange.

Entrance to the Afek Park: from Rte 483 (Petah Tikva–Rosh Ha'ayin), next to Afek Junction.

Best season: year-round

Length of visit: 2 hrs to a day

Tel.: Visitors' Center: 03-9348463; Tel Afek: 03-9030760; Yarkon Park: 03-9348462

Same-day, single admission fee to both parts of the park

And Me-jarkon and Rakkon, with the border before Joppa. (Josh 19:46)

Antiquities	Outdoor recreation	Lookout point
WC	Telephone	Picnic site

Accessibility Rating

♿ 3	👤 3
P ✓	👥 ✓

The Yarkon National Park consists of two adjoining sectors, each with a separate entrance. One sector encircles Tel Afek—access is from route 483 between Rosh Ha'ayin and Petah Tikva; the other sector is northwest of here, around the bends in the Yarkon River—access is via route 5 on the road leading to the Baptist Village. Both sectors contain extensive areas for rest and recreation. Whoever intends to visit only the park sites should allocate a few hours, but those who intend to spend time relaxing on the grass and among the trees might consider staying for much longer.

SOURCES OF THE YARKON RIVER

The headwaters of the Yarkon are in the mountain highlands of Samaria and Benjamin. Here one finds its main tributaries: Nahal Kana, Nahal Raba, and Nahal Shilo, but these are intermittent streams which carry water only in winter. There are small, picturesque springs in Nahal Kana but their water soon peters out after a short distance. The real riverbed only begins at the major springs of Rosh Ha'ayin, and from here the river flows until it spills into the sea, and crossing it was once difficult and almost impossible. Evidence of this occurred as late as WWI when the British army under

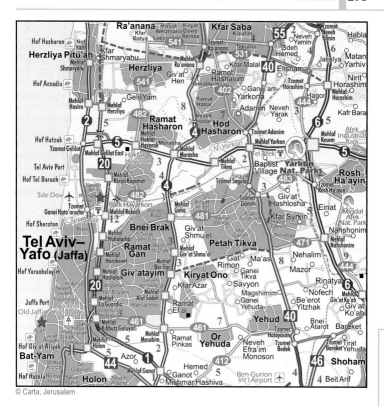

© Carta, Jerusalem

General Allenby was forced to halt at the southern bank of the river for several months. Crossing the river was considered an important military operation and 3 memorial monuments are testimony to this.

Since ancient times, the river has traversed all the routes coming from the south; the only area where the river could be forded was at Tel Afek, between the Yarkon Springs and the mountains. Over the generations, military convoys passed through this point and even today there are vestiges of fortifications designed to defend the passage: Afek Tower, also known as Yaveh Tower or Tzedek Tower on the east, and Tel Afek fortifications beside the springs to the west. The town of Rosh Ha'ayin is situated exactly at the Tel Afek passageway. The name Rosh Ha'ayin is a translation of the Arabic 'Ras el-Ain', which is also applied to the springs and to the train station nearby. Most of the stream water was channeled southward to the Yarkon-Negev water carrier resulting in today's springs being but a shadow of their former volume.

TEL AFEK

The first indications of settlement at Tel Afek date from the Chalcolithic period more than 5,000 years ago. In the Early Bronze period (about 3000 BCE) Afek (biblical Aphek) was a large, fortified city. It was close to Aphek that the Philistines launched their military campaign against the Israelites which resulted in the latter's defeat and the destruction of Shiloh.

> Now Israel went out against the Philistines to battle, and pitched beside Eben-ezer; and the Philistines pitched in Aphek.... And the Philistines fought, and Israel was smitten, and they fled every man into his tent; and there was a very great slaughter; for there fell of Israel thirty thousand footmen. And the ark of God was taken; and the two sons of Eli, Hophni and Phinehas, were slain. (1 Samuel 4–11)

Herod built a city here and there are visible remnants. He called the city Antipatris, after his father. Excavations have exposed the floor of the main street (the *Cardo*) and the commercial quarter of the city. The city was destroyed by an earthquake in 363 CE. Over the centuries, the city declined in size and was confined only to the hilltop of Tel Afek.

The Ottoman Fortress Binar Bashi

This building is the central element at Tel Afek. For a long time it was mistakenly identified as the Antipatris fortress. In fact, it was built by the sultan Selim II,

Afek fortress.

YARKON NATIONAL PARK AND TEL AFEK

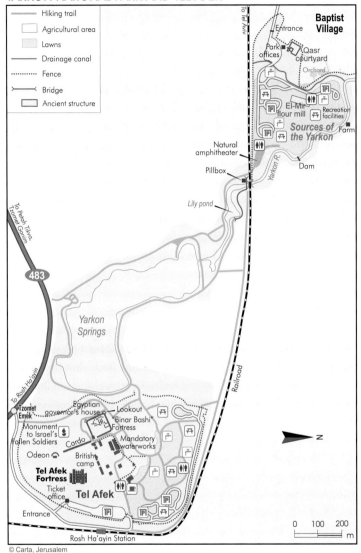

Legend:
- Hiking trail
- Agricultural area
- Lawns
- Drainage canal
- Fence
- Bridge
- Ancient structure

Baptist Village

To Tel Aviv

Entrance

Park offices

Qasr courtyard

Orchard

El-Mir flour mill

Recreation facilities

Sources of the Yarkon

Farm

Natural amphitheater

Yarkon R.

Dam

Pillbox

Lily pond

To Petah Tikva, Tzomet Gannim

483

Yarkon Springs

Railroad

To Rosh Ha'ayin

Tzomet Emek

Egyptian governor's house

Lookout

"Binar Bashi" Fortress

Monument to Israel's fallen Soldiers

Cardo

Mandatory waterworks

Odeon

British camp

Tel Afek Fortress

Ticket office

Tel Afek

Entrance

Rosh Ha'ayin Station

0   100   200 m

N

© Carta, Jerusalem

in the 16th century, and was given the nickname Binar Bashi—the head of the spring. Despite the destruction, the structure is still impressive today, especially its walls and towers, in particular, the corner watchtowers. The northwest tower affords a beautiful view of the surrounding area.

The Egyptian Governor's House

This structure was built in the middle of the 2nd millennium BCE. It is the most complete of the Afek castles and served as the residence of the local Egyptian ruler.

The Water System and the British Army Camp

In the 1930s, the British built a water system that brought the flow from the Yarkon springs near the coastal plain to Jerusalem in the Judean hills. Close to the facility there was an army camp for British soldiers who were assigned to its defense. In the War of Independence (1948) the facility ceased to operate after pipes in the pumping system burst. In 1955, the Israeli National Water Company, Mekorot, dammed the area of the springs and renewed flow in a new direction, from the Yarkon springs south to the Negev. With the establishment of the National Water Carrier, a pumping station also delivered water to the center of the country, to Jerusalem and to the Negev.

There is a path connecting the Tel Afek sector of the park to the sources of the Yarkon sector. It passes by a large pond, continues to the Tel Aviv–Rosh Ha'ayin railway tracks, and reaches an oval structure, a pillbox. The marked path is part of the trans-Israel Trail.

SITES ALONG THE YARKON

The Pillbox

This was a guard post built beside the Yarkon River bridge in 1937 during the Arab disturbances in order to protect the rail line and the bridge from sabotage. The

Tel Afek — the fortress.

guards, who were called "the Railway Gendarmerie Corps," were mostly Jews.

Lily Pond

Below the railway, there is a narrow gate which leads to a large grassy area surrounded by the Yarkon and its tributaries. Here the main subject is the river, with a natural lily pond whose flowers float on the water's surface, various bank plants and tall trees.

This is a tranquil area except for the occasional passing of a train. The chirping of birds fills the air with sound, perhaps the descendants of the birds which sang to Joel Moses Solomon, one of the founders of Petah Tikva. It is pleasant to stroll along the length of the river with the hope of catching a glimpse of the animals living on its banks or simply to gaze upon the flowing water.

El-Mir Mill

This flour mill, powered by the current of the Yarkon, was built by the Romans and renovated in the Mamluk and Ottoman periods. It continued to function during the early years of Petah Tikva (founded in 1878). In the past, the mill site had 13 power stations where flour was ground.

Qasr Courtyard

This agricultural farm was built by Salim Qasr during the rule of Mohammed Ali (1832–1840). In 1845, the land was sold to Baron de Rothschild and eventually he placed the land at the disposal of the first residents of Petah Tikva.

Yellow water lily.

The Yarkon Ecology Education Research Center

The Center conducts training courses in the vicinity of the Yarkon River, integrating research programs with topics bearing on the interaction of man with the river environment.

OUTSIDE THE NATIONAL PARK AREA

Nahshonim

At Kibbutz Nahshonim there is a Motor Park (Nahshonit). It offers water games and various attractions for children and adults.

Migdal Afek

There are remains of an ancient settlement at this site. It was known from the late Second Temple period at the time of the great Jewish revolt against the Romans when Jewish military forces attempted to delay Roman troops advancing from Caesarea to Jerusalem. Remains of a Crusader fortress, Mirabel, built upon the remnants of a former ancient fortress, may also be seen here. It was destroyed by Saladin. On a nearby hill, a hewn burial cave in the style typical of the Second Temple period has been exposed. Based on the dating of various pottery fragments, the site was settled from the Hasmonean period up

Common rush.

to the Middle Ages. In the 19th century, an Arab village sprang up—Majdal es Sadeq, named after the sheikh, Sadeq el Jamini, who exercised control over the area. The village was abandoned in the War of Independence.

Mazur Ruin (Mausoleum)

This is a Roman mausoleum from the 2nd or 3rd century CE that has been preserved in its entirety. According to Arab folklore, the place was called Makam en Nabi Yehiye, which means "the holy place of the prophet Johanan," referring to John the Baptist. With the establishment of the National Water Carrier, a pumping station also delivered water to the center of the country, to Jerusalem and to the Negev. From the roof of the mausoleum one has a good view of the surrounding area.

Yarkon River.

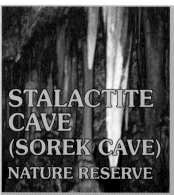

STALACTITE CAVE (SOREK CAVE) NATURE RESERVE

Location: W slopes of the Judean Hills, S of Nahal Sorek. From Route 38 (Sha'ar Hagai interchange–Beit Shemesh road), turn onto Route 3855, N of Beit Shemesh.

Best season: year-round

Length of visit: ¾ to 1 hour

Tel.: 02-9925756

Fax.: 02-9990215

Entrance fee

Yet I planted thee a holy vine (*sorek*)... (Jer 2:21)

Outdoor recreation | Lookout point | Picnic site | Sound & light show
WC | Snack bar | Restaurant | Souvenir shop

Accessibility Rating

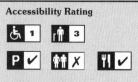

The cave was discovered quite by chance when a bulldozer, chipping away at the walls of a stone quarry in the Beit Shemesh area, suddenly exposed a hole in the solid rock formation. On closer inspection, workers were stunned to find a magnificent stalactite/stalagmite cave, now known as the Sorek Cave

Stalactite caves are not rare phenomena and are found in mountainous limestone areas in various countries. Caves of this type are formed through a karstic process—the name "karst" comes from an area in Yugoslavia where this active process is widespread and was first scientifically examined. As rain falls through the atmosphere, it picks up CO_2 which dissolves in the droplets. Once the rain hits the mountainous terrain, it percolates through the soil and picks up more CO_2 to form a diluted solution of carbonic acid [$H_2O + CO_2 = H_2CO_3$]. When this acidic water comes into contact with limestone, diversified processes begin to take place. In this case, the water seeped through to the bottom of the mountain exploiting every possible opening and emerged as springs. The bedrock on the surface begins to dissolve—that is, the water "eats through" large quantities of limestone leading to the formation of subterranean caves.

If the water continues to drip lightly from the roof of the cave, drop after drop, something

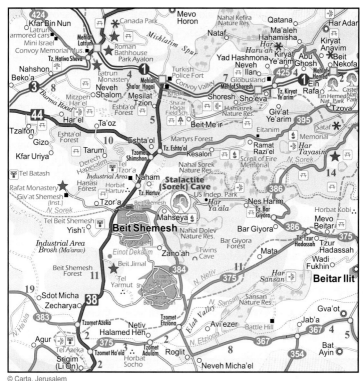

© Carta, Jerusalem

from the dissolving material sticks to the roof of the cave, and if this process continues, the water continues to drip from the protruding formation, enlarging it. Every drop leaves a miniscule portion behind on the emerging formation and after a great length of time a full pillar forms called a stalactite. If this process takes place along a crack or crevice in the roof of the cave, a "curtain" of stalactites forms. From the drops that fall on the floor of the cave there also emerge pillars, growing in an upward direction to form stalagmites. This process also takes place over a long period of time. On occasion, a stalactite and a stalagmite meet and join together in a "kiss," eventually becoming one. These stalactite and stalagmite formations are exceedingly varied in their contours and colors.

If the process of dripping stops, either through climatic changes or some other cause, the development of the stalactites and stalagmites ceases, and the cave, which may still be picturesque, becomes in effect a "dead" cave. If the process of dripping continues, the pillar formations take on varying colors depending upon the nature of the material through which the water penetrates, and then the cave is said to be "living." Sorek is a "living" cave; water continues to drip from the roof and this makes for a colorful display of stalactites and stalagmites. The cave area is small, a little more than an acre, but its varied content ranks with the best caves in the world, and among the prettiest.

As soon as word leaked out about the discovery of this cave, it became a destination for unplanned and unguided visits. Destruction ensued as irresponsible visitors took away "souvenirs." The cave was then gated and closed to the public; facilities such as walking paths and lighting were installed and visiting quotas were put into effect. The carbon dioxide exhaled by humans mixes with the pervading high humidity in the cave and this has a deleterious effect on the processes of dissolution and productivity.

The Valley of Sorek is where Samson lived. The Bible mentions that Samson "loved a woman in the valley of Sorek, whose name was Delilah"

"Curtain" in Sorek Cave.

(Judges 16:4). Some visitors have claimed to have discerned her visage among the gnarled shapes of the limestone cave. Since then, other karst caves have been discovered at different locations in the country, but in the meantime none of them compare in beauty and uniqueness to the Sorek Cave.

OUTSIDE THE RESERVE

The Martyrs Forest

The trees in this grove were planted along both banks of Nahal Kesalon in memory of the holy martyrs of the Holocaust. The Nahal begins in the vicinity of Mevaseret Tzi'on and ends where it enters into Nahal Sorek.

Stalactites in Sorek Cave.

In the heart of this forest, close to Moshav Kesalon, is the Scroll of Fire monument. It was sculpted in bronze by Nathan Rapoport and rises to a height of 8.5 m. The monument is in the form of two Torah scrolls and each scroll is filled with reliefs that relate the history of the people of Israel from the days of the Temple's destruction to the Holocaust and the establishment of the State of Israel.

On the south side of Nahal Kesalon but north of route 395 is the B'nai Brith, or Martyrs', cave. This is a natural formation that was widened in order to enable people to enter and commune with the victims of the Holocaust. Beside the cave there is a place for parking and drinking water is available. A large number of memory plaques with the names of communities that were annihilated in the Holocaust have been placed along the length of the Nahal.

Beit Jimal

This is an Italian monastery established by monks of the Salesian Society in 1919. The monastery itself was built in 1881 on the foundations of an earlier Byzantine church. According to tradition, this is the location of the ancient village of Gamla where Rabban Gamliel the Elder, president of the Sanhedrin at Jabneh, held court in the first century CE. Christians accord him honor because he is remembered as the teacher of the disciple Paul. In addition, he was the advocate of St. Stephen who was stoned

Beit Jimal Monastery.

to death in Jerusalem because of his beliefs and became the first Christian martyr. Tradition holds that Rabban Gamliel and his son are buried in a crypt in the monastery's church.

Today, as part of its cultural activities, the Society hosts concerts of liturgical and classical music. Wines, various types of cheese, and other items of a religious and non-religious nature are sold by nuns who live on the premises.

Stalagmites in Sorek Cave.

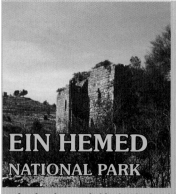

EIN HEMED NATIONAL PARK

...for the pleasant fields, for the fruitful vine. (Isa 32:12)

Location: from Route 1 (Tel Aviv–Jerusalem), turn off at the Hemed interchange, about 7 km W of Jerusalem.

Best season: year-round

Length of visit: 1/2 hour to a day

Tel.: 02-5795274

Entrance fee

Christian site · Antiquities · Outdoor recreation

WC · Telephone · Picnic site

Accessibility Rating

♿ 2 · 🚶 3

P ✓ · 🚻 ✓ · 🍴 ✗

The Jerusalem Hills are not blessed with perennial streams that flow year-round. Moreover, the springs of this region yield a low volume of water and do not develop into streams. However, they have been exploited since ancient times. During the Second Temple period and later, there were installations by these springs which utilized every drop of water for irrigation of orchards and vegetable gardens. Some of these springs still exist today and a small volume of water still emerges from them. Groves of trees containing Kermes Oak (*Quercus calliprinos*), Pistachio, Carob, and Almond have developed on either side of the streambed of Nahal Kesalon. The Parks Authority has regulated the flow of water, expanded the grove, and planted grassy areas. There has also been some archaeological reconstruction at this site. Despite its modest size, it is an important national park in the Jerusalem environs.

CRUSADER STRUCTURE

During the period of Crusader rule in the 12th century, in the reign of King Fulk V of Anjou (1131–1143), the Knights of the Order of St. John (the Hospitalers) built a fortified farm here. The place was given the name Aqua Bella ("Beautiful Water"). When it came under Arab control, the name was changed to Deir el Banat (Daughters' Monastery), even though the place was not used

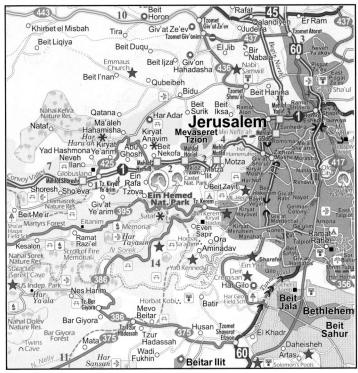

© Carta, Jerusalem

as a monastery. The fortress, partly destroyed, is still standing. The fortress was built to guard the water source.

OUTSIDE THE NATIONAL PARK AREA

Ein Bikura (Sataf)

About 5 km west of Jerusalem, on the right side of the road that leads from Ein Kerem to Bar Giyora, a green-covered slope descends into Nahal Sorek. Before the War of Independence, the Arab village of Sataf occupied this site; its inhabitants fled during the War.

In 1949, Jewish immigrants attempted to settle here. They named their colony Bikura, but abandoned it soon after. The site contains remains of large buildings from the Roman period, a terraced slope used for agriculture, two springs (Ein Sataf and Ein Bikura), an aqueduct, collection pools, and irrigation channels. All these structures and installations have been restored by the Jewish National Fund (JNF). The JNF also built hiking paths to allow visitors ample access to all sections of the Park. Visitors now enter an entire area

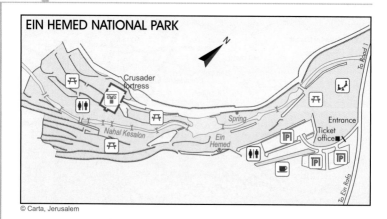

EIN HEMED NATIONAL PARK

Crusader fortress

Nahal Kesalon

Spring

Ein Hemed

Entrance

Ticket office

To Road 1

To Ein Rafa

© Carta, Jerusalem

which recovers the ambiance of a mountainous agricultural plot in biblical times. To bring this restoration to life, the JNF has offered Jerusalem and area residents the opportunity to work small plots of the terraced land, growing vegetable and fruit gardens that were indigenous to the biblical period for home consumption.

St. John in the Desert Monastery

This picturesque monastery, run by the Franciscans, is situated at the edge of Moshav Even Sapir. It is named after John the Baptist who, according to Christian tradition, was born in nearby Ein Kerem in the early 1st century CE. The monastery is built over a tiny grotto with a small spring alongside. Christian tradition relates that Elizabeth, mother of John, isolated herself in this place and then disappeared. The monastery is built on a steep incline 550 m above Nahal Sorek and provides a splendid view of the valley below and the village-like Jerusalem neighborhood of Ein Kerem.

Because John the Baptist first went into seclusion in the "desert" area of Ein Kerem, this area is called "the first desert" to distinguish it from the expansive region of the Judean Desert to the southeast, "the second desert," where John the Baptist isolated himself later for the second time in his life.

Ein Kerem

Ein Kerem is a residential neighborhood situated in the southwest of Jerusalem. It acquired its name from the vineyards (*kerem*, in Hebrew) and olive trees found in its environs, as well as after the spring that flows among its dwellings. There are 5 churches and monasteries in the village: the Church of St. John the

Crusader fortification in Ein Hemed.

Baptist, the Monastery of St. John the Baptist, the Church of the Visitation, the Sisters of Zion Convent, and the Russian Orthodox monastery.

The Arab village that once stood here was taken by IDF forces in July 1948 in "the ten-day battle" and its inhabitants fled.

Abu Ghosh

The residents of this village are descendants of a Muslim clan who settled here in the 16th century and earned their keep by extracting tolls from pilgrims making their way to Jerusalem. During the War of Independence in 1948, village residents did not interfere in the military campaign over control of the road to Jerusalem and there were even residents who actively supported the Jews in their struggle against the British Mandate. Within the village, remains of a settlement from the Neolithic period have been found. A church built in 1924 was constructed over the remains of an ancient Byzantine church; a Benedictine monastery was established on the foundations of a Crusader monastery from the 12th century, and there are remains of an inn from the early Arab period.

Wild daisies.

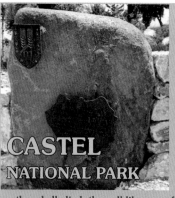

CASTEL NATIONAL PARK

Location: at the approach to Jerusalem, from Route 1, turn off at the Har'el interchange to Mevaseret Tzi'on.

Best season: year-round

Length of visit: about 1 hour

Tel.: 02-5330476

Entrance fee

...they shall climb the wall like men of war... (Joel 2:9)

Jewish site

Lookout point

WC

Picnic site

Accessibility Rating

 1   1

P ✓   ✗   ✗

The Castel is a hill which rises to the south of the main highway entering Jerusalem from the coast (route 1). An Arab village by the same name was located at its summit and is derived from the Latin *castellum* (camp), an indication of its Roman origin.

HISTORY

This location was of special significance during the War of Independence. The United Nations General Assembly Resolution 181 (II) of 29 November 1947 recommended a Partition Plan for the division of British-mandated Palestine into a Jewish State and an Arab State. The city of Jerusalem, with its 100,000 Jews (c. 60 percent of the city's population), was to be under a special international regime administered by the United Nations. Jerusalem would have been an isolated salient in the midst of Arab territory and totally cut off from the Jewish State. The Arabs, however, did not accept the Partition Plan, and immediately after passage of the Resolution they launched attacks against the Jewish sections of Jerusalem and cut off the Jewish settlements west of the city to the coast from any access to the Holy City. In the Judean Hills there were only a few scattered Jewish settlements; the Arabs, in effect, had control over the entire range of hills and a strategic hold on the only road leading up to Jerusalem from Sha'ar Hagai.

© Carta, Jerusalem

The Castel was one of the Arab positions in the Judean Hills that overlooked the road to Jerusalem. Snipers entrenched on the hill endangered Jewish traffic. In March 1948, vehicular passage was completely blocked. At the beginning of April, the Haganah command launched "Operation Nahshon," designed to break the blockade and forge a route to Jerusalem. A force of 1,500 Haganah combatants was mobilized for this assignment. Their task was to seize the Arab positions along the hilly ridges overlooking the road, thereby opening up Jewish access to the city. On the night of 2–3 April, the Harel brigade of the Palmah overran the Castel position and handed it over to the Moriah battalion of the Etzioni brigade stationed in Jerusalem.

The Arabs, who understood the military significance of the capture of the Castel and its importance for battle morale concentrated hundreds of soldiers for a counter-attack on the position and its new defenders. The battle, accompanied by rainy weather, lasted 5 days with the Arabs shelling and continually launching attacks while snipers attempted to disable Jewish resistance. The Jewish soldiers defended the Castel from three points on its immediate perimeter—"Nahshon," "Boaz" and the eastern command post. Between 3 and 5 April, the defenders retreated from the Nahshon command post. Between 5 and 7 April, they retreated from the Boaz and eastern command posts and thus found themselves surrounded on the village hill. On 6 April, hundreds of Arabs attacked the Castel under the district command of Abd el-Qadr el-Husseini. Husseini was killed, although the Arab fighters at the time thought he had been captured and charged the hill with fierce dedication. The defenders were given an order to retreat and during the withdrawal 17 Palmah soldiers and 21 infantrymen were killed. Thus, the Castel again fell into the hands of the Arabs.

On the 9th of April a decision was made to capture the Castel at all costs. A Palmah unit was despatched from Kiryat Anavim. To their great surprise, the Castel was completely abandoned—the Arab combatants had been called to participate in the funeral of their commander. Again, the Castel returned to the Jews.

Castel Hill.

OUTSIDE THE NATIONAL PARK

Tzova

Kibbutz Tzova is on route 395 (Kerem Junction–Ramat Razi'el). The ruins of the abandoned village of Tzova are northeast of the kibbutz, on a summit that rises above its surroundings. During the Crusader period, there was a fortress called Belmont built to secure the route to Jerusalem. In 1187, the stronghold was conquered by Saladin and in 1191 it was partially destroyed. In 1834, Abu Ghosh and his cohorts hid here in their rebellion against the Egyptian regime. The Egyptian ruler captured the place

Memorial for those who fell in the battle on Castel Hill.

THE BATTLE ON CASTEL HILL, 3–9 APRIL 1948

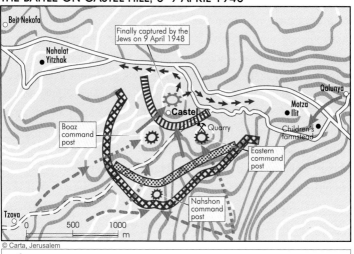

© Carta, Jerusalem

◄─ ─ Arab attack, 3 April 1948	Area under Jewish control
◄···· Arab attack, 5 April 1948	✕✕✕ 1–3 April 1948
◄── Arab attack, 4 August 1948	▨ 3–5 April 1948
◄ ◄ ◄ Jewish retreat from Castel Hill, 4 August 1948	▥ 5–8 April 1948

Relief of the area and memorial to the armored corps that tried to breach open the road to Jerusalem.

and destroyed the remaining standing structures of the fortress. In the War of Independence, the Arabs used this village as a base for their efforts to block the route to Jerusalem until they were overcome by units of the Harel brigade in "Operation Dani."

Today, Kibbutz Tzova offers 3 attractions for children:

Inflatable castle park ("Kiftzova")

Huge inflatable installations where children can bounce around, ride battery-operated cars and bumper cars, and engage in other activities in an open but roofed area. There is a giant enclosed games hall which is open also in winter, a skating rink, and an archery range.

Wildlife park

Children may pet small animals. There are also fawns, peacocks, alpacas, and other wildlife.

Spring

A hike to an underground spring system, 40 m long, and lit up. The walk continues to the Tzova spring, the water supply source for the now-abandoned Arab village of Tzova.

Har Tayasim

This site lies beside the Ein Kerem–Tzova–Kesalon road. At the summit, 795 m above sea level, is a monument to the pilots who fought in Israel's military campaigns. The mountain (*har*) is named after 2 pilots and 4 crew

Crested lark's nest.

whose plane crashed in this area during the War of Independence.

Cassidony (in Hebrew, "Maccabeans' blood").

Kennedy Monument

This memorial, beside Moshav Aminadav, is dedicated to the memory of John Fitzgerald Kennedy, President of the United States, who was assassinated in 1963. The site was opened in 1966. The monument is an oval structure, 7 m in height, and in the form of a trunk of a felled tree. Its construction consists of 50 pillars extended outwards at the bottom like roots symbolizing the 50 states of the American union plus a 51st pillar above them at a higher level, representing the District of Washington, the nation's capitol. Inside the structure is a bust of Kennedy and around the inner perimeter the seals of the 50 states.

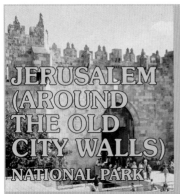

JERUSALEM (AROUND THE OLD CITY WALLS) NATIONAL PARK

Location: around and including the Old City walls of Jerusalem. Access to Jaffa Gate from Route 1.

Best season: year round

Length of visit: 2½–3 hours

Tel.: 02-6250143

Do good in thy good pleasure unto Zion: build the walls of Jerusalem. (Ps 51:18)

Jewish site Christian site Muslim site

Antiquities Telephone

The route on top of the Old City walls (entered from Jaffa Gate) is not accessible for individuals with disabilities.

The wall which encircles the Old City of Jerusalem was built in 1536 by Suleiman the Magnificent. The Ottoman Empire, then at the peak of its development, was interested in establishing strategic strongholds in different places within its domain. The foundation for Jerusalem's walls, a city that was conquered and laid waste time after time, existed and it was determined more or less by the contours of the terrain. Suleiman's walls were built principally on this basis. Today, the Old City is encircled by built-up urban areas on all sides, but at the time of the building of the Ottoman wall and for 300 years afterwards the Old City constituted Jerusalem in its entirety—the territory immediately beyond its walls, a wilderness.

THE GATES OF JERUSALEM

Jaffa Gate

From the middle of the western section of the wall a road led to the port of Jaffa on the Mediterranean, hence the gate's name. The Arabs refer to the gate as Bab el Khalil (Hebron Gate) because a road also departs from here south to the city of Hebron.

Damascus Gate

In the middle of the northern wall stands the most important and splendid gate of the Old City. A road from here leads to

Jaffa Gate.

Damascus, from which it derives its name. In Arabic it is called Bab el Amud (the pillar gate) after a pillar that was erected in the gate's inner square during the Roman-Byzantine period. In one of the alcoves of the wall there is a museum exhibiting the history of the city's gates.

Herod's Gate (Flower Gate)

This gate is located near the northeast corner of the wall. In Arabic it is called Bab ez Zahara.

Lions' Gate

This gate, also known as Gethsemane Gate and St. Stephen's Gate, is situated in the eastern section of the wall. On one side there are reliefs of lions, hence its name. In Arabic it is called Bab Sitt Maryam (Our Lady of Mary Gate), because of its propinquity, according to Christian tradition, to the birthplace of the mother of Jesus. In the Six-Day War in 1967, IDF paratroopers broke into the Old City through this gate and advanced to the Western (Wailing) Wall.

Dung Gate

This gate is found in the southern section of the wall and is mentioned in the Bible (Nehemiah 3:13–14).

Zion Gate

This gate is farther up the hill in the southern wall. The Arabic name is Bab en Nabi Da'ud (the prophet David's Gate). It is on Mount Zion, and obtains its name from the geographical location. Palmah forces broke through this gate to the besieged Jewish Quarter during the War of Independence.

All the above gates were actual entrances to the Old City with doors that closed every evening.

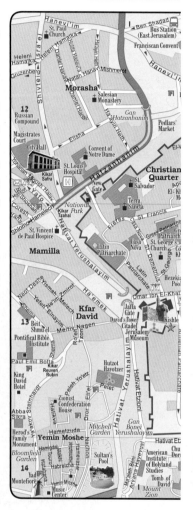

There was a seventh gate, the Gate of Mercy, or the Golden Gate, which was closed and sealed up from the time it was built. The New Gate, which provides a separate entrance to the Christian Quarter in the northwest corner of the Old City wall, was opened at a later date.

A new city outside these walls began to emerge, neighborhood by neighborhood, beginning in

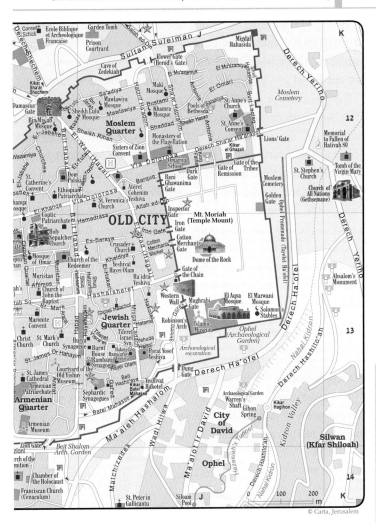

© Carta, Jerusalem

the middle of the 19th century. There was no residential linkage between the Old City and the new residential areas, and even when the new construction approached the city walls, an unbuilt space remained between it and the city wall. This empty area, which varies in width along the different sectors of the Old City walls, has been designated a National Park.

From Jaffa Gate southward, the wall follows along the top of a declining slope. The area between the wall and the Jerusalem Brigade Road (Hativat Yerushalayim) reaching to the southwest corner of the wall has been landscaped. The southern wall, up to the Valley of Hinnom, including the south bank of the Valley, constitutes a large part of the Park. Here, a concentration of structures and other elements of religious and historical significance have been found and are integrated into the Park.

The process of creating the Park was complex and lengthy because of the sensitivity that accompanied every plot of land and every structure along this corridor. Now completed, the Park adds immensely to the venue of the Old City wall, both separating the Old City from the New more clearly, as well as providing a bridge between them.

"David's Tower" (Citadel)
This former stronghold, immediately south of Jaffa Gate, was built by Herod at the time of the Jewish Revolt against the Romans. It served as a fortress in the Roman, Crusader and Ottoman periods. During the period of Jordanian control (1948–1967), it was used as a military post. Most of its remains date from the Middle Ages, but remnants of the original wall may be discerned, as well as remnants from the Hasmonean period.

The structure was separated from the city by a deep moat. A section of this moat was filled in the 19th century and became the main entrance to the Old City for transportation vehicles, leaving Jaffa Gate immediately beside it for pedestrian traffic and ornamental effect. Today, the citadel is an antiquities site and a place for exhibitions and public events. On display is

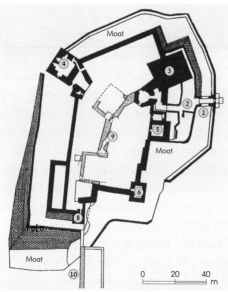

THE CITADEL (DAVID'S TOWER)

1. Bridge
2. Entrance
3. David's Tower (Phasael's Tower)
4–6. Towers
7. Mosque
8. Minaret of the mosque
9. Building remains from Second Temple period
10. Old City wall

© Carta, Jerusalem

a permanent exhibit about the history of the city of Jerusalem.

Mount Zion

This hillock is situated at the southwest corner of the Old City. During the Second Temple period it was part of the Upper City. The mount draws Jewish pilgrims to:

David's Tomb. According to an ancient tradition, King David is buried here.

Chamber of the Holocaust. This room is next to David's Tomb and is a remembrance site for victims of the Holocaust.

There are also several places here which are regarded as holy to Christians:

"David's Tower."

Temple Mount wall (southeast corner), the archaeological park, and the Mount of Olives.

The Coenaculam (also called the Cenacle, or the "Last Supper Room"). Here Jesus ate his last meal with his disciples before his crucifixion. It may have been the Passover meal (Luke 22:7,8,15; also John 13:12,2 and 18:28).

The Basilica of Holy Zion. A Byzantine church considered by some to be the location of the first Christian church.

Church of the Dormition. This church was built in 1910 on the remains of earlier structures. Its name is derived from the Christian tradition that Mary fell asleep here and, like Jesus her son, was taken up to heaven. The Church contains a beautiful mosaic of the zodiac, Christian symbols, and images of the prophets.

The Church of St. Peter in Gallicantu. This church was built in 1931. According to Christian tradition, this is the place where Peter heard the cock crow (*in galli cantu*—Mark 14:68; Luke 22:60).

The Armenian Church. This building is situated near the Zion Gate. According to the tradition, this is the house of the High Priest, Caiaphas, where Jesus was held after he was arrested (Matthew 26:57). The church was damaged in the War of Independence and was restored after the Six-Day War. A new church was erected beside it.

Cemeteries

There are Jewish, Christian Orthodox, and Protestant cemeteries. The last was in use for over a hundred years and closed at the end of the British Mandate.

Archaeological Excavations

The most important archaeological section of the Park is located between the Old City wall and the wall of the Temple Mount. Here remains from the First and Second Temple periods up to the Umayyad period have been found.

Just south of the Temple Mount, between the compound wall and Derech Hashilo'ah (Silwan Road), is the area of the biblical Ophel, a hill located north of the "City of David." Herodian remains of a monumental stairway leading up to the Hulda, Double and Triple Gates of the Temple Mount were uncovered here.

The Ophel Archaeological Garden

This archaeological park is directly south of the Temple Mount. It was dedicated in 1983. This unique site affords a view of remains from all the periods, from the First Temple period to the Ottoman period.

The Muslim Cemetery

This cemetery is spread along the length of the eastern wall, almost from the impressive southeast corner to the Stork Tower (Burj Laqlaq) in the north.

On this east side, the Park extends from the wall and the cemetery down to the Kidron Valley.

The Hinnom Valley

This valley lies to the east and to the south of the Old City. The

The Temple Mount wall, looking west.

origin of its name is not known. In ancient times it was a scene of horror where human beings were sacrificed to the pagan god Moloch. During the period of the Israelite Kingdom, altars to false gods were set up in this Valley (Jer 7:31). A Hebrew derivative of Hinnom, *Gai-hinnom*, entered the lexicon as the equivalent of "Hell"—a place of torture for evil persons in the next world.

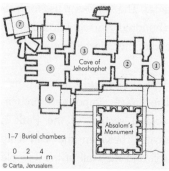

Plan of Absalom's Monument and the Cave of Jehoshaphat.

THE IMPRESSIVE TOMBS IN THE KIDRON VALLEY

Absalom's Monument

A splendid tomb built in the Second Temple period, partly hewn from existing stone and partly constructed, opposite the southeast corner of the Old City. According to popular tradition, this is the monument that Absalom, son of King David, built for himself (2 Samuel 18: 18). Legend relates that the hand at the head of the tombstone was cut off because the son had raised his hand against his father. In the past, passersby customarily threw stones at the monument as a sign of denunciation until it was finally covered in its entirety. In 1925, it was re-exposed.

Absalom's Monument in the Kidron Valley.

The Tomb of Hezir's Priestly Family (left) and the Tomb of Zechariah in the Kidron Valley.

The Tomb of Zechariah

This large tomb, carved out of the surrounding rock, dates from the Second Temple period. Tradition has it that this is the burial site of Zechariah, son of Jehoiada the priest, who was stoned to death in the courtyard of the Jerusalem Temple at the orders of King Joash (2 Chronicles 24:20–21).

SITES ALONG THE NORTHERN WALL

The Sultan Suleiman and Hatzanhanim ("the Paratroopers") streets run so closely along the northern Old City wall that in places space is left only for a long garden. Sites of interest (from east to west) include Herod's Gate, Zedekiah's Cave, and the Damascus Gate plaza. This section ends with the protuberance of the wall up to the New Gate.

The Cave of Zedekiah

This is a large cave situated between Damascus and Herod's Gates. It is about 300 m long and about 100 m wide. According to legend, King Zedekiah escaped from Nebuchadnezzar, king of Babylon, via this cave and was caught at the other end of the cave on the plains of Jericho (2 Kings 25:4–6). In the opinion of scholars, this is a quarry from the period of Herod and its stones were used to build the Temple.

1. Entrance
2. "Tears of Zedekiah" spring
3. Lowest point in cave
4. Entrance to lower floor

Plan of Zedekiah's cave.

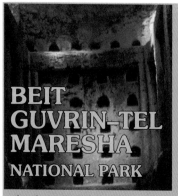

BEIT GUVRIN–TEL MARESHA NATIONAL PARK

Location: (1) from Route 1, turn to Route 38 (Beit Shemesh–Kiryat Gat), c. 35 km to the S; (2) from Route 40, turn at Plugot junction to Route 35 (Kiryat Gat–Hebron), c. 17 km to the E.

Best season: year-round

Length of visit: 1–5 hours

Tel.: 08-6811020

Fax: 08-6812957

Entrance fee

...then the people did hide themselves in caves, and in thickets, and in rocks... (1 Sam 13:6)

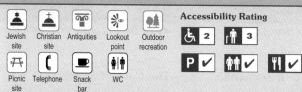

Jewish site   Christian site   Antiquities   Lookout point   Outdoor recreation

Picnic site   Telephone   Snack bar   WC

Accessibility Rating

♿ 2   🚶 3

P ✓   🚻 ✓   🍴 ✓

The National Park of Beit Guvrin–Tel Maresha covers 1,250 acres. This large area is well-known, and justly so, for its many caves and archaeological remains. Tel Maresha occupies the highest point in the Park.

Geologically, the rock in the area is a thin layer of hard limestone with lower bedrock of soft chalk limestone which is malleable and can be easily cut. The early masons would hew a small hole in the ceiling of the hard limestone and remove the lower layer of soft and moist limestone according to their needs. At the conclusion of every operation of this sort, a bell-shaped cave with an aperture at the top would be formed. There are hundreds of caves of this type throughout the area, some of them isolated, and others forming an interconnected system. Many were later converted into living quarters, the soft limestone being hollowed out to create additional subterranean rooms. Initially, they were locations for olive oil manufacture, cisterns, and burial caves. The number of caves is very large but only a few of them have been opened to the public.

In the summer months, the countryside is dry and yellow. In winter and spring, the landscape is green and the ruins and slopes are covered with flowers. The Beit Guvrin floral display, with its carpets of red Crown Anemones (*Anemone coronaria*), is a real visual delight.

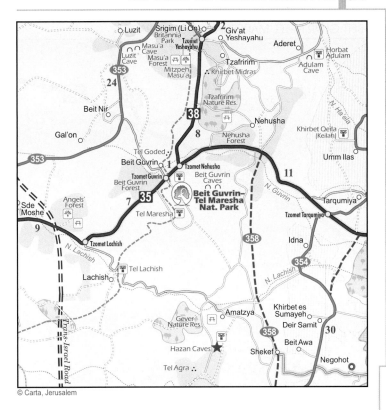

© Carta, Jerusalem

THE HISTORY OF MARESHA

Maresha(h) appears among the list of cities of Judah in the Book of Joshua (15:44). Rehoboam fortified it against an impending attack of the Egyptian pharaoh Shishak and King Asa annihilated the Ethiopian invader, Zerah. After the Babylonian Exile, Edomites settled throughout southern Judea, and the area was called Idumea. Marisa, as it was then called, was a Gentile city with a cosmopolitan population—Edomites, Sidonians, and in the Hellenistic period Greek-speaking peoples. John Hyrcanus conquered the city in 112 BCE and converted its population to Judaism. According to one tradition, the family of Herod originated from here. After the conquest, the population was considerably reduced and it was completely annihilated by the Parthians in 40 BCE.

THE HISTORY OF BEIT GUVRIN

Beit Guvrin was a new town and the successor to Marisa. Its history may be charted both through

BEIT GUVRIN–TEL MARESHA NATIONAL PARK

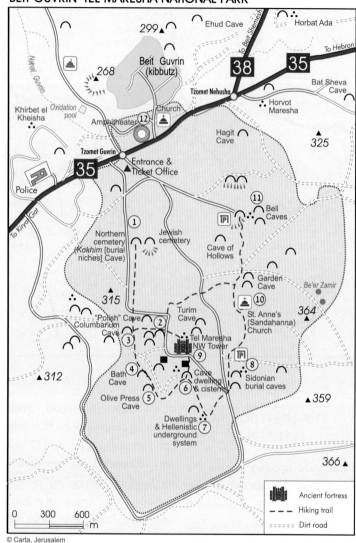

© Carta, Jerusalem

historical documents and through many archaeological findings. The Romans and Byzantines called the city Eleutheropolis, which means "city of freedom." It was the largest city in the south and had a Jewish community several of whose members are mentioned in the Talmud and Jewish commentaries: Rabbi Yonatan and Rabbi Judah bar Ya'akov. After the Arab conquest, it resumed its former name in the form "Beit Jibrin." In the period following, the Crusaders thought the city was

Beersheba, but nicknamed it "Beit Jiblin" and built a fortress there. Archaeologists have found remains from all the periods.

SITES IN THE PARK

The Park is divided into two sectors: the south, where the biblical and Hellenistic city of Maresha is located; the north, where Beit Guvrin, the Roman and Byzantine city is located.

1. The Northern Cemetery

This cemetery dates from the 3rd–2nd centuries BCE. Two caves with rock-cut burial niches were discovered, which are open to the public.

2. The "Polish" Cave

This was a cistern which at a later stage was hewn to house a dovecote installation for raising pigeons. The cistern was hewn in the 4th–3rd centuries BCE. In 1943, Polish soldiers, who visited the site, carved the words "Warsaw, Poland," along with the Polish eagle, that country's national symbol, on the cave wall, and the name "Polish Cave" stuck.

3. The Columbarium Cave

This is a large cave in which 2,000 niches were carved as nesting places for the breeding of pigeons. Their meat was used for ritual and eating purposes, and their feces for fertilizer. The columbarium ceased operation towards the end of the 3rd century BCE and the niches were re-utilized as storage areas.

4. The Bath Cave

This cave contains two

Mosaic with depiction of a fox and grapes.

subterranean alcoves into which water was channeled for bathing and ritual purposes.

5. The Olive Press Cave

At Maresha, 22 underground olive presses were found dating from the 3rd–2nd centuries BCE. The cultivation of olive trees and the manufacture of olive oil were important economic enterprises during this period.

6. The Cave Dwelling and Cisterns

The cave's living quarters, built at ground level, date to the Hellenistic period (3rd–2nd centuries BCE). Its approximately 150 sq m consist of a central courtyard surrounded by rooms. A staircase leads to a second floor. The dwelling was apparently destroyed in 112 BCE at the time Maresha was conquered by John Hyrcanus I.

Below the living quarters are cisterns which gathered rainwater. The water was channeled through canals and clay pipes. One of the cisterns allowed passage through a hewn stone quarry to an additional residence.

7. Dwellings and an underground system from the Hellenistic period

The residential structures here are similar to those described above. The northern house allows descent to a well-preserved and beautiful room with a bath. An underground path leads to a columbarium, rooms and additional cisterns.

8. The Sidonian Burial Caves

This system of burial caves dates from the 3rd–2nd centuries BCE. In cave no. 8, the rectangular

Mosaic of a lion.

niches (triangular-shaped at top) were restored, and the original paintings were also restored on the basis of the sketches made by the archaeologists who excavated the site. The inscriptions, as well as the paintings found in the cave, shed light on the ethnic origin of those buried here—Edomites, Sidonians, and Greeks—as well as on the mythology and art of the period.

9. The Northwest Tower, the Shops and the Dwellings

The hilltop of Maresha is flat. A fortress was built there and the visitor has a panoramic view of the countryside. North of the fortress were dwellings, and shops or workshops were built close to the fortress wall.

10. St. Anne's Church

This church was built in the Byzantine period and was partly renovated in Crusader times. The name of the church, St. Anne, was corrupted by the Arabs to Sandahanna.

11. The Bell Caves

These caves were hollowed out during the Byzantine and Early Arab periods. About 80 caves make up a single linked system. Flocks of screaming jackdaws swarm above these caves. The jackdaw is a smaller member of the raven family, also completely black. These birds nest in the caves. They are concentrated in two places in the country: around Nablus and here at Beit Guvrin.

12. The Amphitheater

This impressive structure was discovered in an area north of route 3. It is a common error to apply the term amphitheater to all the semicircular Roman theaters in which artistic performances

Sidonian tomb.

were held. The Beit Guvrin edifice, which is circular and entirely closed, is a genuine amphitheater designed for gladiatorial combat, and perhaps even for water games. The high walls, roofs and entrances of this structure are still standing and the visitor can get a good feeling for the days when it was packed with spectators attending the games and spectacles. A large fortress stands beside the amphitheater.

OUTSIDE THE NATIONAL PARK

Hazan Caves

About 8 km south of the Park is an enormous number of rock-hewn caves that were used as a refuge and hiding place by Jewish combatants in the Bar Kochba revolt against the Romans. The site now offers a mix of activities for children and adults.

Angels' Forest

This forest of planted pine stretches over an area of 1,750 acres. The project was undertaken by the Jewish National Fund with the generous assistance of the Jewish Federation of Los Angeles. There is an observation tower, picnic tables, recreational facilities, and hiking trails.

Britannia Park and Mitzpeh Masu'a

This site was financed by the British Jewish community, hence its name. At 10,000 acres, this is a very large Israeli park. It is situated between Beit Guvrin and the Yeshayahu junction. A track, which is part of the trans-Israel Trail, traverses the length of the park from north to south. There are directional arrows etched into erected stone markers and the track provides access for all types of vehicles. It crosses the Srigim–Agur road (route 353) and climbs to Mitzpeh Masu'a. This is a forested lookout (372 m above sea level) which offers

Amphitheater.

Mosaic of a fruit basket.

a magnificent view of the coastal plain to the west, the western slopes of the Hebron hills and the Jerusalem hills to the east, and the expanse of Britannia Park. Nearby are picnic tables, drinking fountains, and service facilities. There is also a mule farm, restaurant and kiosk.

Khirbet Midras

Among the ruins of this ancient settlement are various structures, a columbarium, and refuge caves from the Hellenistic, Roman and Byzantine periods.

Bell cave.

Location: on the Mediterranean coast, S of Ashkelon, Route 4.
Best season: year-round
Length of visit: 1 hour
Tel. (park office): 08-6711768, 08-6739660
Tel. (ticket office): 08-6736444
Fax: 08-6734227
Entrance fee

Tell it not in Gath, publish it not in the streets of Ashkelon... (2 Sam 1:20)

The origin of the word "Ashkelon" is apparently derived from the word *shekel*, an appropriate name for a city which was over the centuries an *entrepot* (commercial port).

The National Park is situated to the south of the city on an ancient tel, where antiquities from all periods were exposed. The quantity of standing and strewn pillars is immense and if one takes into consideration the number of pillars removed from the ancient city, one gets a good idea of its former greatness.

HISTORY

The city has a rich history from its very beginnings thousands of years ago. The rampart that served as a wall for the Canaanite city is about 4,000 years old and approximately at this period it is mentioned by name in the Egyptian Execration Texts. Because of its location on the *Via Maris* leading from Egypt northward, it was an important location for invaders and rulers. Thus, it was conquered many times, and rebuilt just as often.

Ashkelon is mentioned in the Book of Joshua as part of "the land that remained" that the Israelites did not conquer. However, it was conquered after the death of Joshua, then retaken by the Philistines and became one of their five principal cities. On the death of Saul and his son, Jonathan, in their battle against the Philistines, David lamented:

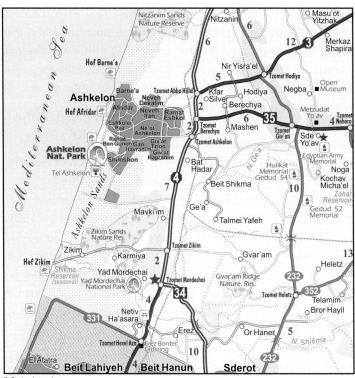

© Carta, Jerusalem

*Thy beauty, O Israel, upon thy
    high places is slain!
How are the mighty fallen!
Tell it not in Gath,
Publish it not in the streets of
    Ashkelon.* (2 Sam 1:19–20)

During the period of the Judges, Samson's exploits took him to Ashkelon. Samson paid off a bet by killing 30 local men, stripping them of their garments and giving them to the Philistines who had answered his riddle. When Philistia came under Assyrian sovereignty beginning in 734 BCE, the king of Ashkelon, Sidqa, joined Hezekiah, king of Judah, in an alliance against Assyria. The Babylonian king Nebuchadnezzar destroyed the city to its very foundations, but it was re-established and flourished in the Persian period.

Alexander the Great turned it into a Hellenistic city, and it became a center of independent Greek culture, even though Jews and other ethnic communities dwelled there. The city maintained its independence throughout the Hasmonean and Herodian dynasties. During the Great Revolt against the Romans, there were fierce battles between the Jews and Gentiles.

The Jews, who gained the upper hand at the beginning, suffered heavy losses. During the Roman period, the city rose to greatness and counted among its citizens several scholars and Jewish sages. The city continued to prosper in Byzantine times and its name appears on the renowned Madaba map and in other mosaics. The Arabs conquered the city in the early 7th century and called it Ascalon. Through all these periods up to the Crusader Kingdom a Jewish community was present. The Crusaders only conquered the city in 1153 and following this the city changed hands several times until the Mamluk sultan Baybars totally destroyed it in 1270.

In the 19th century, the Arab town of Majdal and the village of Jora were founded near the ancient city, many stones of which were used in their construction. Many stones and pillars also ended up in Gaza and Jaffa.

On 15 May 1948 the Egyptian army invaded the newly-declared State of Israel, advanced up the Mediterranean coast, and on 24 May arrived at Majdal. The Egyptian forces remained entrenched there until 5 November at which juncture the Israeli forces of the Yiftah brigade cut off the coastal road from Majdal and the Egyptians withdrew. The Arab residents of Majdal surrendered and then abandoned their town. The new Jewish city of Ashkelon arose north and east of the tel.

SITES IN THE NATIONAL PARK

1. The Rampart and Gate of the Canaanite City

Archaeologists exposed an earthen rampart from the Middle Canaanite period (2000–1550 BCE) more than 2 km long, 15 m high and 30 m wide at its base. All that is left is a gate with its arch intact, estimated to be about 4,000 years old.

2. The Canaanite Sanctuary

This is an important finding which is not readily apparent at first glance. It is situated beyond the Canaanite gate on the slope facing the sea. A statuette of a silver-coated bronze calf, 10.5 cm in height, was found here and is now on exhibit at the Israel Museum in Jerusalem.

3. The Roman Basilica

This impressive 3rd century structure, in the center of the Park, is 110 m long and 35 m wide. In the center is an open courtyard surrounded by pillars, many of which have been restored. To the south is a semicircular hall with rows of seating that was probably used by the city council and court.

ASHKELON NATIONAL PARK

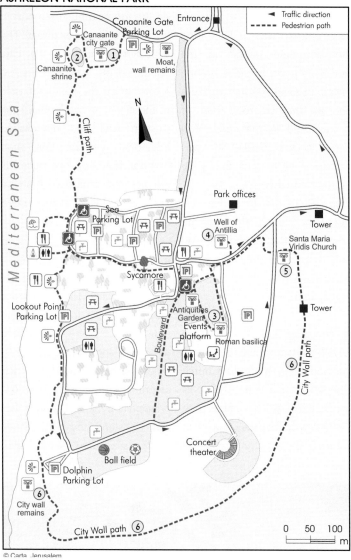

© Carta, Jerusalem

Excavations exposed marble statues that adorned the semi-circular hall. Today, the place exhibits a statue of the winged Nike—the goddess of Victory—and a statue of Isis, the Egyptian goddess that appears here in the form of Tyche, goddess of Fortune for the city.

4. The Well of Antillia

This is located north of the road. The device used to draw water from the well was operated by a beast of burden. The water was used for irrigation.

5. The Santa Maria Viridis Church

This church was built during the Byzantine period in the 5th century CE. It had 6 granite pillars, used to support a gallery and an inclined roof. Part of it was used in the early Arab period (638–1099). In 938 it was destroyed in a mass frenzy by Muslims and Jews.

In 1153, the Crusaders restored the church, changing the original structure and leaving only 4 pillars. They decorated the ceiling and added paintings to the walls.

6. The City Wall

A path leads from the remains of the Santa Maria Viridis Church along the length of this wall to its end by the sea. The wall as seen today was built by the Fatimids in the mid-12th century. It was built as part of a fortified compound on the top of a huge rampart in face of the Crusader threat. The Crusaders conquered the city, reinforced the wall, and erected a fortress on the southwest side of the city. The sea battered the western wall and demolished additional sections that man had not destroyed, but much still remains. It is a massive structure and granite pillars were inserted at the time to reinforce it.

FLORA

The Park has been planned not only for a short visit, but also for those who wish to spend some time there. There are grassy areas, walking paths, and many other facilities. There is a rich assortment of natural vegetation, principally trees and bushes that can withstand the salty winds off the sea—date palms, olive,

False Sycamore Fig.

False Sycamore Fig bearing good seedless fruit, Christ's Thorn Jujube, and many shrubs. The flora are a memento to ages past and a contemporary delight.

HISTORY OF THE JEWISH COMMUNITY

A Jewish community resided in Ashkelon for several decades before the Great Revolt against the Romans (66–71 CE). According to Josephus Flavius, 2,500 Jewish residents of the city were slain during the uprising. Among the findings which indicate a Jewish presence in Ashkelon are two dedicatory inscriptions from a synagogue: one on a chancel screen and the other on a stone column. Also, a stone chancel was found engraved with a seven-branched candelabrum (*menorah*), another inscription listing the 24 priestly divisions, a dedicatory inscription in Aramaic, and the pedestal of a marble column bearing a relief of a *menorah*, *shofar* (ram's horn), and *ethrog* (citron).

Ashkelon as described in the 12th century by the Crusader pilgrim, William of Tyre

[Ascalon] lies upon the seacoast in the form of a semicircle, the chord or diameter of which extends along the shore while the arc or bow lies on the land looking toward the east. The entire city rests in a basin, as it were, sloping to the sea and is surrounded on all sides by artificial mounds, upon which rise the walls with towers at frequent intervals. The whole is built of solid masonry, held together by cement which is harder than stone. The walls are wide, of goodly thickness and proportionate height. The city is furthermore encircled by outworks built with the same solidity and most carefully fortified. There

Ashkelon — antiquities.

are four gates in the circuit of the wall, strongly defended by lofty and massive towers. The first of these, facing east, is called the Greater Gate and sometimes the Gate of Jerusalem, because it faces toward the Holy City. It is surmounted by two very lofty towers which serve as a strong protection for the city below. In the barbican before this gate are three or four small gates which one passes to the main entrance by various winding ways. The second gate faces west. It is called the Sea Gate, because through it people have egress to the sea. The third to the south looks toward the city of Gaza, whence it takes its name. The fourth with outlook toward the north is called the Gate of Jaffa, from the neighbouring city which lies on this same coast.

(William of Tyre, *A History of Deeds Done Beyond the Sea* [tr. E. A. Babcock and A. C. Krey], New York 1943, pp. 17, 22)

OUTSIDE THE NATIONAL PARK

KIBBUTZ YAD MORDECHAI
Battlesite Reconstruction (1948)

In 1948, Egyptian army units also attacked Yad Mordechai. Defending forces withstood the advances for 5 days and then withdrew. The delaying action allowed Israeli forces in the north to organize and counterattack. Six months later, the kibbutz was retaken and renovation commenced. The kibbutz has on display a model of the battle marking where engagements took place, replete with model soldiers, model vehicles and weaponry. The water tower, pockmarked by shell-fire has become a symbolic site recalling the battle during the War of Independence. Beside the destroyed water tower is a memorial to Mordechai Anielewicz, commander of Jewish

Reconstructed model of the battlefield at Kibbutz Yad Mordechai.

Christ's thorn jujube.

resistance fighters in the Warsaw Ghetto, after whom the kibbutz is named. Today, the site has been declared a national park. At the Yad Mordechai intersection, there is a shopping center and road service station.

Holocaust Heritage Museum

The museum contains photographs and models of the Jewish *shtetl* (village or urban quarter), descriptions of life and event during the period of the Holocaust and the revolt in Europe, "illegal" immigration and pioneer settlement. There is a section on the stalwart defense of the northern Negev settlements during the War of Independence.

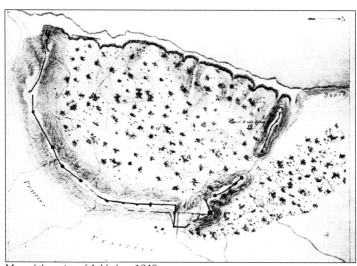

Map of the ruins of Ashkelon, 1848.

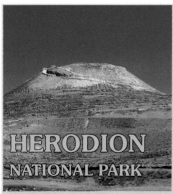

Location: from Route 356 (from Jerusalem via Har Homa to Teko'a), turn SE.

Best season: year-round

Length of visit: about 2 hours

Tel.: 03-7762251

Entrance fee

A Psalm of David, when he was in the wilderness of Judah. (Ps 63:1)

Jewish site

Christian site

Antiquities

Lookout point

Souvenir shop

Snack bar

WC

In the western foothills of the Judean Desert, towering above its surroundings and seen from every direction, stands Tel Herodion. The tel has a natural foundation but its peak was fashioned by man. In order to build a city on the mound, it was necessary to create an expansive flat surface and this entailed leveling the summit.

This tel, with a fortress at the top and an entire complex built below, was undertaken at the instigation of one man, King Herod, who made this site into a palace, a stronghold, and a personal mausoleum.

Herodion, however, is far more than a burial tomb. The tel that one sees from a distance is only a part of the actual site.

The second part extends over the lower region of the tel and contains structures which are not less impressive. The base of the tel was apparently a natural prominence, but a huge amount of material was placed upon this to give it the conical shape that one sees today. A fortress was built at the head of the promontory whose near invincibility was demonstrated by the fact that it was one of three fortified positions that remained standing following the Roman destruction of Jerusalem in 70 CE. In the end, it was handed over to the Romans without a fight.

HISTORY

This spot was chosen on the

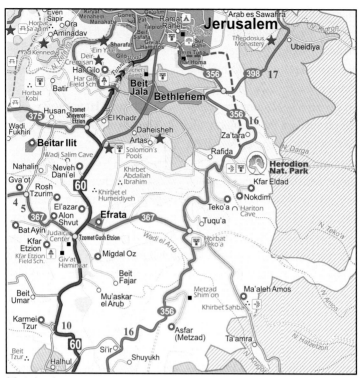

© Carta, Jerusalem

basis of an event in the life of the young Herod. In 63 BCE, the Romans conquered the territory ruled by the Hasmonean dynasty and appointed John Hyrcanus II as governor. Hyrcanus' advisor was Antipater, a Jew of Edomite extraction, and on Antipater's recommendation his son Herod was appointed as governor of Galilee in 47 BCE. Several years later, the Parthians defeated the Romans. Mattathias Antigonus, the nephew of Hyrcanus and his rival, had formed an alliance with the Parthians and he was subsequently appointed king and High Priest of the land. Herod regarded this appointment as a threat to his life and fled with his family from Jerusalem into the desert. Antigonus pursued him, and at the mound which would later become Herodion, a battle ensued between the two camps and Herod emerged victorious. The entire episode was traumatic for Herod, and when he established his kingdom he decided to erect his tomb at the battle site. Herodion was built between 23 and 20 BCE. It is not clear if Herod was finally buried here, and perhaps he was interred in Jerusalem.

And what happened after Herod? About 70 years after the construction on the hill, the fortress was partially destroyed in an earthquake. During the Great Revolt against the Romans, the Zealots took refuge at Herodion for 4 years and then handed the stronghold over to the Romans without any bloodshed. Between 132 and 135 CE, the forces of Bar Kochba built tunnels and cisterns, but with the suppression of the Revolt they abandoned the location and settlement was not resumed here until the Byzantine period. Remains of 3 churches from this period have been identified. Herodion was again abandoned with the onset of Arab occupation in the 7th century.

Today, both the elevated area and the city at its base are part of the national park.

SITES TO VISIT

UPPER HERODION
1. The Mountain Palace-Fortress

This is a circular structure consisting of two walls: the outer wall is much thicker than the inner wall and there is a gap between them. The walls reached a height of 15 m and the space between them was used for storage and corridors. Three semicircular towers, and one circular tower, extend outwards from the exterior wall. Only the sealed base of the circular tower remains and rises 20 m above bedrock. It is estimated on the basis of similar structures at

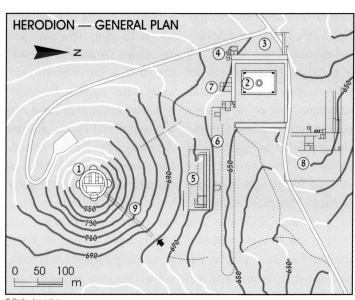

HERODION — GENERAL PLAN

© Carta, Jerusalem

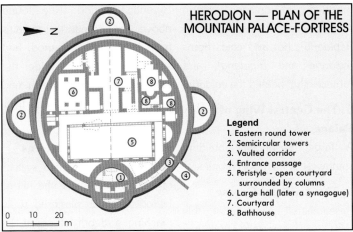

HERODION — PLAN OF THE MOUNTAIN PALACE-FORTRESS

Legend
1. Eastern round tower
2. Semicircular towers
3. Vaulted corridor
4. Entrance passage
5. Peristyle - open courtyard surrounded by columns
6. Large hall (later a synagogue)
7. Courtyard
8. Bathhouse

0   10   20
|___|___| m

© Carta, Jerusalem

Herodion that its original height was approximately 45 m.

Within the fortress, archaeological excavations have exposed the lower parts of the principal structures: the palace, including a hall and sleeping quarters, a Roman-style bath, and an ornate courtyard. On the basis of the many columns and other remains, it would appear that the inner structures were several stories high. When the Zealots captured Herodion during the Revolt, they built a synagogue inside the hall. The lower city, which was built north of the summit fortress, supplied water to the latter.

THE LOWER CITY

The following structures have so far been exposed:

2. The Pool Complex

The pool was 75 × 45 m. At its center stood a round tower and

on three sides there was a garden. Support pillars were built around the garden for a length of 350 m. Based upon the ornamented remains that were exposed, it must be assumed that the entire complex was extravagantly decorated.

3. Wings of the Large Palace

Most of the Herodion construction in the lower city is concentrated to the south, west and north of the pool complex. These were wings or auxiliary buildings of the palace. At the northwest exterior of the pool complex, part of a large storage area was exposed that included a long, narrow room filled with identical storage jars.

4. Roman-Style Bathhouse

This is the largest of its kind discovered so far in any of Herod's palaces. This complex included a dressing room, entrance rooms, warm rooms (*tepidaria*), hot and cold rooms (*caldaria* and *frigidaria*), and furnaces that heated the *caldaria*.

5. The Central Wing of the Palace

A large, rectangular building southwest of the pool complex.

6. The Artificial Course

Researchers believe that this path was especially built for Herod's funeral procession. An extensive description of the funeral is provided in the writings of Josephus Flavius.

7. The Monumental Building

This structure is partly cut out of the bedrock but otherwise built of ashlars. It may have been the mausoleum built for Herod.

8. The Byzantine Churches

Remains of 3 churches from the Byzantine period were found above or alongside remains from the Herodian period, and some were found inside the Herodian structures, which had been cleared of debris and their remains reused.

9. The System of Cisterns

There is a sophisticated system of cisterns dug inside the hill of Herodion. Four plastered wells reaching a depth of about 15 m were found below the palace floor. Several rock-hewn steps led directly down from the palace to these water sources.

OUTSIDE THE NATIONAL PARK

Solomon's Pools

This is a system of large pools situated about 4 km south of Bethlehem, beside the Jerusalem–Hebron road. The pools

LOWER HERODION: PLAN OF THE NORTHERN CHURCH

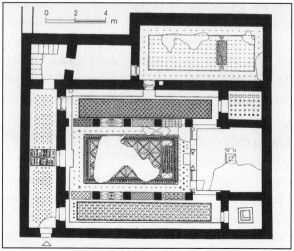

© Carta, Jerusalem

collect rainwater and water from nearby springs; their combined volume is 180,000 cubic meters. From here, water was channeled to Jerusalem, via aqueducts or in pipes, powered by the force of gravity. They were apparently built in the time of Herod in order to improve the water supply to Jerusalem. There is a fortress built by the Turks in 1617 which stands beside the pools in order to guard this water resource.

Hariton Cave

This cave, 450 m long, is the largest karst cave in the country. Its entrance is on the northern side of a cliff overlooking Nahal Teko'a. Spelunkers should enter with strong lantern light and rescue equipment. The passageway between the chambers and the niches sometimes requires a tight crawl.

Gush Etzion

Before the War of Independence there was a bloc of 4 Jewish settlements in this area: Kfar Etzion, Masu'ot Yitzhak, Ein Tzurim, and Revadim. With the outbreak of war in 1948, these settlements were cut off from the rest of the Jewish Yishuv and all efforts to bring in reinforcements failed. These settlements fell on 14 May 1948 after a long siege. Arab forces killed 151 of the defenders and took 320 prisoners. In the Six-Day War (1967) this area was retaken by IDF forces and the settlements were renewed. Today, there is a Center for the Arts in the field of Judaica, cherry-picking (in season), a mushroom farm, winery, a dairy farm open to visitors, and a zoo.

Herodion, viewed from Mt. Gilo.

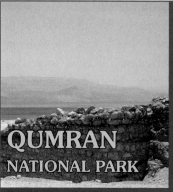

Location: close to Route 90, N Dead Sea.

Best season: year-round. The area is extremely hot during the summer, especially at midday.

Length of visit: 1 to 2 hours

Tel.: 02-9942235

Entrance fee

...the vale of Siddim, which is the salt sea (Dead Sea). (Gen 14:3)

 Jewish site
 Christian site
 Antiquities
 Sound & light show

Accessibility Rating

 2   3

 WC
 Telephone
 Snack bar
Restaurant
Souvenir shop

 P ✓   ✓   ✓

The rock cliff in the north Dead Sea area is neither high nor overly impressive. For many years tourists passed through this stretch of the Dead Sea to bathe in the nearby freshwater springs of Ein Feshkha or continued on to the springs of Ein Gedi without noticing this cliff and its caves or knowing what treasures were hidden there.

The story is as follows: in 1947, a Bedouin youth from a local tribe, chasing after a goat from his herd, entered a cave in the cliff and found a jar with three parchment scrolls inside. Following this discovery, other parchment scrolls were found. The scrolls found their way to the religious leader of the Syrian Christian-Orthodox community (Assyrian), who transferred them to America. The existence of these items became known to the archaeologist, Professor E. L. Sukenik, and he immediately understood their historical value: handwritten script from the Second Temple period, unknown until then. In an intricate transaction, the first seven scrolls were purchased; they included, among other writings, the nearly complete text of the Book of Isaiah, Commentary on Habakkuk, portions from the Psalms, and the Scroll of the War Between the Sons of Light and the Sons of Darkness. Additional excavations, as well as fragments that were saved from cave theft, enriched the findings.

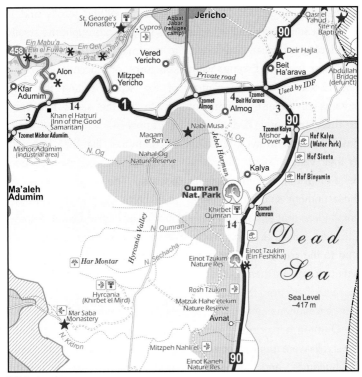

© Carta, Jerusalem

It appears that a group of people, who may be designated as the "Dead Sea sect," settled in the area and hid the writings important to them in caves either on the eve of, or during, the Great Jewish Revolt against the Romans. Because of the dry desert climate, these writings were preserved for about 19 centuries. The main writings are today kept in the Shrine of the Book, a building specially built for these scrolls on the premises of the Israel Museum in Jerusalem. It may be assumed that a large portion of the writings has been lost or is in private hands. The findings created a worldwide sensation. Research of the scrolls and their contents has been the subject of thousands of books and articles and has generated intense debate among scholars and men of religion. Why has this been the case?

Despite the vast amount of written material, it is not clear who transcribed and wrote these works. In the opinion of many scholars, they belonged to the sect of the Essenes, described by Josephus Flavius. On the other hand, others claim that some of the ideas presented in these findings cannot be identified with the ideology or beliefs of this sect. It is clear that the Essenes were not associated with the central streams of Judaism prominent at this time, and fled to the desert in order to live according to their values. Many Christians have great difficulty in accepting these findings since the writings entail ideas that are akin to early Christian beliefs and this would lead to the conclusion that Jesus did not formulate them, but rather received them from the sect.

In excavations undertaken at the Qumran ruins close to where the scrolls were found, a complex of buildings and installations was exposed, and items were found that lead to the conclusion that the sect's scribes dwelled here (or that this location was their center), that they were the possessors of the scrolls and it was they who brought the scrolls to the caves. On the basis of the structures, and according to one of the scrolls setting the way of life for the sect's followers, it appears that they had a communal life that imposed a regimen of humbleness and poverty. The large number of ritual baths suggests that physical purity was highly valued. A large structure was apparently used as the scriptorium. Here were found writing desks, ink-wells, and other items. A channel brought torrential rainwater from the nearby ravines to the settlement; spring water from the cliffs supplemented the water supply. A structure which appears to have been used for skinning and tanning hides was found; another installation seems to have been a workshop for manufacturing jars

Aerial view of Qumran.

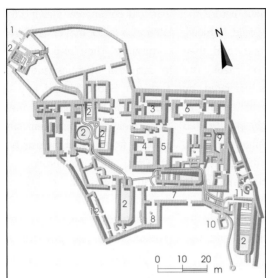

1 Entrance to aqueduct
2 Pools
3 Tower
4 Room lined with benches
5 Scriptorium
6 Kitchen
7 Assembly hall
8 Pantry
9 Ritual baths
10 Potter's workshop
11 Kiln
12 Cattle pen

QUMRAN — PLAN

© Carta, Jerusalem

of the type into which the scrolls were placed.

The finds from the Qumran caves stirred research in the various gullies that descend from the rock cliff to the Dead Sea. Groups of researchers who went to these sites dug up a vast number of items and writings dating from the Chalcolithic period in the Cave of the Treasure, in Nahal Mishmar, to the letters of Bar Kochba. The Qumran site is the starting point for all the above.

The "Dead Sea Sect" in the Way of the Essenes

Members of the Essene sect were monks who lived a communal life isolated from the rest of society. Their daily ritual included

Rumex cyprius.

a sunrise ceremony; before the first repast they would immerse themselves in water, and then begin the common meal. The simple food was prepared by priests in order to assure its purity. No stranger participated in their meals. After the meal, the priest would utter a blessing and then each one returned to his daily work. Towards evening, after completion of work, a similar routine of immersion took place, and then the second and last meal was eaten.

The sect members followed a life of humility, celibacy, and strict adherence to laws of purity; they distanced themselves from war and commerce, viewing the latter as a factor that engendered corruption. They also objected to sacrificial offerings and kept a stricter Sabbath than any of their Jewish contemporaries. Since their calendrical year was different from that of mainstream Israelites, their celebration of Jewish festivals fell on different dates.

Acceptance into the sect required a two-year novitiate. In the first year, they were required to live according to the rules of the sect while still retaining their own property. In the second year, the novice continued the required rituals but had to release

THE WINTER PALACES OF HEROD THE GREAT

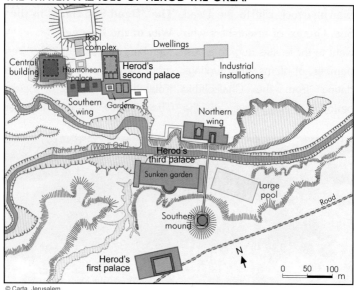

© Carta, Jerusalem

Legend

- ▩ Hasmonean palace
- ▨ Palaces of Herod
- ▨ Dwellings/service wing
- ▨ Pools

his property to the community before being accepted as a member on the sworn condition that he would not reveal the secrets of the sect.

OUTSIDE THE NATIONAL PARK

Herod's Winter Palaces (Tulul Abu el Alayiq)

The winter palaces of King Herod were recognized at a site west of Jericho embracing both banks of Nahal Prat (Wadi Qelt). In Arabic, the place is called Tulul Abu el Alayiq. The remains of one palace, a garden, and a pool were found on the southern bank. On the northern bank were the remains of a second palace and a splendid bathhouse. The two palaces were guarded by a fortress called Cypros, named after Herod's mother.

Nahal Prat Reserve

This is a nature reserve which surrounds a part of Nahal Prat (Wadi Qelt). Several of its sections are narrow, steep canyons. In its lower section, there are 3 large springs—Ein Far'a, Ein Fuwar, and Ein Qelt—as well as a few smaller springs. They gather to form a powerful stream and pleasant bathing pools in several sections. The channel is awash with water plants and plants native to the desert. Animal life is plentiful and varied, especially species of fowl, among them quite rare predators. In the Nahal bed and alongside it are many antiquity sites such as aqueducts, caves where monks lived in solitude, and monasteries. Two monasteries are active: Firan and Mar Jaris (Saint George).

Winter palace of Herod.

356

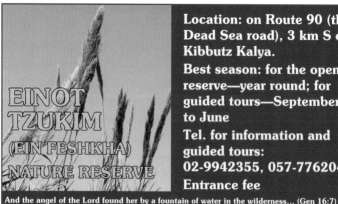

Location: on Route 90 (the Dead Sea road), 3 km S of Kibbutz Kalya.
Best season: for the open reserve—year round; for guided tours—September to June
Tel. for information and guided tours: 02-9942355, 057-7762046
Entrance fee

And the angel of the Lord found her by a fountain of water in the wilderness... (Gen 16:7)

Antiquities | Lookout point | Picnic site | Swimming | Showers

Telephone | Snack bar | Restaurant | WC

Accessibility Rating

♿ 2 🚹 3

P ✔ 🚻 ✘ 🍴 ✔ ≈ ✔

Along the coast of the Dead Sea, from Einot Tzukim to Ein Bokek, are a number of springs. The source of their water is rainfall in the Judean Mountains which percolates into the nooks and crannies of the range. Below the hard layer of limestone, which absorbs water, there is an impervious layer which does not absorb water; here, the water travels along the surface of the rock until it arrives at fissures in the cliff or emerges below it. Except for Ein Gedi, the majority of these springs are saline and not suitable for drinking. Plant life prospers around these springs, and the green spots beside the water contrast sharply with the desert landscape and most of the Dead Sea coast

which is void of vegetation. The Einot Tzukim Nature Reserve extends from the northern coast of the Dead Sea to the foot of the cliff faults. It is wide in its northern sector and gradually narrows as one proceeds south until it reaches Rosh Tzukim (Ras Feshkha). Before the water level of the Dead Sea dropped, the summit of these cliffs formed the edge of the Sea with no possible foot passage at their base. Today, the drastically reduced water level has created a very narrow terrestrial plain between the sea and the cliffs and there is a road which runs along the coast. Below Rosh Tzukim there is a huge boulder marked "PEF" (Palestine Exploration Fund). The boulder is situated 1½ km

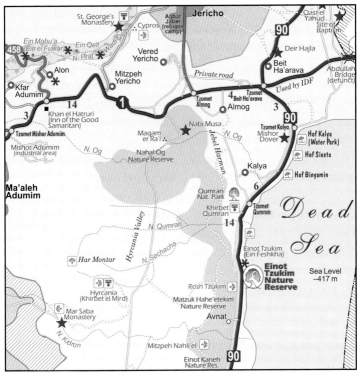

© Carta, Jerusalem

from the entrance to the Reserve, rising 3 m above route 90. Members of the British Palestine Exploration Fund marked the sea level of the Dead Sea on this monument in the 1880s. Einot Tzukim was the natural bathing spring for Jerusalemites, and to accommodate them the area was divided into three sectors:

The Northern Sector

This area, almost 700 acres, is only open to the professional staff of the Nature and National Parks Authority who make inspections to ensure that no damage

has been done to the natural environment and that it remain and develop in its pristine state.

The Central Sector

This 125-acre area is open to the public and contains manmade pools that are fed by "fault springs," that is, those springs which emerge from the Syrian-African Rift in this area. The springs at Einot Tzukim generate more water volume than other springs along the coast. The water is quite saline, making it unsuitable for drinking, but suitable for bathing. Plant life abounds around the springs, mainly thickets of Common Reed (*Phragmites australis*) and Arundo or Giant Weed (*Arundo donax*). Water temperatures reach 30° Centigrade (86° F). There are adequate bathing facilities by the pools including thatched shade structures, showers, and picnic tables.

The Southern Sector

This area of approximately 375 acres is referred to as "the hidden reserve." Guided tours are provided. Walking along the shade of the tamarisks allows one the chance to peek at the various insects that feed from this tree, in particular the weaving ant and its symbiotic relationship to the tamarisk. In addition, there is breathtaking desert vegetation such as the Common Reed and Egyptian Sugar Cane, as well as animal life—invertebrates that live in water alongside fish and amphibians, water fowl, song birds, and others.

Mules were brought to the Reserve to help in reducing damage from fires. They thin out the reed vegetation, especially after a blaze, and thus allow natural vegetation to resuscitate. The current mule population is estimated at 100–150.

The drop in the level of the

Einot Tzukim.

Dead Sea during the past decade has exposed layers of soft clay that constitute the seabed. The waters that flow from the springs towards the Dead Sea have created canyons that become deeper each year as the sea level drops. The waters flow beneath the surface so that it does not wash away the salt from the land. This is the reason that nothing grows on this section of land.

ARCHAEOLOGY

An archaeological site from the Second Temple period was found in the central sector of the Reserve. Current assessments believe it to be an Essene farm settlement whose inhabitants engaged in agriculture and livestock breeding. Recently, a large complex from the Herodion period was exposed which contained a farmhouse, irrigation pond and garden, and a large installation (the only one of its kind found so far in the country) that manufactured balsam perfume.

BALSAM CULTIVATION

The balsam bush, which grew in abundance in the Jericho–Dead Sea area, is not related to the persimmon that is grown today. According to tradition, the aromatic resinous substance

Bathing in Einot Tzukim.

Aerial view of the cliff facing Einot Tzukim (Ras Feshkha).

flowing from the bush, used as a healing ointment, was cultivated in the days of King Solomon, who obtained the plant, according to Josephus, from the Queen of Sheba. The secrets surrounding its cultivation were well kept by its Jewish growers and it proved to be the most expensive product in the country. The original shrub has vanished from the area and the riddle of its exact genetic composition has engaged many researchers.

The balsam bush yielded two types of perfume: an ointment that was manufactured from the stalk and was applied as a medicinal herb and a disinfectant, as well as burned for its incense and for anointing the heads of the Kings of Judah; an aromatic formed by cooking a concentrate of the plant with olive oil. This perfume was considered among the best and was sold throughout the Roman Empire.

ROSH TZUKIM

Opposite the entrance to the Reserve, there is a black-marked trail that ascends to Rosh Tzukim (meaning "cliff top"). From the top of the cliff there is a magnificent view of the Moab Mountains and the Dead Sea and their point of juncture with the Jordan River in the north.

OUTSIDE THE NATURE RESERVE

The Martyrius Monastery

This is the ruins of a monastery (in Arabic, Khirbet el Murasas) located in the center of the town of Ma'aleh Adumim. It was built in the 5th century CE by the Byzantine monk, Martyrius, who was appointed priest of the Church of the Anastasis (the Holy Sepulcher) in Jerusalem, and later patriarch of Jerusalem (478–486 CE). This complex covers an area of approximately 2½ acres (about 10,000 sq m) and contains remains of the monastery, a church compound with fine mosaics, an escape tunnel to the exterior, and a deep and quite impressive cistern.

In the 8th century, during the Early Arab period, part of the grounds was used as an herb garden, now partially restored.

There is an entrance fee.

Khan el Hatruri ("Inn of the Good Samaritan")

This site contains the remains of an ancient wayside inn, which, according to the Christian tradition, was the place where

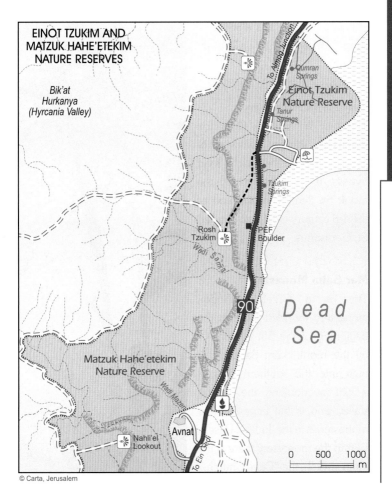

© Carta, Jerusalem

Jesus gave an account to his disciples of how a Samaritan came to the rescue of a passerby descending from Jerusalem and set upon by a band of robbers. The "Good Samaritan" bandaged, clothed and fed him. The remains seen at the site today are from the Umayyad period (late 7th century). The meaning of the Arabic name, Khan el Hatruri, is "Inn for the Hungry." The structure was used by the Turkish army and was destroyed during WWI.

Today, the site has a souvenir shop oriented to Christian pilgrims.

Deir Hajla Monastery
This is a Greek Orthodox monastery situated southeast of Jericho, close to the Jericho road bypass. It was founded by the monk St. Jerome at the end of the 4th century CE. It is also called St. Gerasimus.

Mar Saba Monastery
This is a Greek Orthodox monastery founded towards the beginning of the 5th century CE by the monk Saint Sabas. It is built into the southern face of a cliff overlooking the Kidron Valley and is the largest of the monasteries in the Judean Desert. Within the monastery there is the main church, the "Cave Church,"

Reed.

a large burial niche holding hundreds of skulls of monks who were slaughtered by the Persians and the Arabs. A cave consisting of steps leads north from the monastery to a spring that empties into Nahal Kidron. Beside the spring is a cave where St. Sabas presumably lived prior to founding the monastery. There are many caves along the walls facing both banks of the Kidron where monks lived a solitary life only gathering together on Sunday for communal prayer. Entrance to the monastery is restricted to males only.

Nabi Musa

This is a large inn (khan) distinguished by its white cupolas. According to Muslim tradition, Moses is buried here. Until the War of Independence (1948) there were annual processions to Nabi Musa where celebrations took place over a period of seven days. During the period of the British Mandate, Arab agitators exploited these gatherings to drum up incitement against the Jews. In 1920, the anti-Jewish provocations spread to the Jewish Quarter of the Old City of Jerusalem. Denunciations of Jews in these processions continued over the years but the number of participants diminished with a resultant devaluation of their impact. After the establishment of Israel, these processions and the pageant at Mar Saba ceased.

The site may be visited today, but modest dress should be observed.

*Tristram's Starlings (*Onichognathus tristrami*).*

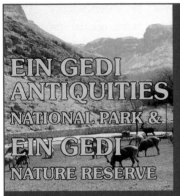

Location: on Route 90 (the Dead Sea road), about 1 km N of Ein Gedi. Reserve extends between the Mt. Yishai ridge and Mitzpeh Ein Gedi in N, to Nahal Hever in S, and from the Nahal Arugot reserve in W to the Dead Sea shore in E. **Best season: fall to spring** **Tel.: 08-6584585** **Entrance fee.** Combined ticket to Park & Reserve may be purchased.

...Behold, David is in the wilderness of En-gedi. (1 Sam 24:1)

Ein Gedi Antiquities

| Jewish site | Antiquities | Lookout point | WC |

Ein Gedi Nature Reserve

| Lookout point | Outdoor recreation | Hiking trail | Picnic site |

| WC | Restaurant | Telephone | Souvenir shop |

Accessibility Rating

 2   3

P X WC X Restaurant X

Accessibility Rating

 1 1

P ✓ ✓ ✓ ≈ X

Ein Gedi, an oasis on the western shore of the Dead Sea, is known since the days of the Bible. Apparently, it acquired its name from the herds of goats or gazelles (in Hebrew, *gedi*) that graze in the area. It is mentioned in the list of the cities of Judah among those in the wilderness (Joshua 15: 62). Pursued by King Saul, the young David found refuge here, as related in the Book of Samuel where "the wilderness of En-gedi" and "the rocks of the wild goats" are mentioned (1 Samuel 24:1–2). The walled camps at the top of the mountains appear as "the strongholds of En-gedi" (1 Samuel 24: 1). It is also identified with Hazazon-tamar (2 Chronicles 20:2). In the Song of Songs (1: 14), the author (traditionally, Solomon) compares his relation to his beloved "as a cluster of camphire (henna) in the vineyards of En-gedi," and this is the first mention of this perfume (and others) whose cultivation and production was the main economic resource of the town.

HISTORY

The special conditions characterizing the oasis of Ein Gedi

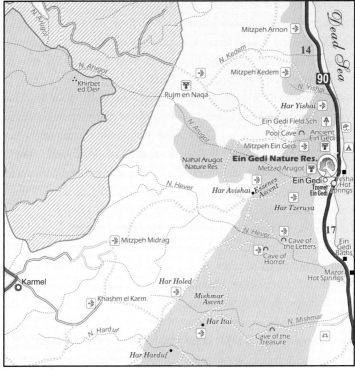

© Carta, Jerusalem

have drawn inhabitants from the earliest of times. Excavations have shown that the area of ancient Ein Gedi, situated between Nahal David and Nahal Arugot, was already settled in the Chalcolithic period. Various items dating from the period of the Israelite kingdom to the Roman-Byzantine period were found at Tel Goren. During the reign of King Jehoshaphat, the Ammonites and Moabites invaded this site and used it as a base for attacking the Kingdom of Judah. It appears that the settlement was destroyed during Nebuchadnezzar's siege of Jerusalem, but was renewed after the Babylonian exiles returned, and was a flourishing community in the Second Temple period. With the suppression of the Bar Kochba revolt (132–135 CE), Ein Gedi's residents fled and the town was destroyed.

Ein Gedi was able to survive thanks to the growing of balsam that was used for medicinal and cosmetic purposes. According to one tradition, King Solomon received this plant from the Queen of Sheba, and balsam quickly became the most cherished product in the country. The secret of its cultivation was well-guarded by Jewish farmers.

The spring of Ein Gedi and the surrounding area were seized by the Alexandroni Brigade in the War of Independence (1948).

THE SYNAGOGUE

An ancient synagogue, discovered during earthworks that were carried out northeast of Tel Goren, is evidence for the continuity of Jewish life in Ein Gedi for hundreds of years, from the 4th–6th centuries CE. Among the findings: a bronze seven-branched candelabrum (*menorah*), more than 5,000 coins stashed in a niche (apparently, the charity collection of the synagogue), an exquisite mosaic floor which is considered one of the earliest synagogue mosaic floors found in the country, and a later mosaic floor with inscriptions in each of its four panels:

The first panel. A list of 13 generations of biblical family heads from Adam to the sons of Noah.

The second panel. This is a list of the 12 zodiac signs, the 12 months of the year, the 3 Patriarchs (Abraham, Isaac, and Jacob), the 3 companions of Daniel, and the blessing "Peace unto Israel."

The third panel. Considered to be the most important, this inscription, in Aramaic, begins with a line dedicated to the donors. This is followed by "All those who sow discord between their fellow men, or speak evilly of their comrade to a stranger, or steal what belongs to another, or disclose the secrets of the city to a stranger — the one whose eyes roam over the entire earth and see what is concealed will uproot this person and his seed from

Mosaic floor from ancient synagogue at Ein Gedi.

under the sun and all the people will say Amen, Amen, Selah."

The fourth panel. This is an Aramaic inscription extolling Rabbi Yose bar Halfi and Hezekiyo bar Halfi for building the fashionable staircase "on behalf of the Merciful One, Peace."

The Jewish settlement and the synagogue were destroyed in a fire. Apparently, the destruction of the settlement was connected to the suppression of the non-Christian minorities during the reign of Justinian (527–565 CE).

THE CHALCOLITHIC TEMPLE

A temple from the Chalcolithic

Mosaic inscriptions from ancient synagogue at Ein Gedi.

EIN GEDI ANTIQUITIES PARK AND NATURE RESERVE

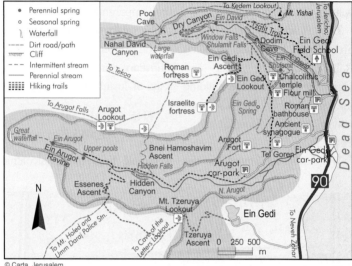

© Carta, Jerusalem

period was found on a hill slope above one of the springs. There were no further items exposed at this site. Some scholars have asserted that the objects found inside the Cave of the Treasure at Nahal Mishmar belong to this temple; the assumption is that the temple was in danger and its occupants hid their treasures in this cave.

THE NATURE RESERVE

The Ein Gedi Nature Reserve is the finest, largest and most important desert reserve in the country. It is formed by two Nahals: Nahal David and Nahal Arugot, both of which are perennial streams. The source of their water is rainfall on the Judean Hills which seeps into the terrain until reaching an impermeable layer, at which point the water flows along the surface until it arrives at the cliff of Matzuk Hahe'etekim, above the Dead Sea, where it pours forth as springs. Their waters flow through a crevice, but are swallowed up before reaching the sea. There is one spring in Nahal Arugot and several in Nahal David.

The contrast between the sectors of the Nahal in which water reaches them—whether it is water flowing along the surface or underground—and the desert landscape where no water is present, is quite stark; there is no transition area. Because the water comes from heights above the coastal plain, waterfalls pattern its course. Nahal Arugot has one main waterfall and a number of small ones; in Nahal David there is one large waterfall, and below it an additional 5 smaller falls. The noise of the rushing water and the thunder of the falls are special features of this Reserve.

In winter, these Nahals, as well as others in the Judean Desert, are subject to flash floods. A tremendous amount of water accumulates in a flash flood, pushing boulders and everything that stands in its way, sometimes even dramatically forcing open a new course of descent. Vegetation in the path of these torrents of water is destroyed and revival often takes a long time.

VEGETATION

Water and high temperatures in this area produce a variety of plant life. Some of the vegetation growing by watered areas may be found in other regions, while other vegetation is native to oases. From the south of the Arava to the Jordanian steppes the vegetation is part of the Sudanese tropical zone and reaches its zenith here. Among the noteworthy trees are the Cordia (*Cordia sinensis*) bearing succulent fruit which provides food for birds; the Toothbrush Tree (*Salvadora persica*); the Bean Tree (*Moringa peregrina*) which has small leaves and in which photosynthesis is performed by the green stems; the Egyptian Balsam *(Balanites aegyptiaca)*; and the Christ's Thorn Jujube (*Ziziphus spina-christi*). These trees grow beside the Acacias which are an inseparable part of the desert landscape.

Nahal David.

The Reserve is also filled with various types of bushes, dwarf shrubs, and various Hemicryptophytes. Here also is one of the solitary refuges of the Large-leaved Helleborine (*Epipactis helleborine*) from the orchid family; it is the only plant from this family that strays from its Mediterranean environment into the desert regions. Beside the waterfalls, and especially at the Dudim Cave, next to the large waterfall, grows the Common Maidenhair (*Adiantum capillus-veneris*). The Hoary Nightshade (*Solanumincanum*) bears fruit that looks like tiny eggplants. At the lower end of the Nahal may be found thickets of Common Reed (*Phragmites australis*) and Giant Reed (*Arundo donax*).

Wild mountain goat.

Hyrax.

ANIMAL LIFE

The plants and water attract various forms of animal life. Among the water fowl are Tristram's Starling (*Onychognathus tristamii*) identified by a copper-colored spot on its wings in flight and by its calling note; the Red-rumped Wheatear (*Oenanthe moesta*) with its black tail; and the Sand Partridge (*Ammoperdix heyi*), related to the turkey. The latter nests here while its young keep to the ground and disappear from sight. One may also see Bulbuls and Desert Sparrows.

The words of Psalm 104:18 provide an apt description of the fauna encountered in the landscape:

> The high mountains are for
>   the wild goats;
> The rocks are a refuge for the
>   conies [hyrax].

The goats, that until 1948 were almost never seen in the area, and were on the verge of extinction, have revived since the enactment of laws to protect desert life. They wander in the Reserve and its periphery without fear from humans. All aspects of an animal's life may be observed in this setting: eating and resting, the clash of the antlers of males during rutting season, and the females with their kids, whence originates the name Ein Gedi

(Spring of the Kid). Hyraxes sit and rest on the rocks or climb trees to eat their leaves. With the natural increase of the hyrax and goat population, the small leopard population, which lived in hidden recesses of the desert, revived for a short period. For a few years, leopards were seen in the vicinity of Ein Gedi, but

Waterfall in Nahal David.

following a number of tragic accidents, the last leopards vanished. It is possible that they will be renewed by leopards that still roam the Negev.

RECOMMENDED HIKING TRAILS AT EASY AND INTERMEDIATE LEVELS IN THE RESERVE

The Ancient Synagogue
See above, p. 366.

Nahal David
This is a circular trail which ascends on one side of the Nahal and returns on the other side. It begins beside the ticket booth at the entrance to Nahal David. The trail passes by waterfalls and pools until it reaches David Falls. Length of the walk is about an hour. Above the waterfalls is the karstic Dudim Cave. One should begin one's exit from Nahal David not later than 3:30 pm.

The Hidden Waterfalls in Nahal Arugot
The entrance to Nahal Arugot from the west is about 10 km south of Bethlehem. It flows southeast until it empties into the Dead Sea, north of Ein Gedi. An ancient route followed its bed from Bethlehem to Ein Gedi. Part of the upper section of the Nahal, which has a number of canyons, is included in the Reserve. The Nahal cuts through chalk and hard limestone, creates a clifflike ravine about 500 m high and about 1,000 m wide. The Nahal has a constant flow of clean and sweet water. The Nahal's source is the Arugot Spring and along the length of the Nahal there are additional smaller springs.

Hikers in the Ein Gedi Nature Reserve.

From the ticket office at the entrance to the Nahal a red-marked trail leads east to the Hidden Falls. The trail passes through wild landscape which has plenty of water all year round. The hike takes between 2 and 3 hours and is graded at the intermediate level. One should depart from the Hidden Falls on return to the entrance not later than 3:00 pm.

Kibbutz Ein Gedi

On the premises of the kibbutz there is a botanical garden, cactus garden, and artists' workshops: quilting, ceramics, carpentry (magic wood). Artists allow visitor participation in their workshops.

Apart from the Kibbutz there is a Field School of the Nature Protection Society located in the vicinity of the Reserve. Many activities and recreational facilities have also been established in this area and supplement any visit to the Reserve.

Maidenhair fern in Nahal David.

Flash flood in Nahal Arugot.

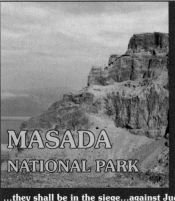

MASADA NATIONAL PARK

...they shall be in the siege...against Judah... (Zech 12:2)

Location: from Route 90 (Dead Sea road), turn W; also accessible from W (direction of Arad), by walking up the rampart.

Best season: year-round

Cablecar: 8 am–4 pm; on Fridays and eve of Jewish holidays, until one hour before the site closes

Tel.: 08-6584207/8
Sound & light show: 08-9959333

Fax: 08-6584464

Entrance fee

Jewish site | Muslim site | Antiquities | Lookout point | Picnic site | Camping

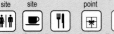

WC | Snack bar | Restaurant | Souvenir shop | Telephone

Accessibility Rating

♿ 2	👤 3	👁
P ✓	👫 ✓	🍴 ✓

Masada, which up to now was a national Jewish site, has been declared a World Heritage Site by UNESCO. It thus joins three other Israeli sites in the same category: the Old City of Jerusalem; the Old City of Acre; and the "White City" in Tel Aviv. Altogether, this distinguished list numbers about 700 sites throughout the world.

Masada was built, subjected to military siege and attack, and finally destroyed vanishing from history. From the Jewish writings at the time of its construction or shortly thereafter (late 1st century BCE–1st century CE), Masada finds no mention, except in the writings of Josephus Flavius. Without his description, what occurred here would have been subject only to conjecture. Almost 18 centuries had passed before research unveiled, step by step, the story of this place.

Masada is first and foremost a geological formation. On the east, this isolated rock cliff falls in a sheer drop to the Dead Sea. Its northern side comprises the southern bank of Nahal Ben Ya'ir, the southern side comprises the northern bask of Nahal Masada, and the western side was formed by a geological fault that separates the Masada precipice from the surrounding Judean Desert. In this fashion, a natural fortress was created.

The high priest Jonathan, apparently referring to the Hasmonean king Alexander Yannai, had already given his

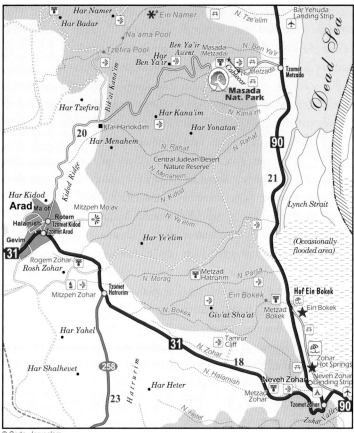

© Carta, Jerusalem

opinion on the strategic value of this place. He fortified the elevated plateau and perhaps laid the foundation for the intricate water system at the site. A number of years later, King Herod continued the work of his predecessor, and made major improvements. Masada became a combination "winter palace," refuge in time of need, and perhaps a way station for travelers and caravans heading east before traversing the Dead Sea. The Lynch Strait, a narrow stretch of water which connected the northern basin of the Dead Sea from its southern basin, was shallow and easy to cross. In the opinion of geologists it was, in fact, dry land at the time, making it a convenient route to Transjordan and beyond.

In Herod's accustomed manner, Masada was constructed from its foundations in a splendid fashion. The detailed description of the place was provided by the contemporary Jewish historian, Josephus, and until Masada was thoroughly excavated, several scholars regarded his account as exaggerated. Today, we think that the description was authentic and accurate. Masada was surrounded by a wall, fortified, and almost invincible. The official palace stood in the west and another, elaborate, three-tiered palace-villa, completely separate from the fortress, was situated on the northern edge of the cliff. One of its unique installations was the water system which secured it a voluminous amount of water in an arid climate: two channels brought flood waters from Nahal Masada and Nahal Ben Yair to two rows of gigantic collection cisterns which could hold thousands of cubic meters of water. From there, the water was hauled up a winding path by mules to the summit of the fortress.

The emotional value of Masada was acquired through the courageous stand in 74 CE of the Zealots, who for months heroically contended with the sophisticated Roman siege until their bitter demise. Details of the Roman siege have been exposed, particularly in the studies of the German researcher A. Schulten in the 1930s. The Roman cordon around Masada was one of the most exhaustive efforts of its kind up to contemporary times and the findings in the field supply realistic evidence backing the story told by Josephus. The eight Roman camps at the base of the fortress hill are still visible; each one had a specific assignment in the siege, and were laid out with exactitude over a distance of more than 4 km, encircling the entire plateau, and thus preventing anyone from leaving.

Mosaic floor in the Western Palace.

Masada — on the ascent to the summit.

To the most vulnerable sections of the wall, the Romans brought their siege batteries. On the top of the plateau remains of buildings from the Herodian period are evident, as well as dwellings of the Zealots including a synagogue close to the fortification wall.

The visitor does not have to use too much imagination in order to sense life under the siege and its tragic finale. The Zealots fought to the very end and it is not for us to judge their choice of suicide rather than suffering the fate of Roman captivity and physical abuse. There is no idealization of mass suicide, and it is not an example for future emulation. If Masada has a didactic message, it is the heroic military stand and not the choice of death as the last option. Justifiably, this cliff, this solitary sentinel in the heart of the desert, has become a pilgrimage site for thousands of Jewish youth and a site of world interest.

DAILY LIFE AT MASADA

Living space was a central problem at ancient Masada. The

well-to-do families lived in palaces and ornate buildings, whereas the rest of the population found lodging in chamber rooms of the fortress's walls. Every family brought to their cell-like abode their belongings and utensils and built the needed facilities for daily life: a stove, baking oven, small pantry and the like. Workshops were integrated into some of the watchtowers along the wall. The family unit functioned as a basis for the allocation of provisions, and the name of the family head was written on the cooking utensils placed in the storage rooms. For distributing supplies they used small "tags" inscribed on pottery shards (ostraca).

RELIGIOUS LIFE

Much attention was devoted to the religious life at Masada. A synagogue, attached to the wall and facing Jerusalem, was built inside a spacious public building. Fragments of two scrolls kept by the synagogue were found in the back room under the synagogue floor. Two ritual baths were also built: one was inside and adjoining a casemate (double fortification wall) in the south, and the other was in a courtyard west of the storerooms. A special effort was made to collect rainwater that was not pumped from a source. There was also

a study hall (*beth midrash*) to perpetuate study of the Talmud. Priests and Levites carried out the religious duties. There were also Torah scrolls, several fragments of which were found in the excavations.

SOUND & LIGHT SHOW

Using up-to-date technology, there is a presentation of what life was like in the Second Temple period.

ALONG THE WALKING TRAIL

1. The Western Gate
The gate presently visible is of Byzantine origin. The Romans breached the walls at a location slightly north of here.

2. The Tanners' Tower
Inside this tower in the Herodian wall, the Zealots manufactured basins to store liquids; apparently, this was an industrial installation for tanning hides. In the liquid refuse that filled the room, a portion from a composition close to the Book of Jubilees, in Hebrew, was found.

3. The Western Palace
Excavations showed that this was the main administrative and ceremonial palace. Its total area is 3,700 sq m.

Its western wing contains storerooms and a kitchen, and,

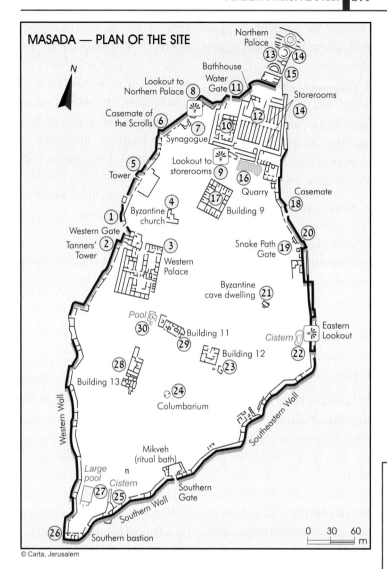

MASADA — PLAN OF THE SITE

© Carta, Jerusalem

to the north, two courtyards surrounded by rooms. Beneath the floor is a network of cisterns.

In the northern wing is a large central courtyard, north of which are dwellings for servants and guards. The other sides of the wing contained workshops; in one, a pottery kiln was found.

The southern wing contains the royal apartments, built in great splendor and munificence.

4. Byzantine Church

This church, built in the 5th century CE, consists of a hall and 3 rooms.

5. Tower

The tower was built from dressed sandstone. In the walls are spaces between the stones that appear in the shape found in columbaria (dovecotes).

6. Casemate of the Scrolls

Inside this casemate items of great value were found from the time of the Zealots: scroll fragments, ostraca, silver shekels, bronze coins, and the like.

7. Synagogue

This is one of the earliest excavated synagogues in the world, and among the very few which existed at the same time as the Temple in Jerusalem. Scroll fragments were found, including one from the Book of Ezekiel of the "vision of the dry bones" (37: 1–14).

8. Lookout from the Northern Palace

From this vantage point, one can see Ein Gedi, Nahal Tze'elim, Mt. Ben Ya'ir, and Mt. Kana'im. In addition, immediately below one can see the places where the Romans set up their siege camps, as well as Masada's reservoirs, water channel, and the northern palace.

9. The Storehouse Lookout

From here one can see the storehouse area and building 9.

10. The Administrative Building and the "Lottery" Square

This is a building from the time of Herod. The Zealots built a ritual bath in the central courtyard. North of this building is the "lottery" square identified by the inscriptions on the ostraca, among them 11 names. One of the names found is that of Ben Ya'ir, a leader of the Zealots at Masada, and it is possible that these were the fateful lots that decided who would kill whom in the final suicide killing.

11. The Water Gate

The gate is covered with stone slabs, and along its walls are benches for those waiting to fill their water jugs.

12. The Bathhouse

This facility was built by Herod in typical Roman style. It consists of a courtyard surrounded by pillars, an entrance chamber and changing room, a cold room (*frigidarium*) with a stepped pool, a warm room (*tepidarium*), and a hot room (*caldarium*) serviced by a double-layered floor allowing for a flow of hot air from below. The bathhouse is decorated with mosaics floors and frescoes. The roof serves as an excellent location to view the storerooms and the plaza entrance of the northern palace.

13. The Northern Palace

This is one of the most elaborate buildings built by Herod. Josephus Flavius gives a detailed description. It is built in 3 tiers of rock with a differential height of 30 m from level to level.

14. The Storerooms

These very large storage facilities for food, supplies and weaponry contained enough provisions to last for years.

15. Villa Remains

Built in the characteristic style of other dwellings at Masada.

16. Stone Quarry

This quarry provided the building material for the structures at Masada.

17. Building 9

Lodgings for the military officers and their families.

18. Casemate

A parchment was found inside this casemate with verses from Psalm 103.

Masada — the caldarium *of the bathhouse.*

19. The Snake Path Gate

This gate is typical of those found at Masada: the floor is paved with stone slabs, there are benches along its walls of white plaster which give the appearance of marble blocks, and it is adjoined by a guard room.

20. The Eastern Wall

This is a typical wall section. It is a casemate wall, that is, a double fortification wall with partitioned compartments, sometimes used for storage or dwellings. In one of the rooms in the eastern wall catapult stones were found which the defenders probably used to guard the Snake Path.

21. A Cave Dwelling from the Byzantine Period

This was built by monks inside a crater that may have been used as a stone quarry for the manufacture of plaster.

22. An Open Cistern

The cistern has a fence around it with openings for water conduits.

23. Building 12: The Royal Apartment

This stylish building was re-used by the Zealots.

24. Columbarium

This building, dating from the days of King Herod, has small niches in its walls. The structure was used for breeding doves on its ground floor, and the upper floor was used as a guard tower.

25. Cistern

This is a cistern from Herodian times. It was fed by a channel which entered from the southern window.

26. The Southern Bastion

This guarded against access to the plateau from the southern flank.

Masada — the round tower.

27. The Large Pool

This is also a Herodian structure whose function is unclear.

28. Building 13

This is an unfinished building from the Herodian period.

29. Building 11

This is another building typical of Herodian construction.

30. Swimming Pool

This Herodian facility was used both for swimming and for bathing.

OUTSIDE THE NATIONAL PARK

Zohar Hot Springs

A cluster of hot springs emerges from the oasis of Neveh Zohar, south of Masada (route 90). The oasis is 150 m long. The springs yield about 500 cubic meters of heavily saline water daily. Since 1958, this site has been used as a medicinal spa because of the high sulfur content of its waters. Luxury hotels with sulfur baths and pools, massage rooms, and other facilities are nearby.

MASADA AND ITS ENVIRONS

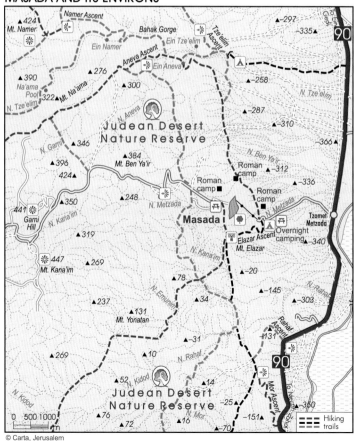

© Carta, Jerusalem

NAHAL BESOR NATURE RESERVE & ESHKOL NATIONAL PARK

Location: entrance from Route 241, next to Urim.

Best season: year-round

Length of visit: 2 hours to a day

Tel.: 08-9985110

Fax: 08-9985267

Entrance fee

So David went…and came to the brook Besor… (1 Sam 30:9)

 Outdoor recreation

 Antiquities

 Lookout point

 Picnic site

 WC

 Snack bar

 Telephone

 Swimming

 Showers

Accessibility Rating

 3

 3

P ✔   ✔   ✔   ✔

NAHAL BESOR

Nahal Besor, including its tributaries, is the largest Nahal in the south of the country. The Nahal begins on the Tziporim Plateau west of Sde Boker and flows north, joined by its tributaries the largest of which are Nahal Be'er Sheva and Nahal Revivim. The former emerges out of the Be'er Sheva Valley and the latter begins beside the Yeroham junction, passing by the Mashabim junction and Revivim and joining Nahal Besor beside Horbat Halutza. The basin and tributaries of Nahal Besor are spread over 3,500 sq km—in effect, most of the Negev region.

In accord with international geographic regulations, each Nahal must have one name only, its terminal boundary being where it empties into a large body of water or into another principal Nahal. The Arabs in the area did not abide by these practices and gave different names to each section of the Nahal. Thus, Nahal Besor acquired different names along its course: the lower section was known as Wadi Ghaza, and the upper parts were called Wadis Shalala, Abu Ghalyon, and so forth; Nahal Revivim was variously called Wadi Dayka, Wadi Asluj, Wadi Tamila, and additional names. This proliferation of names along a single water course caused no end of confusion among visitors

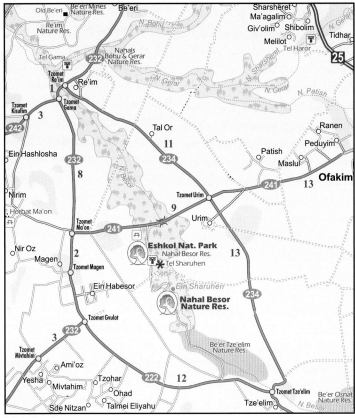

© Carta, Jerusalem

who toured this area in the past.

One of the special features of Nahal Besor is its landscape, in particular its plateaus and hills of loess terrain, through which the Nahal carves its course. Loess is a relatively soft material that is layered through the force of water and wind on the original base of limestone, and the water easily penetrates the porous surface. As a result, for many miles the Nahal forms a deep and wide canyon. For most of its distance it is a dry riverbed, but at various spots there are springs and in several places there is a flow of water even in the summer. In winters with heavy rainfall the Nahal bed becomes a roaring stream sweeping everything in its path. The loess soil rises with the first drops of rain, and the water, even though the amount may be small, skims along the surface to the primary streams, then to the secondary and the tertiary, finally emptying into the Nahal bed where, as mentioned above, it becomes a torrent.

ESHKOL NATIONAL PARK

A large portion of Nahal Besor's banks, from the point where Nahal Beersheva enters it up to the Gaza Strip border, is a nature reserve, and at its center, by route 241 leading from the Gilat to the Ma'on junctions, is the Eshkol National Park, also known as the Nahal Besor Park. This location received the status of a nature reserve not only for its natural landscape and many antiquity remains, but also to give legal sanction for the protection of its banks which are so sensitive to damage.

Eshkol National Park, under the joint jurisdiction of the Jewish National Fund (JNF) and the Nature and National Parks Protection Authority, offers a direct contrast to its surrounding Negev landscape, and it is on this account that it has drawn the attention of local inhabitants as well as visitors from afar. Ein Besor is the spring which makes up the heart of the Reserve, and, as in so many similar cases, furnishes opportunities for the development of recreational facilities. In the area where there is a steady flow of water, there are bridges and a large pool for swimming with a constant water temperature of 20° Centigrade (68° F). This large park, covering 750 acres, accommodates a variety of tastes for vacationers: picnic tables with barbeque grills, many of them tucked away in the immediate landscape granting privacy and solitude. The Park has undergone reforestation

Eshkol National Park.

Besor springs.

and there are broad expanses of grass. The peaks of several summits give a good view of the layout of the area, the Nahal and its environs.

One of the heights is Khirbet Shalala (Shalala Ruins) situated in the northern area of the Park. During World War I, Australian soldiers, who were engaging Turkish forces in the vicinity, discovered a beautiful mosaic floor among the remains of a Byzantine church. The mosaic was removed to Canberra, Australia, and now appears on a wall in that city beside a monument to the unknown soldier.

THE BESOR ROUTE

The Besor Route is a scenic dirt road which follows the west bank of the Nahal for a distance of 18 km from the National Park to the Tze'elim junction. The route offers a view of the Nahal landscape, and animals or fowl such as the Stone Curlew (*Burhinus oedicnemus*) or the Houbara Bustard (*Chlamydotis undulate*). In the bed of the Nahal are two trails, one marked green and the other black; in the southern section of the green trail one can cross the Nahal channel on a long suspension bridge, the only one of its kind in Israel.

Nahal Besor — the badlands.

SITES ALONG THE BESOR ROUTE

1. Badlands Lookout Point

This is a vantage point over-looking the badlands cut by Nahal Besor and towards the farmlands situated on both sides of the Nahal.

2. The Old Railway Bridge

The bridge and parts of a railway track are the sole remains of a British construction effort during WWI. The British army under General Allenby, who came from Egypt to Palestine via the Sinai Desert, sought to gain control over Gaza city by staging an assault from this area. The bridge and track were on a line from Beersheba to Rafi'ah, on the Mediterranean coast.

3. Tel Sharuhen

This is one of many antiquity sites in the area. The tel rises to a height of 50 m above the bed of the Nahal. Excavations uncovered remains of an ancient settlement mentioned both in Egyptian writings as an important base in the Negev, and in the list of cities of Simeon in the Book of Joshua. In addition, important finds from the period of Philistine settlement were found.

Nahal Besor.

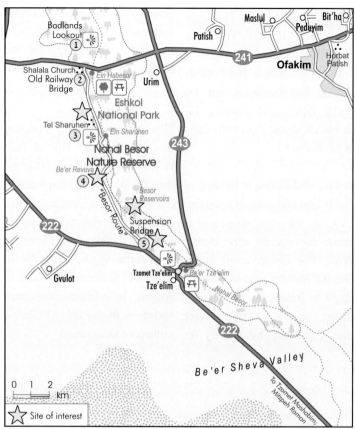

Badlands
Lookout
①

Maslul   Bit'hq
Peduyim
Patish
Ofakim   Horbat
241   Patish

Shalala Church
Old Railway ②   Ein Habesor
Bridge   Urim

Eshkol
National Park
Tel Sharuhen
③   Ein Sharuhen   243

Nahal Besor
Nature Reserve

Be'er Revuva
④

Besor
Reservoirs

222   "Besor Route"   Suspension
Bridge
⑤

Gvulot   Tzomet Tze'elim   Be'er Tze'elim
Tze'elim   Nahal Besor

222

Be'er Sheva Valley

To Tzomet Mashabim;
Mitspeh Ramon

0 1 2
km

⭐ Site of interest

© Carta, Jerusalem

In the opening stages of the Israeli War of Independence, this site served as a base for the Egyptian military incursion. The IDF overcame the Egyptian position in Operation Assaf. Close to the tel, amongst the vegetation of the Nahal, is Sharuhan spring which was the main source of water for local residents.

There is a lookout tower on the summit of the tel giving a view of the surroundings.

4. Be'er Revuva (Well)

At the beginning of the 20th century, upon the initiative of the Turks, a village was established for the Tarabin Bedouin tribe. In order to encourage a sedentary life for the Bedouin, 12 wells were dug in the area and several Tamarisk trees were planted. In the center of the village, called Ru'eiba, was a well which was later restored during the period of the British Mandate. The first pioneers of Kibbutz Gvulot, who arrived in 1943, purchased their drinking water from this well.

5. The Suspension Bridge

The bridge, 80 m long, is suspended over a large, deep pool of water above the Nahal channel. The Tze'elim tower may be reached via the bridge. From the lookout tower, there is a view of the Nahal Besor ravine and its rocky terrain.

OUTSIDE THE NATURE RESERVE

Dangur/Nirim

This is a memorial site to the combatants of Kibbutz Nirim who, few in number, withstood the assaults of the large attacking forces from Egypt at the beginning of the War of Independence. The settlement location at that time was at Dangur. Dangur was totally destroyed, and later the kibbutz resettled at this new location.

Horbat Ma'on (Ruin)

Ma'on (Menois) was established in the Roman-Byzantine period. The remains of a synagogue from the 6th or 7th century with fine mosaic floors depicting Jewish symbols and Aramaic inscriptions was found here. The site, called Khirbet el Ma'in in Arabic, is located close to route 242 beside Kibbutz Nirim and is open to the public.

Horbat Patish (Ruin)

This is the ruin of the Byzantine village, Futis, which appears on the 6th century Madaba map. It is apparently also the site of Patish, mentioned in the list of towns conquered by the Egyptian king Shishak. There are remains of structures, cisterns and remains of an Ottoman fortress (Qal'at el-Futis). Below the fortress ruins, which dominate the surrounding area, is a large cave.

The ruins of Patish (left) and the name as it appears on the Madaba map (below).

TEL BEERSHEBA NATIONAL PARK

Location: c. 2 km E of Be'er Sheva, off Route 60.
Best season: year-round
Length of visit: 1 to 2 hours
Tel.: 08-6467286
Entrance fee

...and they went out to the south of Judah, even to Beer-sheba. (2 Sam 24:7)

 Jewish site Christian site Antiquities Lookout point

Accessibility Rating

 WC   Telephone

Tel Beersheba National Park rises above the confluence of Nahal Hebron with Nahal Be'er Sheva. To the east is the Bedouin village of Tel Sheva, to the north the Jewish town of Omer, and to the northwest, on a hill overlooking the city of Be'er Sheva, is the monument to the Negev Brigade. The identification of the tel with biblical Beersheba was generally accepted, but the excavations which confirmed this were only conducted in the 1970s.

HISTORY

Settlement began here during the Chalcolithic period (c. 4000 BCE). Finds from this period include a few potsherds, as well as several of the cisterns.

According to the biblical account, Abraham, in his wanderings through the Negeb, arrived here: "And Abraham planted a grove in Beer-sheba, and called there on the name of the Lord, the everlasting God" (Genesis 21:33). During the period of the Judges, a fortified city was erected here which lasted until the destruction of the First Temple, and this is the city which was exposed in the excavations.

From the Hellenisic period are remains of a large fortress and a nearby temple. In the Herodian period, a large palace was built on the tel; its deep foundations destroyed a good part of the earlier Israelite city. In the Roman period, Beersheba was at the

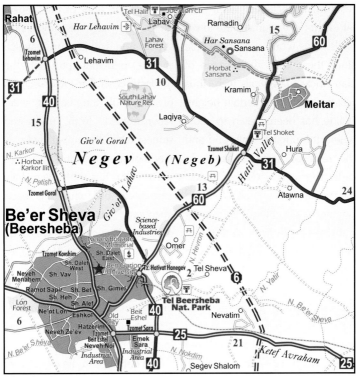

© Carta, Jerusalem

center of *Limes Palaestina* and a Roman fortress was built on top of the earlier Hellenistic structure. In 636 CE, at the time of the Arab conquest, the Roman fortress was still standing. Beersheba was popu-lated during the Byzantine period and a number of churches were built then and later more were added with the arrival of the Crusaders, but all were destroyed in the following centuries.

Only at the beginning of the 20th century was settlement renewed, when Be'er Sheva became the administrative center for the Negev. In 1917, it was captured by the British. On 17 May 1948, the city was taken by Egyptian forces but was then captured by the Negev Brigade of the Palmah and the Eighth Armored Brigade of the IDF on 21 October of the same year.

TOUR OF THE RESTORED ISRAELITE CITY

Of the 15 strata partly exposed at Tel Be'er Sheva, archaeologists chose to restore the stratum belonging to the late Israelite period (8th century BCE). Remains from this period were considered the most important and the restoration included what was left of the city, namely the lower walls. This work was not simple since these walls were made of clay bricks. The walls were thus restored only to a certain height. A line has been drawn to show where the original walls end and the restored sections begin. In order to prevent collapse, a new layer of bricks was built above the original walls, identical in color but different in form so that one can easily distinguish the restored walls from the original.

The findings indicate that the first settlement on the tel was from the Chalcolithic period in the 4th millennium BCE, but these structures were destroyed. Settlement was renewed in the 12th century BCE, that is, in the Iron Age, which coincides with the Israelite period. Three or four centuries later, a well-planned administrative city was built here which apparently had jurisdiction over a wide area of the Negev. It is this city—its dwellings, streets and fortifications—which is the principal part of the reconstruction. The lower sections of most of the houses were reconstructed from undressed stones, while the upper half was made of sundried mudbrick.

The city has not been fully excavated, but what has been uncovered allows for a full overview. The city plan was oval, encircled by a casemate wall, of which parts have remained *in situ*. The wall was built on top of a glacis in order to encumber anyone trying to force their way into the city.

The entrance to the city is from the southeast through a simple **anterior city gate** (1) which has a **deep well** (9) alongside it, outside the city gate. The well served the caravan animals which were not allowed entrance to the city. Beyond this watering place

Tel Beersheba.

TEL BEERSHEBA

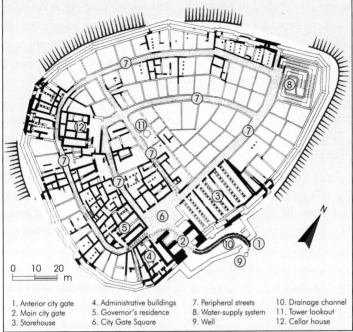

0 10 20 m

1. Anterior city gate
2. Main city gate
3. Storehouse
4. Administrative buildings
5. Governor's residence
6. City Gate Square
7. Peripheral streets
8. Water-supply system
9. Well
10. Drainage channel
11. Tower lookout
12. Cellar house

© Carta, Jerusalem

is the **main city gate** (2) built in the usual fashion: a massive structure with two chambers on either side of the gateway. Upon entering, one arrives at the **City Gate Square** (6), from which the streets of the city fan out.

According to the city plan, peripheral streets running parallel to the wall were laid, thus forming three blocks of structures crossed by two of the streets. Another street cut through the center of the town. The **Governor's residence** (5) was probably situated just off the city square and a short distance away was the **cellar house** (12) with deep foundations. It is likely that there

was a shrine here which was dismantled during the religious reform of King Hezekiah, who sought to center the religious cult in Jerusalem. Thus, it is also probable that the horned altar stood here, of which dismantled remains were found. The large altar, which is similar to those discovered at Tel Arad, has been partly restored and stands at the entrance to the site.

The **large storehouse** (3), north of the city gate, consists of 3 halls, each one divided lengthwise into three rooms. In the city's northern corner is an impressive **water-supply system** (8) that brought water into the city from outside its walls assuring a sufficient water supply in case of siege. It is similar to the water systems found at Hazor and Megiddo: a square shaft with a set of staircases descending to a deep cistern which accesses ground water.

The Parks Authority has erected a **tower** (11) at the center of the site, from which the entire antiquity complex can be viewed, as well as the surrounding area: the modern city of Be'er Sheva, the Negev Brigade memorial, Tel Sheva, the town of Omer, and the countryside.

OUTSIDE THE NATIONAL PARK AREA

SITES IN MODERN BE'ER SHEVA

The Negev Museum

This museum houses its displays in what was once an old Turkish mosque. There is an exhibition of the history of Be'er Sheva from the Chalcolithic period to the present day. Exhibits include findings from the dig at Tel Be'er Sheva and other excavations in the area. There is also a collection of photographs of Be'er Sheva from the Ottoman period.

The Bedouin Shuk (market)

In the past, the *shuk* was held on the northern bank of Nahal Be'er Sheva, but in 1996 it was transferred to roofed structures close by. The *shuk* is held every Thursday from 8 am to 2 pm.

Abraham's Well

This is a Byzantine structure which, according to tradition, was dug by the patriarch Abraham. The well is fed by groundwater originating from a riverbed which filters through the terrain and accumulates at a relatively shallow depth. The well has been restored and the location fenced. There is an entrance fee.

The Negev Brigade Memorial.

Beersheba, as depicted in a 19th century engraving.

The Negev Brigade Memorial

This monument, which covers 100 sq m, was designed by the sculptor Danny Caravan. It is dedicated to the memory of soldiers of the Negev Brigade and members of settlements in the vicinity, who defended the Negev when it was under siege in the War of Independence. The monument consists of 18 elements, each of which has a symbolic meaning: a water tower pock-marked by shell-fire; a structure in the form of a military post; a bunker; a water pipeline which was the life-line for settlements in this area; and other items.

The poets Haim Guri and Nathan Shaham composed verses dedicated to the monument and they are engraved on the sides of the structures.

The Old Railway Station

The old railway station is situated in the northwest corner of the city. It was built by the Ottoman Turks copying the style of German architecture of the time. The building is now used by the Society for the Preservation of Nature in Israel (SPNI) as a center for field studies.

The Turkish Bridge

This bridge was built in 1910 to help the Turkish army on its way to Egypt. The bridge was 190 m in length, and until the 1970s was the longest bridge in the country. It was built by Jewish construction workers from Jaffa and today is considered as a sort of monument to the Jewish laborer.

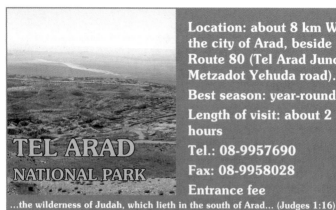

Location: about 8 km W of the city of Arad, beside Route 80 (Tel Arad Junct.–Metzadot Yehuda road).

Best season: year-round

Length of visit: about 2 hours

Tel.: 08-9957690

Fax: 08-9958028

Entrance fee

...the wilderness of Judah, which lieth in the south of Arad... (Judges 1:16)

Jewish site

Antiquities

Lookout point

WC

Snack bar

Accessibility Rating

The Tel Arad National Park has two constituent parts: the Canaanite city in the south (3150–2200 BCE); and the various strata of fortifications on the upper tel in the north, the main one of which is the Israelite stronghold. The Israel National Trail by-passes the tel along its southern base.

The findings at Tel Arad are among the most important in the Negev region, verifying information known from written sources and adding new information.

HISTORY

Arad is mentioned several times in the Bible. Its earliest mention is found in the Exodus tradition where the Israelites failed to conquer the city upon their entrance into Canaan from Egypt. Only later, did this become an Israelite city.

There has been some difficulty in identifying the lower ruins on the tel with the ancient Canaanite Arad because the ancient settlement dates from the Early Bronze Age to the 3rd millennium BCE, long before the Exodus from Egypt. Because the inscription from the time of the Egyptian king Shishak (10th century BCE) mentions two cities named Arad, it is assumed that the Canaanite Arad at the time of the Exodus was located at Tel Malhata, and the greater Israelite Arad was located in the upper section of what is now called Tel Arad.

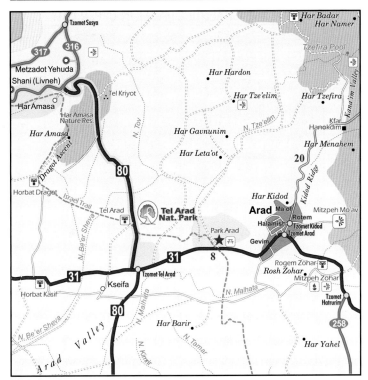

© Carta, Jerusalem

EXCAVATIONS OF THE CANAANITE (LOWER) CITY

Excavations at the lower tel began in 1962 under the supervision of Ruth Amiran, and the dig at the fortress was continued by Yohanan Aharoni.

The Canaanite city was surrounded by a thick wall, a great part of which still remains. It was built of two layers of large stones, with a fill of small stones. On the outer edge are semicircular towers. Among the excavated items of note: the dwelling area in the southern part of this site, the palace and shrines in the central part, and the well. The well is round and deep and supplied the water for the city in an area which is parched and has little rainfall. It was renovated and restored in later periods.

THE ISRAELITE CITADELS (UPPER CITY)

The principal structure on the "citadel mound" dates from the Israelite period. It is located in the northern section of the National Park and was built about 1,500 years after the Canaanite city was destroyed. Archaeologists have

PLAN OF THE ISRAELITE CITADEL IN UPPER CITY

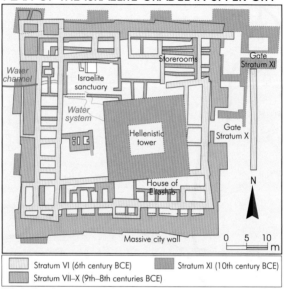

Storerooms
Gate Stratum XI
Water channel
Israelite sanctuary
Water system
Hellenistic tower
Gate Stratum X
House of Eliashib
N
Massive city wall
0 5 10 m

Stratum VI (6th century BCE)
Stratum VII–X (9th–8th centuries BCE)
Stratum XI (10th century BCE)

© Carta, Jerusalem

exposed 12 strata of construction; the earliest stratum is Canaanite. Six additional strata may be attributed to the Israelite period, beginning in the 12th century BCE and continuing until the days of Jehoiakim and Zedekiah in the 6th century BCE. The principal feature is a large fortress that was renovated several times over the generations, and stood until the Early Arab period.

The first Israelite citadel was destroyed in the 10th century BCE during the campaign of Shishak, pharaoh of Egypt. He recorded the conquest of two towns named Arad on a memorial tablet at Karnak. A portion of the citadel remained in the northeast corner of the tel. The impressive structure of the later Israelite citadel was built over it.

This fortress, square in shape, was surrounded by a 4-m-thick wall, with small insets at intervals of 9 to 10 m. Its single gate was in the east. This wall was used in later strata up to the Hellenistic period when a tower was erected in a smaller area in the center of the fortress. All details concerning the structure and information deduced from the findings point to the construction of a royal citadel designed to function as a border stronghold against any incursions from the Negev. There is no evidence that this was gradually built by waves of settlement. The two most important findings from the citadel are the Israelite sanctuary and the hoard of ostraca found in the residence of the governor, Elyashib, son of Eshiahu.

THE ISRAELITE SANCTUARY

The Israelite sanctuary indicates that Yahwistic worship took place here from the earliest period of Israelite settlement until destroyed in the religious reforms initiated by King Josiah. Two incense altars found here are now at the Israel Museum in Jerusalem and replicas have been placed in the holy of holies of the Tel Arad shrine. These findings provide evidence of the dispersion of the religious cult, with similar shrines found in the border cities of the Kingdom of Judah, as well as in Dan and Bethel in the Kingdom of Israel.

THE OSTRACA

The 107 Hebrew ostraca found at this site have special importance because of their inscriptions, most written in ink. Some, dated to about 600 BCE, were letters written to the commander of the citadel, Elyashib son of Eshiahu, whose seal was also found bearing his name. Among the inscriptions are instructions for the distribution of bread, oil and water for the mercenary troops, and an explicit reference to the "House of YHWH."

Among the many other findings are potshards, and the fragment of a bowl with the name "Arad" engraved three times. The other potshards found here may be divided into six categories: storage vessels; cooking pots; serving, eating and drinking utensils; small storage vessels; lamps; and decorated vessels.

THE CITY'S ECONOMY

The findings from the excavations show that the basis for

Tel Arad — the Canaanite well.

the city's economy was quite varied—agriculture, handicrafts, and commerce with Egypt, southern Sinai, and cities and towns in Canaan. This diversification points to specialized professions, social stratification, and the central role Arad played in southern Canaan. Arad was surrounded by small settlements within a short distance of it and there was economic interdependence between the city and these nearby settlements.

OUTSIDE THE NATIONAL PARK

MODERN ARAD—SITES TO VISIT

The town of Arad was founded in 1962 as an urban center for industrial development of the region between the Be'er Sheva Valley and the Hebron Hills. Its picturesque desert landscape is surrounded by cliffs and canyons. Because of its dry and comfortable climate, it has become a place for recuperation by sufferers from asthma and different allergies.

Tourist Center

The Center has its office in the town's commercial center. Information is available about the town of Arad, and many other tourist attractions in the region. From Arad, it is easy to reach Masada from the west and to its audio-visual show that presents the "Masada experience."

Arad Festival

Arad is host to the annual Hebrew Song Festival. The Festival lasts 3–4 days and draws many performers and a large audience. The repertoire ranges from rock to Israeli popular songs and has become a calendar event in the Israeli light music scene.

Tel Arad — the holy of holies in the Israelite sanctuary,

The Arad Visitors' Center

The Center is maintained by the Nature and National Parks Protection Authority. It provides:

- A sound-and-light show screened over a large model of the Judean Desert.
- Simulation of a flash flood in the Judean Desert.
- Exhibition of utensils used 3,000 to 5,000 years ago.
- Models of a Canaanite city and an Israelite fortress, in which desert life of man in ancient times is reconstructed.
- A multi-screen presentation of modern Arad.
- Information on hikes, events, and places of interest in the Judean Desert.

The Center sells maps, hiking trail leaflets, and literature of interest to the hiker and lover of nature.

Deep purple iris.

destroyed in the revolt against the Romans and restored in the 7th century CE. In 1981, a large solar pool whose waters are heated by the sun was built here. This is the first experimental solar pool in the country intended for the production of electricity.

Sites Along the Dead Sea Shore

Ein Bokek

This is an oasis fed by springs of Nahal Bokek. In ancient times, it was a center for the cultivation of fragrant plants. Today, it is a vacation resort, medicinal spa and regulated bathing beach.

Metzad Bokek

Here one finds the remains of a Hasmonean stronghold that was built to guard the oasis. It was

Zohar Hot Springs

See page 383.

Metzad Zohar

This is the remains of a way-station fort from the Roman-Byzantine period situated in Nahal Zohar. It is built on a stone cliff and secured the ancient route that led from Beersheba to the Dead Sea and beyond to the Moab.

Location: on Route 25 (Beersheba–Dimona road), about 8 km E of Dimona.

Best season: spring, fall, winter

Length of visit: about 2 hours

Tel.: 08-6556478

Fax.: 08-6556478

Entrance fee

MAMSHIT (KURNUB) NATIONAL PARK

...the cities that are laid waste shall be desolate... (Ezekiel 29:12)

Christian site · Antiquities · Lookout point

WC · Telephone · Picnic site

Accessibility Rating

♿ 1   🚶 2

P ✔   👫 ✗

The history of human life in the Negev is marked by waves of settlement interspersed with long periods of abandonment and neglect. The factors contributing to this situation may be attributed to climate change, but also undoubtedly to changes that occurred in the lives of people and regimes in the area north of the Negev. To the extent that settlement in the north was well-established and organized, portions of the population could be sent southward to build defenses against the desert and its inhabitants. Whenever political rule in the north weakened, the Negev emptied of its permanent population.

For hundreds of years during the Roman-Byzantine period a complex of settlements formed in the Negev, beginning in the 2nd century BCE with the penetration of the Nabateans, reaching a peak in the Byzantine period, and coming to an end in the 7th century CE. This period saw a flourishing of the incense and spice trade via trade routes from the Arabian Peninsula through the Negev to the Mediterranean coast. For commercial reasons and the need to protect the southern border, six cities were built in the Negev. With the development of a sophisticated water system, agriculture began to thrive in the immediate vicinity of this urban complex. The Nabateans were the first architects of this

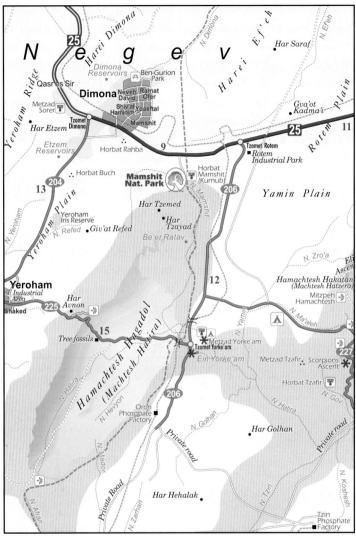

© Carta, Jerusalem

revitalization of life in the Negev. Their kingdom was conquered by the Romans in 106 BCE, but the residents remained and over the years became Latin and Greek-speakers, later converted to Christianity, and then integrated into the Byzantine Empire.

Towns arose along the Incense (Perfume) Route that led west, via Petra to Gaza and the rest of the coastal cities. Mamshit, one of six such cities that are included among UNESCO's distinguished list of World Heritage Sites, stood on the route leading southeast to Be'er Sheva and to Gaza. The name "Mamshit" is speculative:

it appears in the 6th-century CE Madaba map as "Mampsis," and the Arabs nicknamed it "Kurnub." The ruins suggest three strata of occupation. The first is Nabatean dating from the first century CE, and it is covered by a second city, dating from the later Nabatean period, and was finally occupied in the Byzantine period, when it reached its acme. The city was apparently destroyed following a fire prior to the Arab conquest in the 7th century CE. Generally, archaeological evidence reveals that the stones from destroyed cities are taken to build or refurbish a nearby city. In this case, however, the distance to such cities was too great for such undertakings, and thus the ruins of Mamshit remained almost undamaged by man, and its walls, rising to a significant height, are still standing on their original foundations.

Mamshit is surrounded by a city wall, outside of which are two buildings worthy of note: a caravanserai (1), northwest of the city gate, served passersby and caravans that did not enter the city. A large number of coins was found inside this structure.

MAMSHIT (KURNUB) — GENERAL PLAN

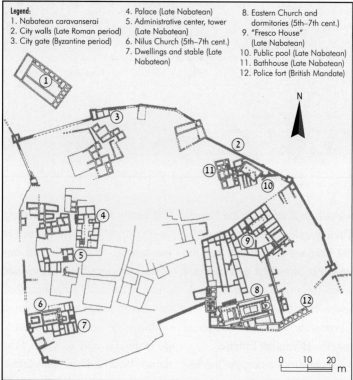

Legend:
1. Nabatean caravanserai
2. City walls (Late Roman period)
3. City gate (Byzantine period)
4. Palace (Late Nabatean)
5. Administrative center, tower (Late Nabatean)
6. Nilus Church (5th–7th cent.)
7. Dwellings and stable (Late Nabatean)
8. Eastern Church and dormitories (5th–7th cent.)
9. "Fresco House" (Late Nabatean)
10. Public pool (Late Nabatean)
11. Bathhouse (Late Nabatean)
12. Police fort (British Mandate)

N

0   10   20
m

© Carta, Jerusalem

A second structure is the dam built in Nahal Mamshit to the west of the city. This is one of three dams and the entire system collected 10,000 cu m of water which was an adequate supply for years of drought. During the British Mandate, when Mamshit served as a station for the Camel Constabulary, a new dam was constructed that was similar to the old one. It has been conjectured that the city was one of the places for the breeding of race horses, and that the large reservoir and cisterns here served these animals.

Within the city, parts of the walls of many Nabatean buildings remain standing, including halls, courtyards and terraces. The palace (4), in the western part of the city, was the most splendid building at this site. The remnants indicate that it was a three-storey building. Beside the palace stood a tower (5), whose base was made of very large stones. Another elaborate building—the "fresco house" (9), a large private house—was found in the eastern part of the city. It had many ornate decorations, and a large hoard of Roman coins (over 10,000!) was found under the floor. Such a hoard points to the economic prosperity of the Nabatean city, and, perhaps, to a remunerative source, horse breeding, which was a highly

Byzantine church at Mamshit.

profitable economic branch.

Two churches, the Western (6) and the Eastern (8) Church, were built in the Byzantine period. Parts of their walls, apses, and mosaic floors remain. In the Western Church, one of the mosaics mentions a certain Nilus, the builder of this church. A beautiful sundial was found in the bell-tower beside the Eastern Church. The fortress stood at the edge of the city.

A tour of the Mamshit ruins provides a feeling for the way of urban life in the heart of a semi-arid region far from other human settlements.

At the site there is a restaurant built in the Nabatean style.

OUTSIDE THE NATIONAL PARK

Metzad Yorke'am and the Yorke'am Spring

The Yorke'am fort (=*metzad*) was apparently built in the Byzantine period. This is one of dozens of strongholds scattered throughout the Negev. They were erected close to ancient trade routes or at vital water sites.

The stronghold is square, measuring about 20 × 20 m in size. The surviving walls are about a meter high. Descending half a kilometer from the stronghold to the wide bed of Nahal Hatira, one arrives at a point where the Nahal bed suddenly deepens and

Arch remaining in its entirety from the main building at Mamshit.

Ancient dam and dam from the British Mandatory period in Nahal Mamshit.

Savigny's agama (sand lizard).

its sides become white, sheer-faced cliffs that enclose ridges and the Yorke'am spring. The descent to the spring is from the northern flank of the Nahal via a series of ancient steps hewn out of the rock. The stairs are as old as the fortress, that is, about 1,500 years. The Yorke'am spring collects water throughout the year, and in the seasonal periods when there are flash floods, pools large enough for swimming are formed.

The Scorpions' Ascent (Ma'aleh Akrabim)

This is an ascent in the Negev highlands, about 20 km southeast of Dimona. The road was paved in the middle of the 1920s by the British Mandate authorities, and at the time was the only road that linked Be'er Sheva to Eilat. In 1950, it was widened and improved by a unit of the Engineer Corps. There is a monument to this feat at the Ascent. In 1953, Arab infiltrators attacked an Israeli bus on its way from Eilat to Be'er Sheva at this point. Almost all the passengers were killed. There is a memorial square to the victims on a hill overlooking the road.

The memorial hill offers a magnificent view of the lower section of Nahal Tzin.

*Euphrates poplar (*Populus euphratica*).*

Location: near Route 40, between Sde Boker and Mitzpeh Ramon.

Best season: year-round

Length of visit: 2 hours to a day

Avdat: Tel. 08-6586391
**   Fax: 08-6550954**
Ein Avdat: Tel. 08-6555689

Entrance fee (combined ticket may be purchased for both parks)

He turneth the wilderness into a standing water... (Ps 107:35)

Avdat National Park

Christian site | Antiquities | Lookout point | Picnic site

WC | Snack bar | Telephone | Souvenir shop

Accessibility Rating

  2   3

P ✔ | ♿ ✗ | 🍴 ✔

Ein Avdat National Park

Hiking trail | Outdoor recreation | Lookout point

WC

Accessibility Rating

  1   1

P ✔ | ♿ ✔ | 🍴 ✗ | 🏊 ✗

AVDAT NATIONAL PARK

The Nabatean–Roman–Byzantine city of Avdat (ancient Oboda) may not have been the largest of the ancient Negev cities, but it was apparently the most important one because it bore the name of the deified Nabatean king, Obodas III. It is also well-known to Israelis who visit the Negev since the entrance branches off from the Sde Boker–Eilat highway, just southwest of the former. Among the cities of the Negev it stands out for its unique urban character. The city was built on a mountain spur, above a plain, as a main station on a junction of the caravan routes and the Incense (Perfume) Route that ran from Petra, cut through the Ramon Crater, ascended Ma'aleh Mahmel and continued to Avdat, Halutza and Gaza. On the plateau between Ma'aleh Mahmel and Avdat, a paved Roman road is still clearly visible.

ARCHAEOLOGY

The Acropolis

Two structures among the ruins of Avdat are prominent: the acropolis, set upon the crest of the spur, and the lower city—a

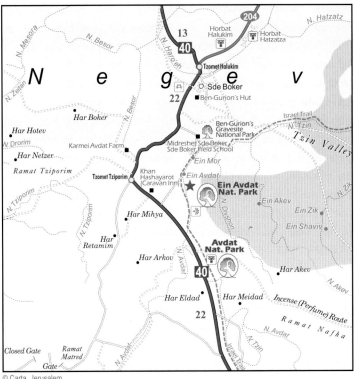

© Carta, Jerusalem

city of caves in the sides of the spur. Parts of the site were excavated under the direction of Avraham Negev and restoration work was done by the National Parks Authority. The acropolis is encircled by a wall of which complete sections still stand, having survived earthquakes and the destructive hand of man. It is a large rectangular complex whose wall was first constructed in the Nabatean period and built upon in the subsequent periods. The complex includes the main public buildings and, in the west, a Nabatean temple whose pillars can be seen from the highway. Two churches are also in the compound, one in the north and the other in the south; there are extensive remains from both: pillars, floors, inscriptions, and the wall of an apse. The North Church is a basilica and the earlier of the two. There is a cistern in the middle of its floor and a baptismal basin beside it. Among the findings in the South Church are important inscriptions that note persons and dates. A large plaza separates the two churches and beyond it is a Byzantine fortress. Important remains were excavated in different parts of the city.

The structure of the acropolis indicates that the city did not grow in an organic fashion but rather was planned by the ruling authority. Below the acropolis, on the western and the northern edge of the spur, sprawls the city of caves, dwelling places for a majority of the city's residents. The entire city was surrounded by a wall. Its fortifications, however, did not withstand assault, and it was captured by the Arabs when they conquered the country in the 7th century CE. After the conquest, trade routes shifted, and there was no longer a justification for settlement in this area.

The City's Water System

Archaeologists and students of hydraulic systems regard the Nabatean water system with special interest. Nahal Tzin and Nahal Avdat, close to the city, are intermittent streams that carry a heavy volume of floodwater in the rainy seasons. Large cisterns were hewn into the banks of the Nahals and they held water for a number of months. City residents could draw water from the springs that flow through the stretch of canyon in Nahal Tzin about 3 km north of Avdat. Water flows all year long at Ein Ma'arif and Ein Avdat; although the descent to them is difficult, it is possible to access the water that gathers in pools at the lower end of the canyon with ropes tied to buckets. Rope marks in the rock provide evidence that this was the method for obtaining water from this source.

Sources of Livelihood

The city was a station on the caravan route and this provided

Agamid lizard (Agama pallida).

Holly Milk-vetch (Astragalus sanctus).

AVDAT NATIONAL PARK

© Carta, Jerusalem

one of the principal sources of income for Avdat. Below the city, beside route 40, there was a caravanserai that accommodated travelers who did not enter the city. The bathhouse, which was an integral part of the inn, is almost completely intact. Beside it is a cistern more than 60 m deep containing water at the bottom. Another source of income which characterized the Nabatean-Byzantine cities was agriculture. The desert climate of this period seems to have been similar to that of the present day and the amount of rainfall was also the same, yet this did not seem to impair a significant and mixed production which included both field crops and orchards. These agricultural achievements must be attributed to the sophisticated system of water collection and distribution developed by this civilization. Low-level dams were built across the width of all the valleys in the vicinity, and these dams blocked the winter flash floods, collected the rainwater which streamed from the slopes and cliffs, and gathered the alluvial topsoil in furrows along the length of the Nahal. Although these furrows made up but a small part of the general area, they received all the water that descended to the ground surface.

The combination of trade, horse-breeding, agriculture, and military service provided the sustenance that drove the local economy for many generations.

NAHAL TZIN

Nahal Tzin is one of the largest river valleys in the Negev. It begins on the north bank of the Ramon Crater (Machtesh Ramon) and ends at the Dead Sea. It is several dozen kilometers long and its appearance changes several times along its course. Each landscape is completely different. It is thus not surprising that the Arabs have a different name for each section of the Nahal—Wadi Nafakh, Ein Mureifiq, Wadi Fuqara, whereas the Israelis adhere to international convention and apply a single name for the entire watercourse. In its upper section, it is one of the Nahals that descend from the rim of the great crater—not into it but from its outer surface. After 20 km, in which it does not differ in any respect from other Nahals that pass through the terrain of the central Negev, it suddenly becomes an impressive canyon. It is this section that has been designated Ein Avdat National Park. From here it continues a gentle sloping descent to the Tzin Desert, collecting on its way the tributaries that come from the Tzin cliffs, passes by the foot of Ma'aleh Akrabim and Mt. Hehalak, and then expands considerably creating a riverbed 3 km wide before emptying into the salt ponds of Sodom. The springs in the Ein Avdat canyon, the tributaries containing Ein Akev and Ein Zik, and the springs at the foot of the Scorpions Ascent are the only permanent water sources for Nahal Tzin. However, several days of winter rain send torrents through the Nahal carrying everything in its

Avdat — view from the acropolis.

Avdat — general view.

path. When the potash plant was first established at the southern end of the Dead Sea, a large part was destroyed by a flash flood emerging from the Nahal. In the past, desert travelers knew where to find puddles of water left by these sudden floods, and this quenched their thirst during their long treks through the arid lands.

EIN AVDAT NATIONAL PARK

Ein Avdat National Park is a distinctive section in the long course of Nahal Tzin. After the Nahal passes the Avdat plateau in a rather level riverbed in a northeasterly direction, it turns north and then, without any warning, it suddenly drops as

Avdat — the southern city wall.

a waterfall several dozen meters into a narrow, deep crevice composed of white limestone. The Nahal continues for 2½ km in this canyon formation and opposite Midreshet Sde Boker and the gravesite of Israel's first Prime Minister, David Ben-Gurion, it turns east, opening up as a wide expanse. The entire cliff section of Nahal Tzin is a nature reserve and the canyon sector and its fringes are a national park.

The canyon has two springs: Ein Ma'arif and Ein Avdat. They create a water landscape of flowing streams, ice-cold pools, and small waterfalls, generating a complete contrast to the desert scenery surrounding the canyon. The high walls are composed of alternate layers of limestone and flint rock which form different shapes of natural sculpture.

These springs were known to the earliest human inhabitants of the area and there is evidence of a Stone Age mill at the top of the large falls. There are also scattered remains from a site that manufactured flint tools. At one point at the head of the falls, the cliff stands prominently above the spring, so that it was possible to haul up water in a bucket tied to a rope. The grooves in the rock at the edge of the cliff were caused by the action of pulling and releasing the rope over time. It is quite likely that the inhabitants of Avdat drew much of their water in this manner from this site. Caves in the walls of the canyon were in the past used as dwelling places by monks.

THE SILK ROUTE

One of the important routes of ancient times passed through

Nahal Tzin and entrance to the canyon of Ein Avdat.

the broad desert section of Nahal Tzin—Darb es Sultan—a branch of the Incense (Perfume) Route. This route came from Edom (present-day Jordan), traversed the Arava valley in the vicinity of Ein Yahav, passed through the Tzin Desert, ascended Ma'aleh Tzin where Midreshet Sde Boker stands today, and proceeded past Shivta to the Mediterranean Sea coast. It is quite likely that the springs, which are not far from the Route, were used by its travelers.

Canyon of Ein Avdat.

THE IBEX AT EIN AVDAT

These springs were not only known to man, but were also, and continue to be, a watering hole for animals in the Nahal area, especially the horned ibex. Ibex must drink at least once every two days, and the existence of springs or backed-up pools are a requisite for their existence in the desert. The ibex tread on the steep cliffs with the ease of humans who walk along a level sidewalk, and a prevalent sight are the males, with their large horns, and females and their young leaping on the walls of the canyon on their way to or from the water source.

FLORA

The canyon vegetation is similar to that found at a desert oasis. Tamarisks and Euphrates Poplar (*Populus euphrastica*) grow in the vicinity of the flowing water, while the Atlantic Pistachio (*Pistacia atlantica*) may be found at the northern entrance to the canyon—perhaps the northernmost habitat for this tree species, which is native to the Negev mountains. A notably rare plant that grows here is the Spear-leaved Dogbane (*Trachomitum venetum*) of the *Asclepiadaceae* (milkweed) family. This is one of the few places in the country where this plant is found. Visitors to the desert, who arrive only at the edge of the waterfall, whether by foot, bicycle or motor vehicle, appreciate this place.

OUTSIDE THE NATIONAL PARK

Sde Boker and Ben-Gurion's Desert Hut

Kibbutz Sde Boker was founded in 1952 by a group of officers and soldiers who had been

Male ibex.

Atlantic Pistachio.

demobilized by the IDF. Israel's first Prime Minister David Ben-Gurion decided to settle here after he resigned from the Government in 1953 (and officially announced his retirement from politics). After he and his wife, Paula, passed away, it was decided to preserve their living quarters exactly as they left it. Adjacent to Ben-Gurion's house, another wooden home, formerly the guards' quarters, now houses an exhibition highlighting Ben-Gurion's diverse, unique feelings for the Negev.

The Ben-Gurion Heritage Institute and Research Center at Sde Boker

This institute houses the archives connected to David Ben-Gurion

Dunn's Lark.

and his political life. It contains thousands of documents, diaries that he wrote, and the like. It was established in 1982. There is an audio-visual presentation of the life of Ben-Gurion.

The Ben-Gurion Gravesite

The tombstones of Ben-Gurion and his wife are located at the edge of the cliff overlooking Nahal Tzin and the National Park. The gravesite has a well-groomed garden. A lookout tower offers a bird's-eye view of Nahal Tzin and the "Little Crater" (Machtesh Hakatan).

The Restored Agricultural Farm

This is an attempt by Professor Even Ari to reconstruct an ancient agricultural farm. A tour of the farm shows how fruit trees were cultivated and how they received an adequate supply of water even if their only source was rainfall.

Khan Hashayarot (Caravan Inn)

A guest house and center for desert activities situated above Ein Avdat, on route 40, about 7 km south of Sde Boker, the caravanserai hosts a wide range of activities that are desert-oriented: a camel trek, rides in a Safari vehicle, bicycle trips, walking hikes, jeep tours on special routes, and rappelling (rope-climbing). Seasonal events, festivals and special shows are held here throughout the year. In the best traditions of the Bedouin, guests are received in spacious tents and treated to various eating fare. There is a coffeehouse. An area shaded by

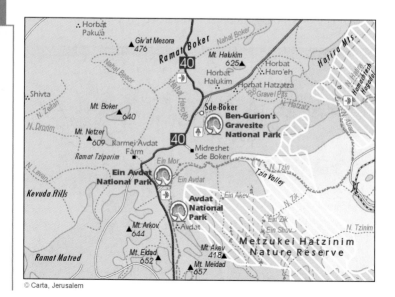

© Carta, Jerusalem

palm trees has been set aside for overnight camping.

Yeroham Lake Park

This park, under the auspices of the JNF and the National Parks Authority, is located west of the town of Yeroham.

The park encloses 4,000 acres. The lake was created by a dam built in Nahal Revivim to collect water from flash floods. Over the years, water accumulated on the eastern side of the dam and became a small lake. A number of hiking paths circle the lake. The lake exists year-round and at its maximum volume it covers about 50 acres. This happens following flash floods in the winter months and the lake maintains itself for several months after such an occurrence. A thick, dense grove of Pistachio trees grows around the lake. Olive, eucalyptus, Atlantic pistachio, pine, and date trees were planted and are nicely distributed over the surrounding slopes.

Within the park there is a reserve of Large Sternbergia (*Sternbergia clusiana*), a Byzantine fortress, and a settlement site from the Middle Canaanite period.

Karmei Avdat Farm

This is one of several Negev Desert farms open to visitors. It has vineyards and a winery. There is also a gallery exhibiting blacksmith and ironworks and pottery made at the farm.

Ein Avdat.

424

Location: from Route 211, about 15 km W of Telalim Junction, turn S.
Best season: year-round
Length of visit: 1 hour
Entrance fee

SHIVTA
NATIONAL PARK

In the cities of the mountains, in the cities of the vale, and in the cities of the south... (Jer 33:13)

Christian site

Antiquities

WC

Accessibility Rating

Shivta (ancient Sobata) is one of six Nabatean-Byzantine cities that were built and flourished in the north-northwestern area of the Negev between the 1st and 7th centuries CE. It is called Isbeita, or Subeita, in Arabic. Whereas the other cities were situated on the ancient caravan routes (e.g., the Incense or Perfume Route) between Arabia and the Mediterranean coast, Shivta was not, nor did it ever have a transportation or security role to play based on its location. Its principal *raison d'être* comes from its agricultural importance.

Large areas around the city are covered with small pebble mounds which the Bedouin call Tuleilat el Anab, that is, "mounds of grapevines," and

some scholars today claim that that these mounds were used for the cultivation of grapes. Evidence for this are the wine-presses found in this area.

THE WATER SYSTEM AND AGRICULTURE AT SHIVTA

Since there were no springs at Shivta and rainfall was sparse, the conclusion must be drawn that the water source for this city must have been based on the collection of the little rainfall and flash floods following the rain. The entire city was covered with private cisterns located in household courtyards and water reached them through the run-off from the roofs and streets, and apparently also from

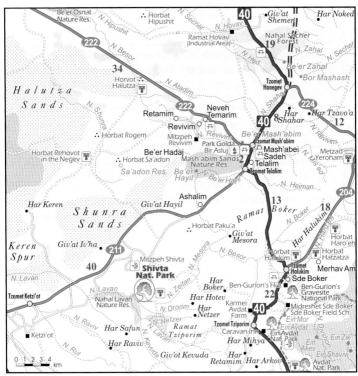

© Carta, Jerusalem

water brought by conduits to the city from distant reservoirs. The city streets followed the path of the conduits and reached a double pool capable of holding a voluminous quantity of water. The double pool was apparently built by the Nabateans and continued to be used in the Byzantine period. Run-off water from the city was channeled to this pool and "notes" were found written or inscribed on pottery shards (ostraca) giving confirmation to those residents who had carried out their obligation of cleaning the pools.

According to another solid opinion, the pebble mounds around the city were intended to increase surface run-off and perhaps also to create alluvial sediment which was then transferred to the valleys. The Negev cities held by the Nabateans beginning several centuries before the Common Era, developed a unique desert agriculture. Because the amount of water was not sufficient to irrigate the entire area, they built low dams across the width of the valleys with a large furrow after every dam. Water coming down the surface of the slopes was directed to these furrows. As a result, small areas received a copious amount of water enabling 4 percent of the general land area to be cultivated. The collection of pebbles above the slope and their assembly into mounds allowed the water to flow freely, as well as perhaps permitting the alluvial soil to progress towards the furrows.

HISTORY

Shivta was a city without walls. An aerial photograph gives a good picture of the city's street arteries and its housing foundations. The structure of the dwellings and the method of construction indicate the stages in the building of the city and the way of life of its inhabitants.

Beginning in the 1st century CE, it was a Nabatean city. In the 2nd century CE, when the Romans conquered the Negev, it became a Roman city. In the 4th century CE, the city reached its peak of development. Its residents accepted the Christian religion, the city expanded its boundaries, and three churches were built of which remains are visible today. In the year 500 CE it was damaged by an earthquake, but not destroyed. Settlement continued after the Arab conquest in the 7th century and a mosque was built. With the change in the fabric of life in the Negev, the city declined and was abandoned by the 9th century.

SITES TO VISIT

After the ruins of Shivta were

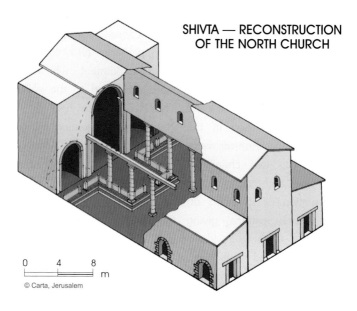

SHIVTA — RECONSTRUCTION OF THE NORTH CHURCH

0   4   8
m
© Carta, Jerusalem

discovered by the British orientalist E. H. Palmer in 1870, several follow-up surveys and excavations were conducted. These efforts weighed in the decision to declare Shivta a national park. Even today, the site is off the beaten path in Israel's northern Negev. The city, whose streets have been cleared of accumulated rubble, has some buildings which are standing in their original location and others which have been reconstructed in part. Among the sites worthy of a visit here:

The Churches

There are three churches, all built to the north of the pool: the South

Remains of Shivta.

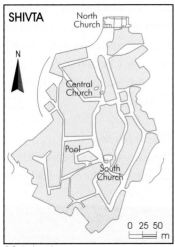

SHIVTA

North Church

N

Central Church

Pool

South Church

0 25 50 m

© Carta, Jerusalem

Church, the Central Church, and the North Church. What remains of all three are the sections that face east: a triapsidal structure divided into a nave and two side aisles, as well as floors and colonnades. A pretty baptismal font was found in one church, hewn out of stone in the form of a cross.

The Colt Mission House

The archaeological mission under the direction of H. D. Colt (son of the inventor of the Colt 45 pistol) excavated at Shivta from 1934 to 1938. The mission took up residence close to the northern entrance of the site. Members of the mission built the residential quarters and inscribed the following in Greek on the lintel: "With good luck. Colt built (this house) with his own money." Mosaic fragments taken from excavated buildings at the site are incorporated in the floor of the house's central hall.

City Dwellings and Streets

Some city houses were multi-storied, and a portion still contain parts of their ground-floor ceiling and second-story walls. The city center was located between the South and Central churches and consisted of several squares and a central plaza that the excavators termed "insulae" (that is, city blocks, usually quadrangular, with multiple dwellings). A large cistern was uncovered here. A workshop quarter was found beside the square. A short inscription appears at the entrance to one of the streets: "As Abraham in faith; as Isaac [inscription erased]; as Jacob in hope; as Moses in modesty; as David in glory; as Solomon in wisdom; as Job in patience."

Egyptian Henbane (Hyoscyamus reticulatus).

OUTSIDE THE NATIONAL PARK AREA

Mitzpeh Shivta

At the top of a hill northwest of Shivta are remains of structures, pools, and a cistern encircled by a wall—apparently the remains of a monastery or church. No excavations have been undertaken here, but around 1990 the site was explored by Professor Yizhar Hirschfeld. Findings indicate that the place was occupied in the Roman-Byzantine period.

This site is located in the midst of an army firing range and is only accessible on the Sabbath and festival holidays.

Shivta Farm

This is a farm that reconstructs Nabatean and Byzantine agri-culture. It has a number of guest houses and is situated about 8 km south of Shivta.

Rehovot in the Negev

This is one of the large settlements established in the Negev in the Nabatean period that flourished in Byzantine times. It was built on a flat hill overlooking the bed of Nahal Shunra (Wadi Ruheibeh), a tributary of Nahal Besor. Excavations unearthed a striking basilica northwest of the city; close by is a large cemetery with scores of tombstones. In addition, dwellings were partially excavated in the southeast area of the city.

Access to the site is via a dirt road running from Halutza, west of route 222 (Mashabim junction–Tze'elim junction).

Shivta — one of the churches.

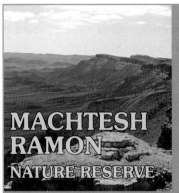

Location: from Route 40, at entrance to Mitzpeh Ramon.

Best season: year-round

Length of visit: 1 hour to a day

Telephone: Visitors' Center: 08-6588691/8; Bio Ramon (Hai Ramon): 08-6588755

Entrance fee to Visitors' Center and to Bio Ramon

They go up by the mountains; they go down by the valleys... (Ps 104:8)

Lookout point · Hiking trail · Sound & light show · WC · Restaurant · Souvenir shop · Telephone

Accessibility Rating for the Albert Promenade

Machtesh Ramon (literally, Ramon Crater) is the largest and most complex crater in the country. This and two others fit the description of "whole craters": Hamachtesh Hakatan ("the little crater") in Mt. Hatzera, and Hamachtesh Hagadol ("the large crater") in Nahal Hatira. Apart from these there is one semi-crater in Timna and two in Mt. Arif, and two partial craters in Sinai. There are almost no comparable geological formations like these in the world and the Hebrew term *machtesh* has entered the international lexicon as a karst erosion cirque. The Machtesh, a sort of giant enclosed saucer with a single exit, resembles a volcanic crater. However, it is not the usual type of crater formed by impact from a meteor. Instead, it was formed by a special and complex geological process at the center of a mountainous ridge. The result: convex layers of rock, a crater rim of hard limestone and a core of soft sandstone, carved out over millions of years by penetrating streams. This occurred during a period when rain was common in this area; today, these craters in the heart of the desert are dry.

Machtesh Ramon is about 30 km long, up to 8 km wide and some 400 m deep. Its outer rim reaches about 1,000 m above sea level. The crater floor has been hollowed down to its earliest geological strata. In the east, it splits into two semi-craters

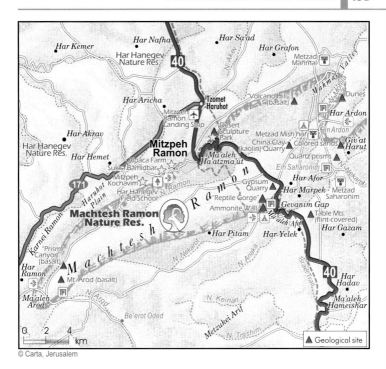

© Carta, Jerusalem

with Mt. Ardon in between; along the southern wall there is a long geological fault. Nahal Ramon, which spills into Nahal Nekarot, drains it toward the Arava. It was once hoped that the Machtesh would yield many natural treasures, but it appears that the only worthy finds are gypsum, china clay (kaolin), and glass sand. Most of the quarries set up here have been abandoned. The importance of Machtesh Ramon today resides mainly in its geology and its scenery.

The top section of the crater's northern wall is of hard limestone whose layers are extended outwards causing rainwater to fall outside the crater rather than into its basin. Landscape to the north is steppe-like and rich in vegetation. The inner wall is steep and its base is comprised of colorful sandstone. The inner part of the crater is dry with little rainfall. The southern wall had crushed in the wake of the geological fault that runs along its side. Its strata of limestone extend sharply to the exterior and create a multi-faulted ridge line in the east nicknamed a "cockscomb." Mt. Ardon rises in the east exhibiting a steep and colorful slope. In the southwest, the crater's base prominently displays black basalt mounds, the products of early volcanic activity.

There are only a few entrances

to the Machtesh. It is possible to descend into the crater from the southwest through the Arod pass, and in the south via the crater wall's fault at the Pitam Gap. An ancient route entered it in the south via the Ramon Gate in the southeast, crossed Ein Saharonim and ascended the height via Ma'aleh Mahmel. The state road (route 40) descends into the crater from the north via Ma'aleh Ha'atzma'ut and exits in the south through Gevanim Gap. The town of Mitzpeh Ramon lies at the top of Ma'aleh Ha'atzma'ut and to the west is the Har HaNegev Field School and Mitzpeh Hakochavim.

FLORA

There is a wide variety of plant species in Machtesh Ramon and the surrounding area due to the great differences in temperature between the basin of the crater and its rim. In the upper areas, the climate is dry and cold, producing vegetation characteristic of the geobotanical Irano-Turanian region, whereas the crater's floor is dry and warmer producing vegetation found in the Saharo-Arabian region.

An additional, special type of growth occurs by the springs—the Common Reed (*Phragmites australis*) and the Narrow-leaved Reedmace (*Typha domingensis*).

FAUNA

The Nature and National Parks Protection Authority chose Machtesh Ramon as the place for Asiatic wild asses (*Equus hemionus*) and Nubian ibex (*Capra ibex nubiana*), which were on the verge of extinction, to be set free to roam the wild. The wild ass, which is of Asian extraction,

Asiatic wild ass.

cannot be domesticated and thus cannot be trained. A few years ago there was some success in breeding these animals at the Yotvata Hai-Bar and they have adjusted well to their new environment and now number about 50.

The ibex has a muscular body, and runs well over rocky and steep terrain. Thus, it is difficult to hunt this animal when it is on the cliffs, but it is easy prey when it reaches its watering spots.

At Mt. Negev and Machtesh Ramon there are additional large animals: leopards, striped hyenas, desert deer, cliff foxes, caracals (lynx), sand foxes, hyraxes, and others. Small rodents and reptiles

Dike at bottom of Mt. Ardon

Haminsara ("The Sawmill").

Rheum palaestinum *in bloom.*

Blue Sinai lizard.

are more difficult to see in nature, but may be seen at the Bio-Ramon mini-zoo.

HIKING TRAILS AND SITES TO VISIT

Ein Saharonim

Ein Saharonim is the only spring in the crater. It used to be a way-station on the Spice Route from Petra to the Mediterranean coast. Thus, an inn was built here for the caravans that passed through. The small quantity of water is sufficient to quench the thirst of a rich variety of plants in the immediate vicinity, and this in turn draws animals to the spot.

HaMinsara (the "Sawmill")

In the center of the Machtesh there is a site of unusual, prismatic sandstone rocks resembling a lumberyard, hence the site's name. The long and narrow "prisms" were created by the crystallization of the sandstone under unique conditions. These pentagonal and hexagonal rocks reach a meter or more in length. They look like wooden slabs, but they are not fossilized wood. A special path was built to reach them in order to avoid their being walked upon and destroyed.

The Ammonite Wall

On the outer southern hillside of HaMinsara, there is a very large concentration of spiral-shaped sea creatures which lived under water 50 to 90 million years ago and became extinct. They ranged from the size of snails to that of tractor wheels. When they died, they sank into the seabed, their skeletal remains inflated, became stone and fossilized.

Bio Ramon (Hai Ramon)

This complex, covering almost 3 acres at the foot of the

Visitors' Center, presents a rich collection of desert plants and animals. It is divided into 2 parts: a reconstructed outdoor desert landscape showing 6 typical habitats found in the Negev hills and Machtesh Ramon; and penned and semi-open enclosures containing about 40 species of animals found in the Negev: reptiles, rodents, spiders, insects and mollusks.

The Visitors' Center, Promenade and Sculpture Garden

The Visitors' Center of the Nature and National Parks Protection Authority is in the shape of a snail, perched on the edge of the Ramon Crater. Here there is a wide variety of literature and an audio-visual presentation about the natural landscape, plant and animal life in the Machtesh. The promenade runs from the Center to Mt. Gamal, where there is a magnificent view of the crater. Observation decks are posted at convenient spots along the promenade. Stone sculptures blending in with the wonderful landscape grace the grounds of the Visitors' Center.

Alpaca Farm

This farm, containing 600 alpacas and llamas, is located southwest of the Visitors' Center. Visitors may walk around the farm, pet the animals, feed them, and ride on them.

Mitzpeh Kochavim

This observation point, south of the Alpaca Farm, was established in 1971 and improvements to the site have been made since then.

Ma'aleh Ha'atzma'ut ("Independence Ascent").

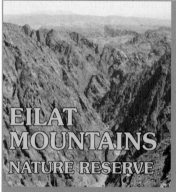

No admission fee

EILAT MOUNTAINS NATURE RESERVE

And when we passed...through the way of the plain from Elath... (Deut 2:8)

Hiking trail

Lookout point

The hiking trails are not suitable for individuals with disabilities.

In terms of geology and scenery, the range of mountains north of Eilat is the most complex and varied area in the country. It is a part of what is called the Arabo-Nubian Massif—a gigantic rock formation that extends over both sides of the Red Sea, most of it bedrock formed during the earliest periods on earth. Since its formation, this geological mass has remained unsettled and subject to many changes, pressures and faults. What is most characteristic of this massif is its crystalline composition. It is not stratified like the limestone found throughout most of Israel. However, not all the massif consists of bedrock. In the changes that this formation has undergone, it has crumbled and reconstituted itself, adding "newer" layers, thereby becoming an extension of the southern Sinai Peninsula that bears no resemblance in form and substance to the geological formations in the rest of Israel.

These mountains never had Hebrew names, either from the Bible or from later sources. When Hebrew names were given, they were chosen on the basis of several criteria: some drew upon Arabic appellations, such as Manaya that became Timna; other names derived from the natural or historical elements in the area, such as Nahal Nehushtan where copper ore (*nehoshet* in Hebrew) is found, or Bik'at Sayarim (the "Patrol Valley"), named

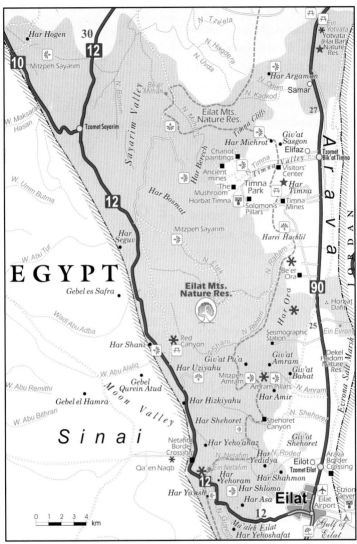

© Carta, Jerusalem

after the Negev Brigade of the Palmah who patrolled the area during the War of Independence. Finally, a number of the more impressive peaks were named after the Kings of Judah—from Solomon, Rehoboam, and up to Hezekiah. "Granite Mountains" is the general name given to this elevated area although granite is only one element from which the mountains are comprised.

All the mountains appear in varying hues according to seasonal light and the position of the sun during the course of the day. The shifting shades are especially sharp for several reasons: in the first instance, there is the contrast between the colors of the water in the Gulf of Eilat, for the most part a deep blue, and the colors of the mountains. The hours of greatest contrast occur at dawn and dusk when the sun is low on the horizon, giving off a range of reddish hues; in the afternoon, yellow-brown is predominant. Because of minimal rainfall, there is no vegetation except in the ravines, and thus no greenish colors are present.

The mountain slopes are very steep and few roads traverse the range. The main one is the "Pilgrim Route" or Darb el-Haj, once taken by Muslim pilgrims from Egypt to Mecca. The route begins in the area of the Suez Canal, crosses Qal'at Nahal to Aqaba, and then turns south towards Mecca. In this section of the mountain range, it reached a pass called Ras en Naqb (Rosh Hama'ala) and then descended via Ma'aleh Eilat to the coast. Trails descend in Nahal Roded and Nahal Gishron. A new road, route 10, follows the Egyptian-Israeli border, linking Eilat with Nitzana. At the Nitzana junction, route 10 continues along the border and route 12 branches northeast to the Uvda airfield. The Israel Nature Trail passes through this area in a north-south

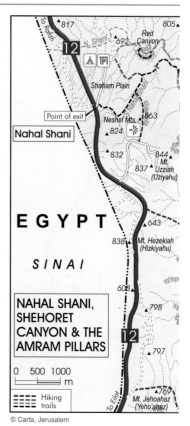

direction from the Uvda Valley to the border crossing at Taba.

FAUNA

The entire area has very little water. There is one small spring, Ein Netafim, which was the only water source for deer, except at Eilat where facilities in the surrounding area now supply water for them. Another interesting animal is the Ornate Spiny-tailed Lizard (*Uromastyx ornatus*), a colorful creature which is only found in this area of the country. Deer roam along the intermittent streams and live

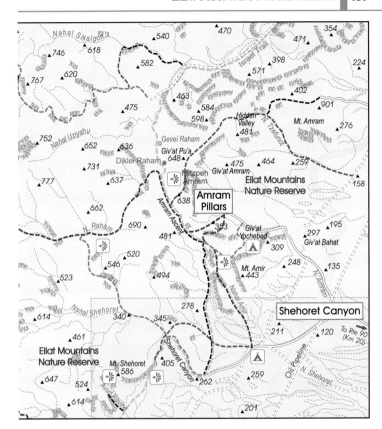

off the leaves of acacia plants, which supply sufficient water for them. The last of a population of Arabian gazelles, numbering only several dozen, live on the margins of the Reserve.

FLORA

Most of the vegetation in the Eilat Mountains is concentrated in the ravines, places where water may be found. Plant life from three distinct geobotanical regions is encountered here: the Saharo-Arabian, where vegetation grows on barren rocky terrain—White Broom (*Retama raetam*), Spiny Zilla (*Zilla spinosa*), and Bushy Bean-caper (*Zygophyllum dumosum*); the Irano-Turanian region, characterized by higher altitudes and colder temperatures —Atlantic Pistachio (*Pistacio atlantica*), Desert Wormwood (*Artemisia desertorum*); and the Sudanese region, with lower altitudes and warmer temperatures—Twisted Acacia (*Acacia raddiana*), Desert Acacia (*Acacia desertorum*), Umbrella Thorn Acacia (*Acacia tortilis*), Doum Palm (*Platanus orientalis*), and Acacia Strap Flower (*Plicosepalus acaciae*).

LOOKOUT POINTS IN THE EILAT MOUNTAINS

Mt. Yo'ash peak, overlooking Ma'aleh Eilat, gives a splendid view of the area, from Mt. Hezekiah and Mt. Uzziah on the Sinai border to the Moon Valley and its surrounding mountains.

Mt. Rehoboam is visibly white in contrast to the dark mountains beside it.

Mt. Tzefahot peak, close to Eilat, offers an excellent vista of the Red Sea, its coastline, and the mountains beyond it.

HIKING TRAILS

Southern Nahal Shani and the Red Canyon

Red Canyon is one of the prettiest in the area of Eilat. The rich assortment of minerals contained in this rock formation creates shapes and images in shades of red, brown, white and purple on its craggy surface. The entrance to the canyon is from route 12 (Eilat–Netafim border crossing) where a dirt road branches north to the parking lot.

The Short Trail. This is a circular route. A green-marked, 600-m-long trail leads from the parking lot to the Red Canyon. At the canyon's edge, a black-marked trail skirts Nahal Shani on its south and returns to the parking lot. Time allocation: about 1½ hrs.

The Long Trail (Southern Nahal Shani). From the starting point on route 12, descend the black-marked trail through a wide ravine. This is the southern half of Nahal Shani. The Nahal has abundant plant life indicating that this ravine draws a respectable quantity of water. A blue-marked trail ascends to Mt. Neshef, where there is a superb view of the Edom Mountains, the Gulf of Eilat, Mt. Shlomo (Solomon), Mt. Amram, and the Moon Valley in Sinai.

The ravine reaches the Red Canyon from the south. Return via the green-marked trail to the parking lot. Time allocation: about 4 hrs.

The Amram Pillars

From the Red Canyon a green-marked trail heads eastward. It continues along the ravine of Nahal Shani, passes through a canyon-like section, and after 2 km turns south towards Gevei Raham, Diklei Raham, and the Mitzpeh Amram lookout. The lookout offers a wonderful view of the Amram Valley, the Arava, the Eilat Mountains, the Edom Mountains, and the Gulf of Eilat. The trail turning south leads to Shehoret Canyon. Another trail, with blue-markers, reaches the Amram Pillars, and from here there is a passage for all types of vehicles, via Nahal Amram, to the Eilat-Sodom highway.

Shehoret Canyon

Access to this canyon and Mt. Shehoret is via a paved road which branches off westward from route 90, about 20 km north of Eilat. Nahal Shehoret drains the eastern slopes of Mt. Hizkiyahu (Hezekiah). In a section east of Mt. Shehoret, the Nahal becomes a canyon built of bedrock 600 million years old. The canyon is 1,200 m long. The continuation of the trail, which is part of the Israel Nature Trail, reaches Mt. Shehoret and from its summit (586 m high) there is a panoramic view of the Arava Valley, Eilat and its Gulf, Nahal Shehoret, the cliffs of Machtesh Amram, Aqaba, and the Edom Mountains.

Red Canyon.

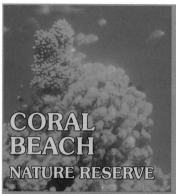

Location: S of Eilat, on the Eilat–Taba road.
Best season: year-round
Length of visit: 1 hour to a day
Tel.: 08-6376829
Entrance fee

CORAL BEACH
NATURE RESERVE

...and they made the ships in Ezion-geber. (2 Chr 20:36)

 Outdoor recreation
 Beach
 Swimming
 Scuba diving
 Showers

 **Accessibility Rating for Coral Beach**

Picnic site | Souvenir shop | Snack bar | Restaurant | WC

Israel is situated between two quite different sea coasts: the Mediterranean Sea and the Gulf of Eilat (Aqaba). The latter is a branch of the Red Sea, which itself is an extension of the Indian Ocean. There is no stream that runs into the Gulf of Eilat; its only water link is with the Indian Ocean. Thus, the Gulf is a sort of "dead end"; whatever is scattered in the Indian Ocean is concentrated in the Gulf. Whoever goes underwater diving in the clear waters of the Gulf cannot but be impressed by the abundant marine life in all its colors and forms.

The Gulf of Eilat is long, narrow and deep—the distance from the Tiran Islands at the entrance to the Red Sea to Eilat/Aqaba is 160 km; it does not surpass 24 km in width, and reaches a maximum depth of 1,850 m. Four countries share its coastline: Saudi Arabia controls the longest stretch of coast on the east side; to the north, Jordan has only several dozen kilometers of shore; Egypt controls the entire western seaboard, and only 11 km in the north belong to Israel.

Israel's short Red Sea coastline has been allocated by the State among a number of land-sea uses: a municipal beach, hotel beaches, a civilian port, a military port, an oil terminal and a smidgen of coast that has been declared a nature reserve.

Because the Gulf of Eilat receives very little organic

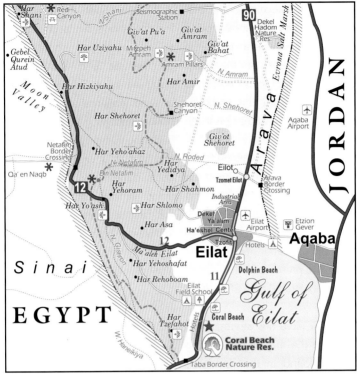

© Carta, Jerusalem

material from external sources, there is very little marine vegetation. The main element which makes up its living content is coral, a form of animal life found on the sea floor. Through its extended branches, the coral collects and thrives on every bit of organic material that comes its way. An entire sub-set of animal life from variegated species feed off the coral formations. These in turn are food for fish and other creatures, and these in turn are nourishment for a fourth sea group, mainly sharks. All these active forms of marine life are dependent for their existence on the basic element in the sea chain, namely the coral.

THE CORAL REEF

The area of Israel's limited Red Sea coast set aside for a nature reserve is occupied entirely by the coral reef. The Reserve is situated along the Eilat–Taba highway. It is 1,200 m long and extends up to 20 m from the shoreline. Along this section of the coastal strip, the sea floor descends very sharply, like a suspended wall, to a depth of 4 m and it is upon this wall-like embankment that the coral colony develops. The reef extends, like an underground island, into the sea from the skeletal remains of the dead coral. This reef, too, is full of coral colonies. Beyond the reef, the sea is quite deep and its principal life-forms are fish.

Until Israel developed its southern port of Eilat, the entire coast was full of wildlife and its remains. Because the Israeli coast had to serve a number of functions for the State, it was difficult to preserve all the wildlife in a concentrated area of a nature reserve.

The Reserve has attempted to preserve the majority of marine species found in the Red Sea. All scuba-divers, and even those snorkeling along the surface, are astounded by the rich forms and colors of fish. Some species live in schools while others are solitary swimmers; some loiter on the sea bed and appear disguised as rocks or curlicues of sand while others swim very slowly displaying their colors or declaring that they are poisonous and that it is wise to maintain one's distance from them. Like many of the country's assets, this marine reserve has unique features which make it a singular visitors' attraction unlike any along the Mediterranean shores.

OUTSIDE THE NATURE RESERVE

Yotvata Wildlife Preserve

Many species of wildlife have become extinct in the wake of geological and climatic changes over the last 20 million years.

Sea anemone.

Moray eel.

Goose barnacles.

But most of the damage has been caused by man during the late 19th and early 20th centuries. Poaching, swamp drainage, deforestation, the paving of roads, agricultural development, construction of settlements, the use of harmful and pest-control material, have polluted the environment and destroyed the natural habitat of animal life—mainly the largest species—found in Israel.

The Yotvata Wildlife Preserve has for its objective the regeneration of endangered species and the rehabilitation of wildlife whose natural environs are the Negev desert terrain. The Preserve is divided into four main parts:

1. An expansive fenced-in open area for herbivorous animals that roam freely and feed on natural plants, but also receive artificial nutrients.

2. A center for large predators from the canine, feline and hyena species which are kept in penned areas. There are also species of desert snakes, lizards, agamas, rodents, and day and night time animals of prey.

3. An enclosure for reptiles and small desert wildlife, as well as birds of prey.

4. A dark room designed to produce night conditions, low temperatures, and high humidity, as well as special lighting for diurnal effects. Here, one can observe the nocturnal activities of rodents such as the southern, rock and desert gerbil, the fruit bat, and others.

Access is via route 90 between Kibbutz Yotvata and Kibbutz Samar, about 40 km north of Eilat. There is an entrance fee.

Gulf of Eilat coast.

Hermit crab.

Sea urchin.

Chiton (coat-of-mail shell).